IMAGES
of America

GREEKS IN HOUSTON

On the Cover: Pictured is the wedding of Nick Voinis and Amalia Coronis on September 24, 1924. Amalia's father thought Nick was the right man for his daughter because he was also from the island of Patmos and had established himself financially in business and in the Greek community. In fact, both families had already discussed a potential betrothal. Nick received his future father-in-law's blessing, and the couple was engaged for a year. The wedding took place in the Coronis family home, and the priest was brought from SS. Constantine and Helen Serbian Orthodox Church in Galveston to officiate because the bride's uncle was having a disagreement with the parish priest in Houston. Relatives, friends, and most of the Greek community were invited to the wedding. (Courtesy of Paul Voinis.)

IMAGES
of America

GREEKS IN HOUSTON

Irene Cassis and
Dr. Constantina Michalos

ARCADIA
PUBLISHING

ISBN 978-1-4671-3029-5

Published by Arcadia Publishing
Charleston, South Carolina

Printed in the United States of America

Library of Congress Control Number: 2013935199

For all general information, please contact Arcadia Publishing:
Telephone 843-853-2070
Fax 843-853-0044
E-mail sales@arcadiapublishing.com
For customer service and orders:
Toll-Free 1-888-313-2665

Visit us on the Internet at www.arcadiapublishing.com

Contents

ACKNOWLEDGMENTS

We would like to thank all of the individuals who contributed invaluable historical photographs and heartwarming stories so that we could write a book that commemorates our ancestors, honors our contemporaries, and inspires future generations. It is a tribute to these pioneers and their descendants and a modest thank-you for the efforts and sacrifices they made.

A special thank-you goes to Fr. Michael Lambakis, dean of Annunciation Greek Orthodox Cathedral, for his love and support.

We are also grateful to Mary Poulos and Carol Vartian of the Archives Committee at Annunciation Cathedral. Mary Poulos augmented our information with her endless knowledge and memories, and Carol Vartian supported and worked side by side with Mary Poulos. We also want to thank Ann Poulos, administrative assistant to Father Michael, for patiently answering our many questions.

Mary Wells Sharpley, with Irene Cassis, coauthored the 65th and 90th Annunciation anniversary histories, which provided source material for this book, and offered her assistance when this project first began.

We thank our families for their support and patience as we worked long days and nights, sorting through pictures and anecdotes, in order to tell the best story we could about Greeks in Houston.

Finally—always and forever—we give thanks to our Lord and Savior Jesus Christ, to whom we prayed daily to guide our hearts and minds to write a worthy tribute.

INTRODUCTION

You will never do anything in this world without courage. It is the greatest quality of the mind next to honor.

—Aristotle

Greece gave the world democracy, philosophy, literature, art, and music. Nowhere is this legacy of wisdom, creativity, tenacity, and grace more apparent than in its immigrants to the United States, who braved physical and cultural obstacles to forge new lives for themselves.

Houston, Texas, was one such destination. When the first recorded Greeks arrived in 1889, Houston was not much more than a swamp, but the entrepreneurial spirit of the fledgling city beckoned with economic promise. Men needed to secure themselves financially, and their hard work and perseverance became the foundation for one of the largest Greek communities in America. Maintaining their cultural identity while becoming good citizens was crucial to these pioneers. Their desire for their own church, where they could worship as Orthodox Christians, motivated the community to build the Evangelismos of the Theotokos (the Annunciation to the Mother of God) at 509 Walker Street.

Once the church was completed, the community established a choir to enhance the services, a Sunday school to teach the tenets of Orthodoxy, and a Greek school to preserve the language of their faith and culture. The formation of Greek American fraternal, social, and educational organizations followed, easing the transition into American society. The most profound demonstration of pride in their new country was the sacrifice of many men during the World Wars as well as the contributions of women here at home to the war effort.

As the community grew, its focus turned, again, to the church. In 1952, the Evangelismos of the Theotokos moved to a larger site on Yoakum Boulevard. In 1967, Houston became the See of the Eighth Archdiocesan District, and the Annunciation Church was elevated to the status of a cathedral. Today, the Greek community of Houston has three churches: the original Annunciation Greek Orthodox Cathedral, St. Basil the Great Greek Orthodox Church in west Houston, and St. John the Theologian near the Clear Lake area. With the addition of the Polemanakos Educational Building, the S.P. Martel Auditorium, and the Steve G. Caloudas Athletic Center, the Annunciation Cathedral complex now encompasses two city blocks.

A major improvement to the complex was the Boozalis Festival Center, a state-of-the-art kitchen for its famous Greek Festival. When the parish celebrated its 50th anniversary in 1967, weekend festivities included a Greek Night. Given the energetic participation and hard work of several hundred parishioners and the enthusiastic response of the Houston community to Greek Night, it was repeated the following year and designated as the second annual Greek Festival. The four-day festival enables the Greek community to share its culture and religion. The profits from the festival help support the church and its charitable ministries in the Greater Houston area. Now in its 46th year, Annunciation's Greek Festival has inspired other ethnic communities in the area to display their heritage in various festivals as well.

Like all ethnic festivals, Annunciation showcases its faith and culture through food, music, crafts, iconography, and church tours. However, the Greek Festival dancers—Parea Hellas—set apart this celebration from others around the country. Choreographed by Panos Papamichalis and Georgia Voinis, the group rehearses the entire year, and the men begin growing their mustaches in the summer so that they will be authentically Greek in time for the October festival. Eventually, Panos moved to Dallas, but Georgia continued, leading the Parea to glorious performances in festivals in Lefkada and Mytilini, Greece. Georgia dedicated herself to this folk dance ministry, exposing *xeni* (strangers) to the Greek spirit and the Orthodox faith while entertaining them until her death in 2003.

Whereas the founders of Annunciation Cathedral began working as fruit peddlers, ditch diggers, dishwashers, cooks, and railroad workers, they assimilated with the Houston community, working, building businesses, and educating their children. Today, the Greek community is composed of restaurateurs, doctors, lawyers, gas station owners, architects, engineers, artists, judges, politicians, teachers, secretaries, and homemakers. There are old-timers; new immigrants; first-, second-, and third-generation Greeks; and converts to Orthodoxy. One consequence of this growth and assimilation was the loss of Greek as a primary language. Nevertheless, because the liturgy was always and forever central to their lives, English was slowly incorporated into services so that the entire community could practice their faith and enjoy their heritage.

Orthodoxy made its presence known in Houston, not only in the Byzantine architecture of the church but also through participation in the Houston Council of Churches, Interfaith Ministries, and, especially, the Philocardiac Ministry in the Houston Medical Center. In 1955, the state of Texas declared the Greek Orthodox Church a major faith, but the immigrants who had arrived less than a century before already knew that. They may have come to escape war and poverty but, in their hearts, they carried the faith of their fathers, which taught them to "do justice, and to love mercy, and to walk humbly with your God" (Micah 6:8).

One

Coming to America

The exodus of the Greeks from their homeland in the 19th century was not entirely by choice. Because much of the land in Greece was too rocky for cultivation and little or no industrial development existed, economic opportunities were limited. Much of Asia Minor was controlled by the Ottoman Empire; Greeks living in those areas were persecuted and had little personal freedom. Many fled these areas, not only for better opportunities but also to save their lives.

Immigrants to the United States braved many hardships. Traveling with immigrants from Italy, they were crowded into the stifling hulls of ships like animals. Some women were pregnant while they made the crossing. All of the immigrants packed their own food for the trip, which included items like bread, cheese, and salami. They took turns sleeping and slept with one eye open because somebody might steal their food. They arrived wearing the same clothes they had on when they boarded.

After crossing the Atlantic Ocean, the immigrants had to overcome one last obstacle before they could enter the United States—Ellis Island. It was alternately called "the golden door" or "the isle of tears." To those who were processed on the island within the usual three to five hours, it was a golden door. It became an isle of tears for those who did not meet US standards for entry and were sent back. Though there were over 12 million people processed into America during the period from 1882 to 1924, about 250,000 were returned home—their hopes for a new life in America shattered. Families were sometimes separated when officials refused entry to those they felt had defects, such as illness or minor physical ailments. However, the immigrants who passed through the golden door of Ellis Island sought jobs in the large cities or on the railroads. Most concentrated in Northern locations, but a few adventurous Greeks, despite the wild reputation of Texas, migrated southwest to the warmer climate with hopes of finding greater opportunities in Houston.

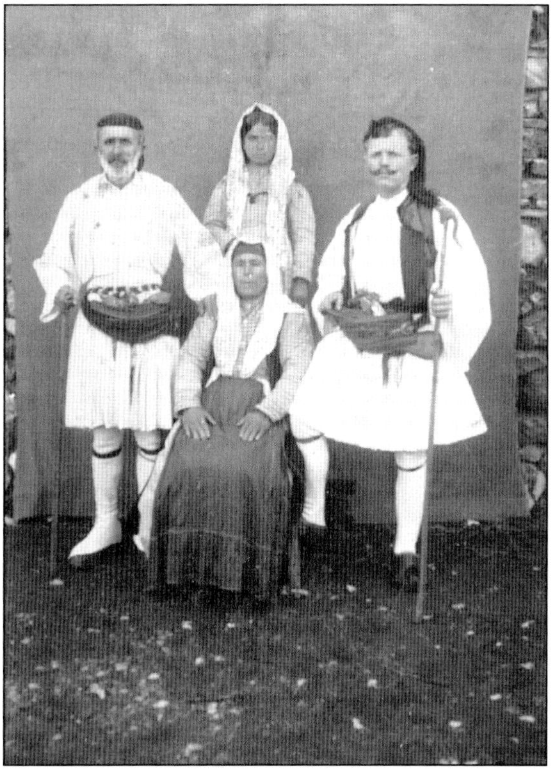

Immigrants to the United States braved many hardships to come to the land of the free. "I have overcome so many obstacles in my life, so many that I would have given up if I were not Greek. Because of my heritage—my belief—my religion has really put me through—it has sustained me," said Demetrios Petheriotes in 1920. Petheriotes is pictured here at far right, with his wife, Katherine, standing at rear. (Courtesy of Houston Metropolitan Research Center [HMRC].)

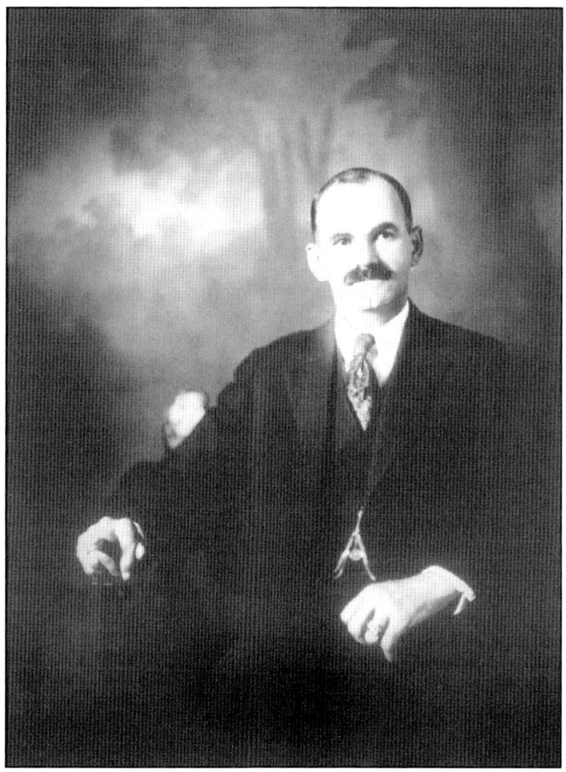

H.D. Pappas, pictured, emigrated from Greece to Dallas and became a restaurateur in 1887. His sons, James "Jim," Peter, Tom, and George, founded Pappas Refrigeration Company in Houston in 1945. In 1967, they expanded their business, opening the Dot Coffee Shop downtown. In the 1970s, Jim's sons, Harris and Chris, joined the family business. Pappas Restaurants, operated by Harris and Chris Pappas, are based in Houston, with more than 85 locations nationwide. (Courtesy of Chris Pappas.)

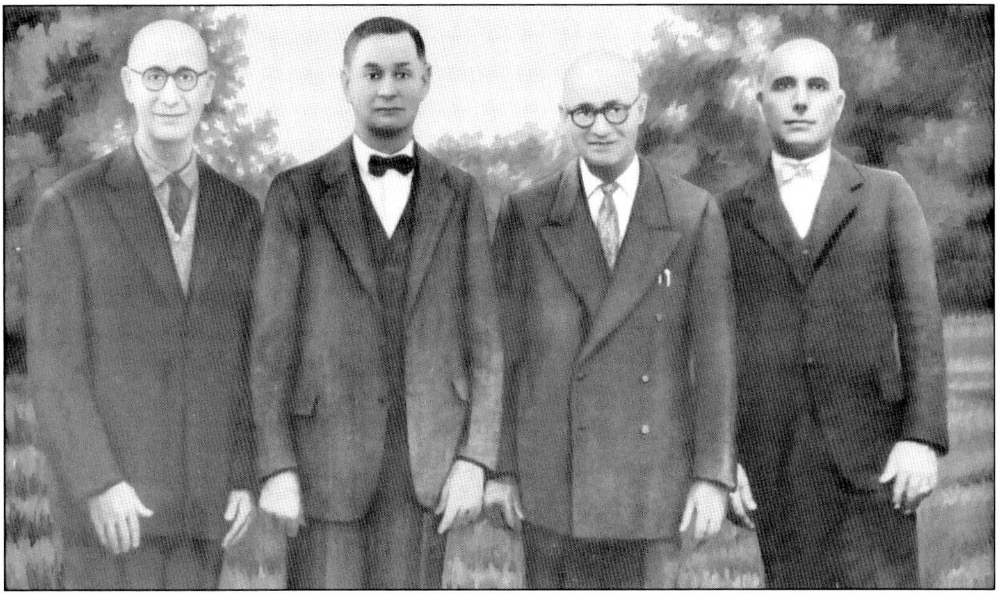

George, Edward, and Peter Polemanakos came from Gerakion, Greece, in 1889, followed by Anthony, John, Theodore (second from right), and Nick (far left). With little education, George, Edward, and Peter worked and saved enough money to buy pushcarts, selling fruits and vegetables. They opened the first confectionery in Houston in 1906 and, later, opened a bakery. Eventually, they bought four movie houses in Houston and five around the state and invested in real estate. (Courtesy of AGOC Archives.)

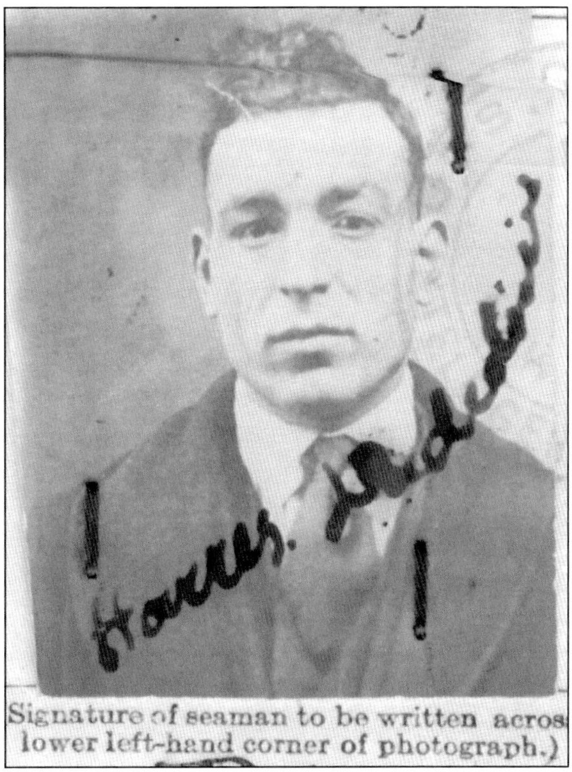

Harres D. Dadinis was born in Istanbul, Turkey, in 1895. Pictured is his entrance receipt to the Port of New York in the early 1920s. He eventually settled in Houston and established a restaurant called Gypsy Village. He later expanded it and renamed it Harbor Lights Club and Restaurant. Harres's wife, Koula, took over the business after his death in 1960. (Courtesy of Dr. Roxane H. Dadinis.)

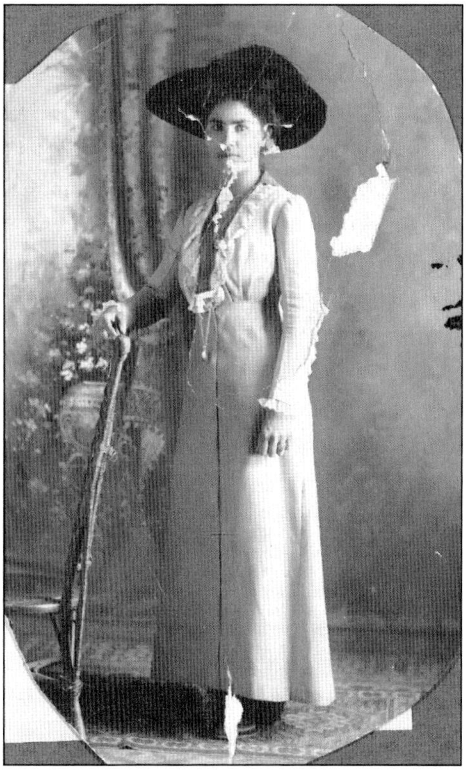

In 1902, Kalliope Vlahos came to Houston from Sparta, Greece, to find her father. Identified as the first Greek woman in Houston, she reunited her family and later married George Kladouris in the first Greek Orthodox wedding performed in Houston. Archimandrite Theoclitos (Triantafilides), from SS. Constantine and Helen Serbian Orthodox Church in Galveston officiated. Father Theoclitos was a Russian priest sent to Galveston by Czar Nicholas. (Courtesy of HMRC.)

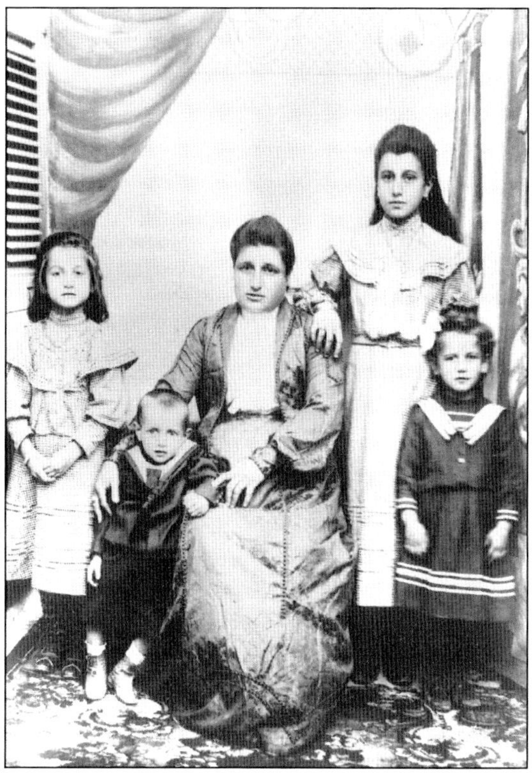

Around 1908, Mary Kontomichali Coronis sent this photograph, taken with her children (from left to right) Amalia, James, Irene, and Katherine, to her husband, Paul, in the United States as "a reminder of us." He had come to America several years earlier and was working in San Francisco at the time, "feeding the gold miners." The family joined him in Houston 10 years later. (Courtesy of HMRC.)

Nicholas Voinis (left) came to Houston in 1910. By 1940, he operated a popular restaurant at 1317 Congress Avenue. Pictured are Nicholas Voinis and business partner Nikita Keffalas in front of the Lone Star Café during the Depression. This photograph was sent to his wife, Amalia Coronis Voinis, in Patmos, Greece, with their children. (Courtesy of HMRC.)

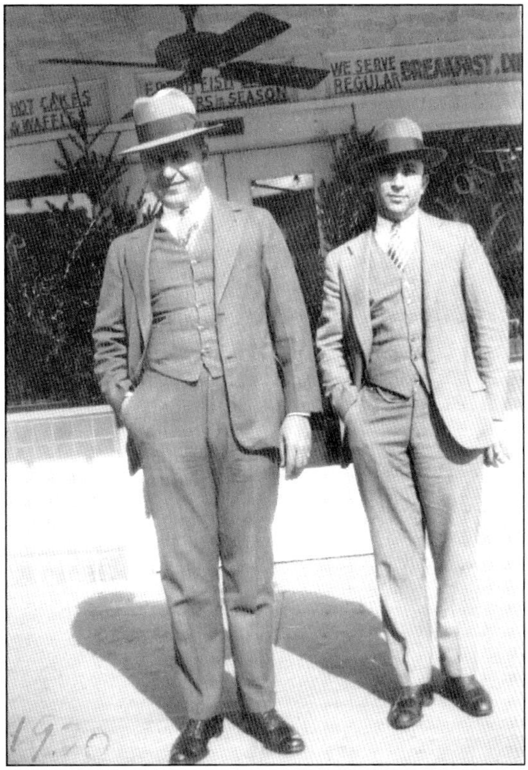

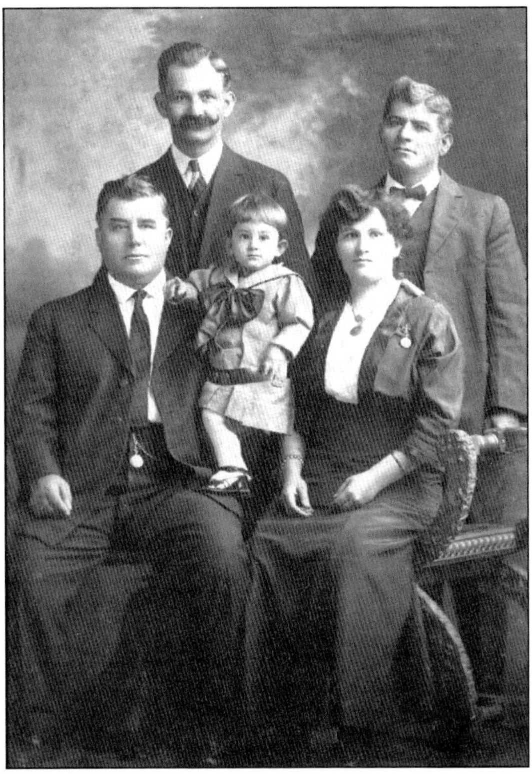

Pictured in 1913–1914 from left to right are (sitting) Chris Malavazou (Malavansos), his son Chris, and his wife; (standing) unidentified and Chris's brother George. Chris was a member of the original Panhellenic Benevolent Brotherhood, whose Greek acronym was ELPIS, meaning "hope." The committee sought a permit from the city of Houston for "the construction of a wooden church on the property of Walker Avenue [sic]" in 1917, according to the ELPIS minutes of August 4, 1917. In 1919, Chris served as president of ELPIS, which later became the parish council. (Courtesy of HMRC.)

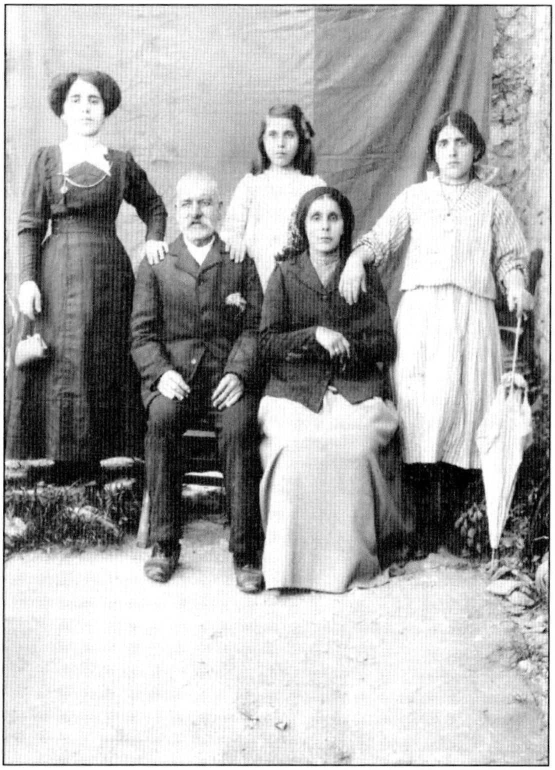

Angelo Mytelinaeos (Mytilen) immigrated to the United States in 1914–1915. He left his father and his mother, Vassiliki, and four sisters in Greece. His sisters were Constantina (Picramenos), Faye (Verges), Anastasia (Kousakis), and Sophia (Petheriotes). Constantina is not pictured in the portrait; Faye, Anastasia, and Sophia are pictured from left to right in the second row. Eventually, all the sisters and their mother immigrated to the United States and were very involved in the early Houston community. (Courtesy of HMRC.)

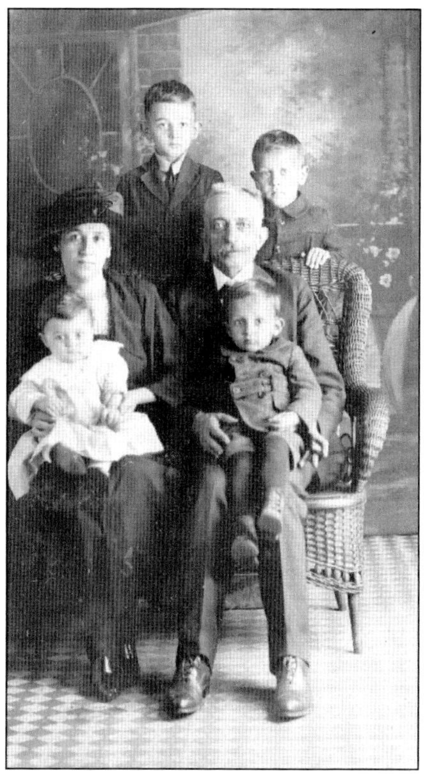

Demetra (née Roupakiotis) Jelson and Athanasios Jelson emigrated from Greece in 1915–1916. Athanasios Jelson first came to the United States to work in 1906 and then returned to Greece to get married. He sold cottonseed oil to restaurants and to his friends. Jelson family members pictured in the 1920s are Demetra holding Cleo, Athanasios holding John, and George and Angelo standing behind them. (Courtesy of HMRC.)

Costa Lardis (far right) came to the United States first and then sent for his sister Maria Lardis (Menutes) in 1916. He also sent for his mother, Argero, and sister Julia Lardis (Mousouliotes), who came together in 1920. Costa became a restaurateur. He and Peter Mousouliotes (Moss) owned the Farmers' Market Café in the Hampshaw Building. (Courtesy of Phillip Moss.)

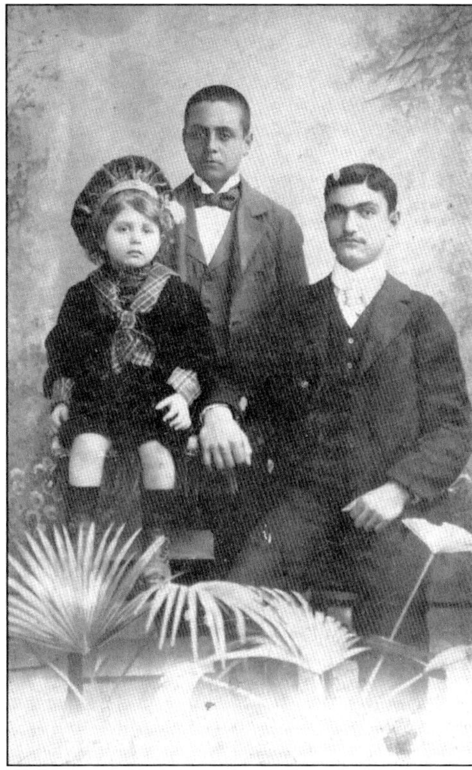

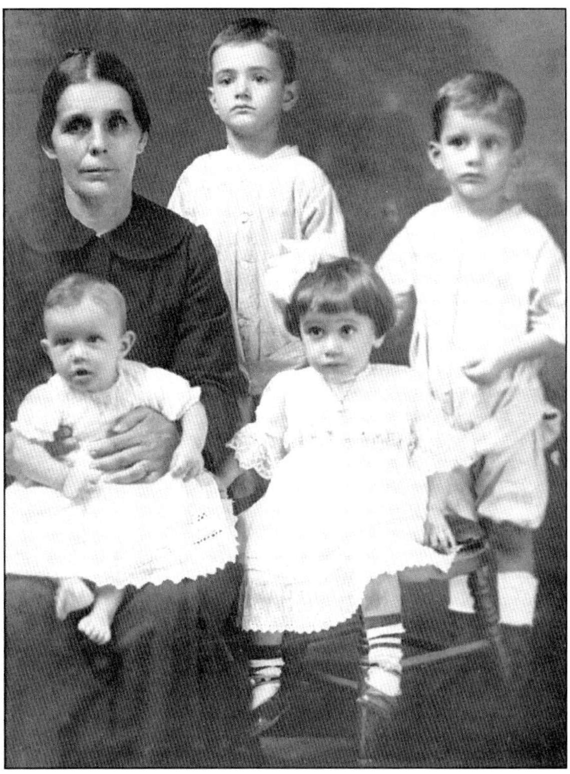

Grandmother (*yiayia*) Vasiliki Mytelinaeos (Mytilen) is with her grandchildren in 1918. Pictured are (standing) Nick and Jim; (sitting) Bessie and Mary Peet. Vasiliki's daughters Aphrodite (Faye) Verges, Sophia Petheriotes, Constantina Peet, and Tacia Kousakis fought over whom yiayia Vasiliki was going to stay with; they all wanted her. She lived until she was well over 100 years of age. (Courtesy of Maria M. Verges.)

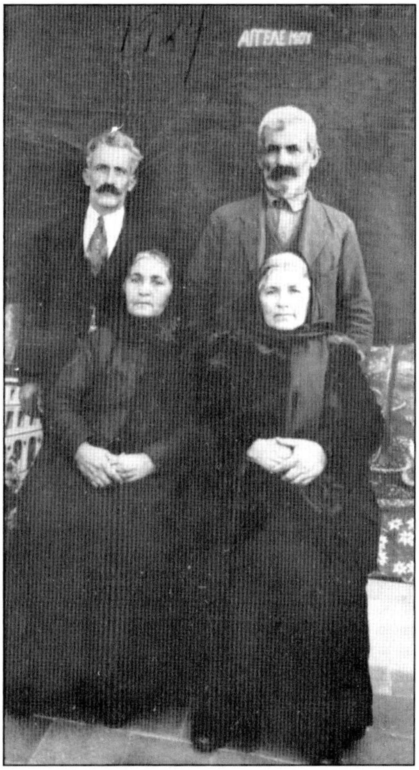

Nick Voinis's family is pictured in Patmos in 1924. Nick came to the United States in 1912 at the age of 15. His father, George, had been here for a while, but Nick thought that it was shameful for his dad to be separated from his family while he, a young man, was at home in Greece. So he came to the United States and sent his father home. (Courtesy of HMRC.)

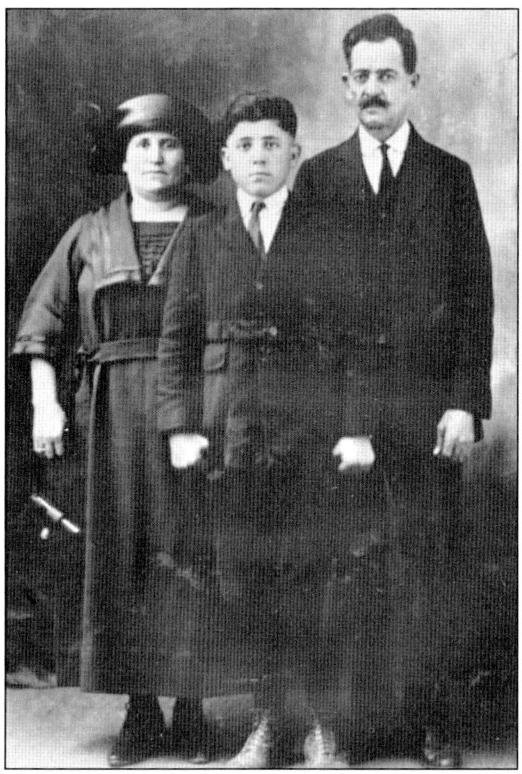

From left to right are Lefkothea Galanos, Theodore Galanos, and Peter Galanos. In 1919, Lefkothea came from Greece with three of her five children, Theodore, age 9; George, age 10; and Stella, age 19. One son, Jimmy, age 13, stayed behind with relatives because he was quarantined with an eye infection; he died in Greece during World War II. Another son, Paul, 20, was already in Houston with their father, Peter. (Courtesy of Despina Denos.)

Two

A New Home in Houston

The Allen brothers founded the city of Houston in 1836, never anticipating a city that would one day become one of the largest in the world. Though it was rich with potential, the Houston that the Greek pioneers found in 1889 was not much of a town at all. George and Peter Poleminacos (later Polemanakos) are listed in the *Houston City Directory of 1889–1890* as the first recorded Greeks in Houston.

More Greek men, single and married, followed. Starting with menial work—shining shoes, washing dishes, mopping floors, selling fruits and vegetables—the Greeks sought economic independence by becoming small businessmen, opening confectioneries and cafés in the downtown area. Always considered foreigners, the Greek men did not gain acceptance easily. Recognizing that learning English was crucial to their success, many were self-taught, and a few were able to go to school to learn English. Some even Americanized their names because their American customers found the long Greek names difficult to pronounce.

For approximately 11 years, the nucleus of Greeks remained totally male. In 1903, Kalliope Vlahos arrived in Houston and, not long after, other women, wives, daughters, and sisters joined the men. Parents or relatives arranged marriages. Dowries, determined by the family's wealth and position, were an important part of marriage arrangements in Greece. The groom also had to show that he had solid prospects as a husband and provider and was of good moral character. The arrival of women transformed the small colony of Greeks into a family-centered community. Besides the clothing and utensils the women had brought with them to set up their new homes, they also brought icons, censers, and candles for the *iconostasis* (home altar). It was in this humble, unobtrusive manner that the light of the Orthodox faith was carried to this city. The arrival of the women and the opportunity for a better life for their families encouraged most to make Houston their permanent home.

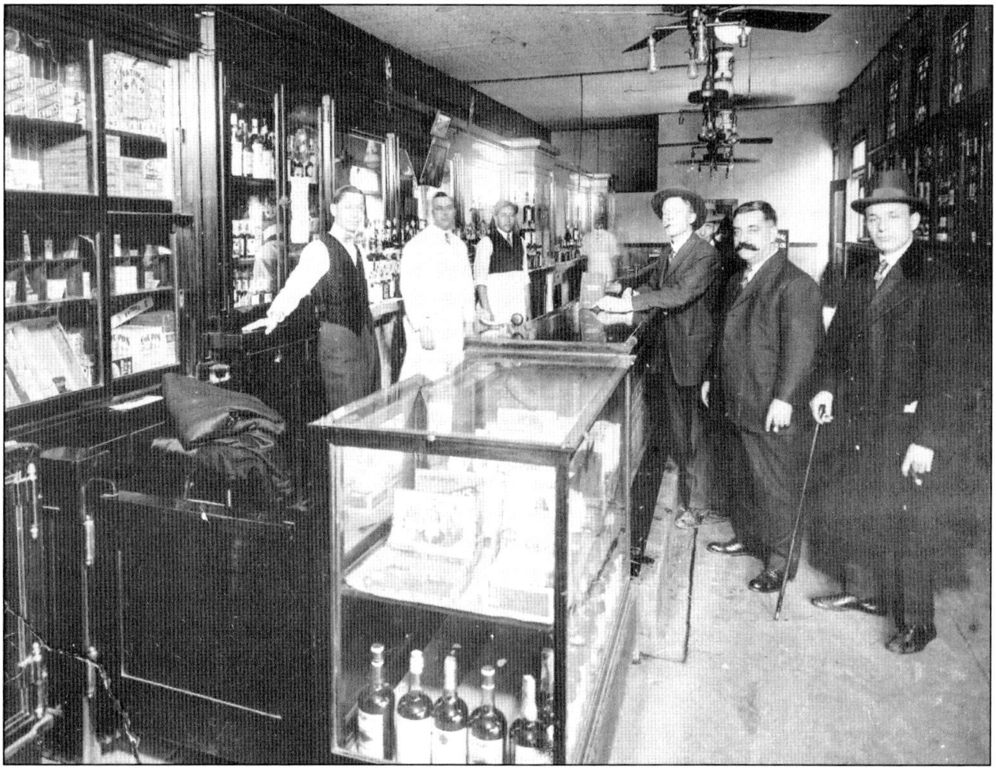

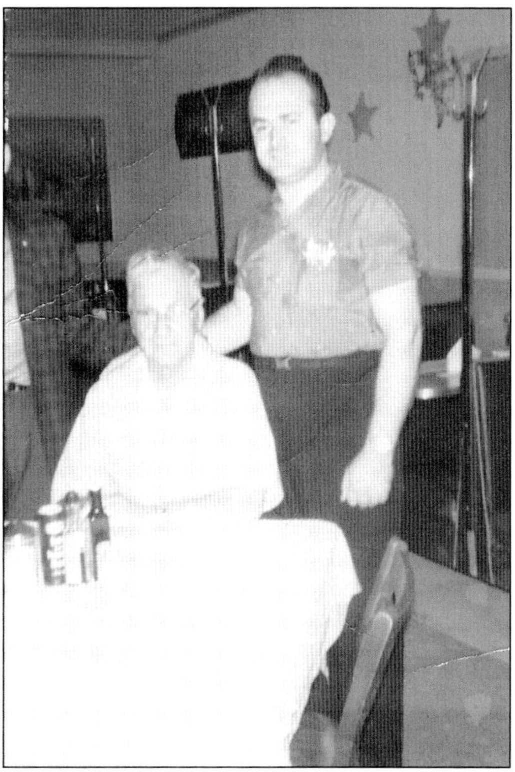

The most common Greek businesses, located downtown, were confectioneries and small cafés, such as the Royal Café, owned by George Picramenos; the Blue Front and the Elite, owned by George Petheriotes; The Presto, owned by Victor Boozalis; and Olympia Candy Kitchen, owned by Theodore Picramenos and Nick Giannoukos. Tom and James Papadakis owned the original James Coney Island, a Houston landmark on Rusk Street. (Courtesy of HMRC.)

From left to right are Theodosios Christofides (Theodore Christie) and James (Priovolos) Christie. Theodore emigrated from Asia Minor to the United States in 1908. He arrived in Houston in 1934 and became a successful restaurateur. James Priovolos and Steve Zoes, cousins, worked for Theodore and, eventually, bought the restaurants. Out of respect, they took the name Christie. James and his family continue to run Christie's Seafood & Steak Restaurant, one of the oldest family-owned restaurants in Houston. (Courtesy of the Christie children.)

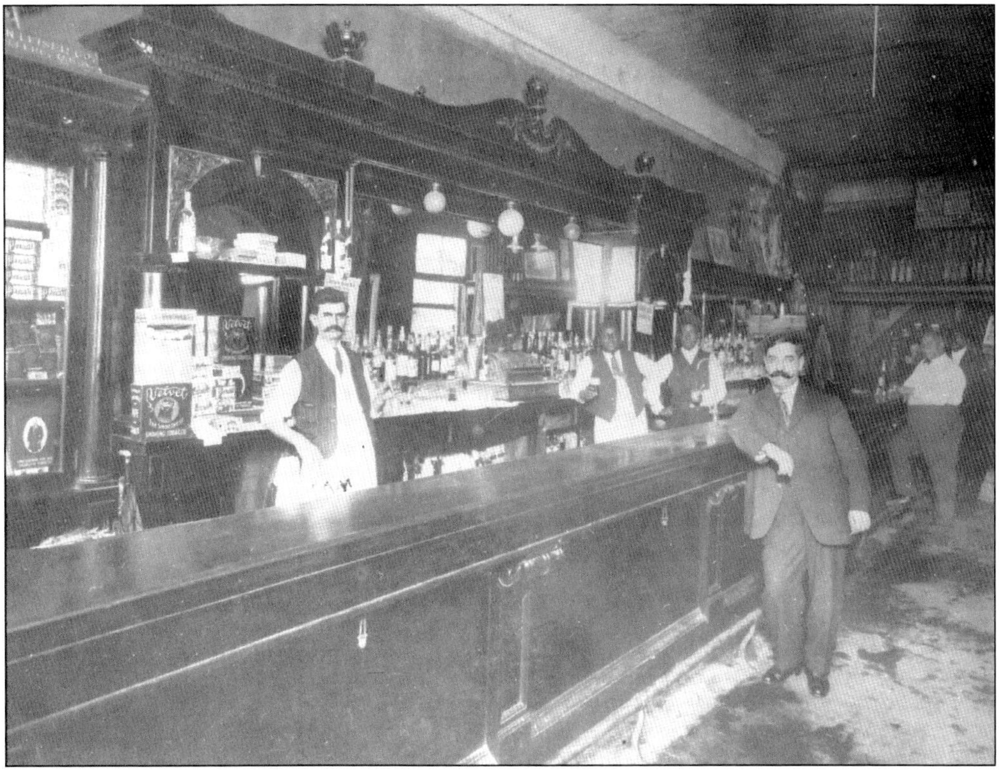

Men came to Houston intending to return to Greece as soon as they had made their fortunes. Starting with menial jobs, they worked themselves up to owning businesses. For example, Pete Menutes opened his saloon in 1914 and later owned several saloons and the National Liquor Supply. Prohibition put him out of business, and he opened a confectionery. (Courtesy of HMRC.)

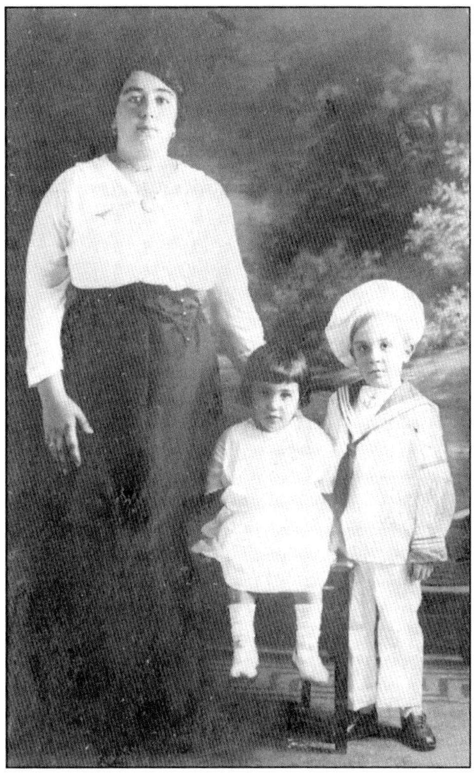

Glykeria (née Kostas) Seitanidis came from Asia Minor to the United States to join her husband Alexander Seitanidis in 1913. He died in 1920, leaving her with three children under the age of six. She later married Nicholas Brailas, a widower, in 1922. She is shown with her children Helen (Sallas) and George Seitanidis (Standish). (Courtesy of Olga Poulos.)

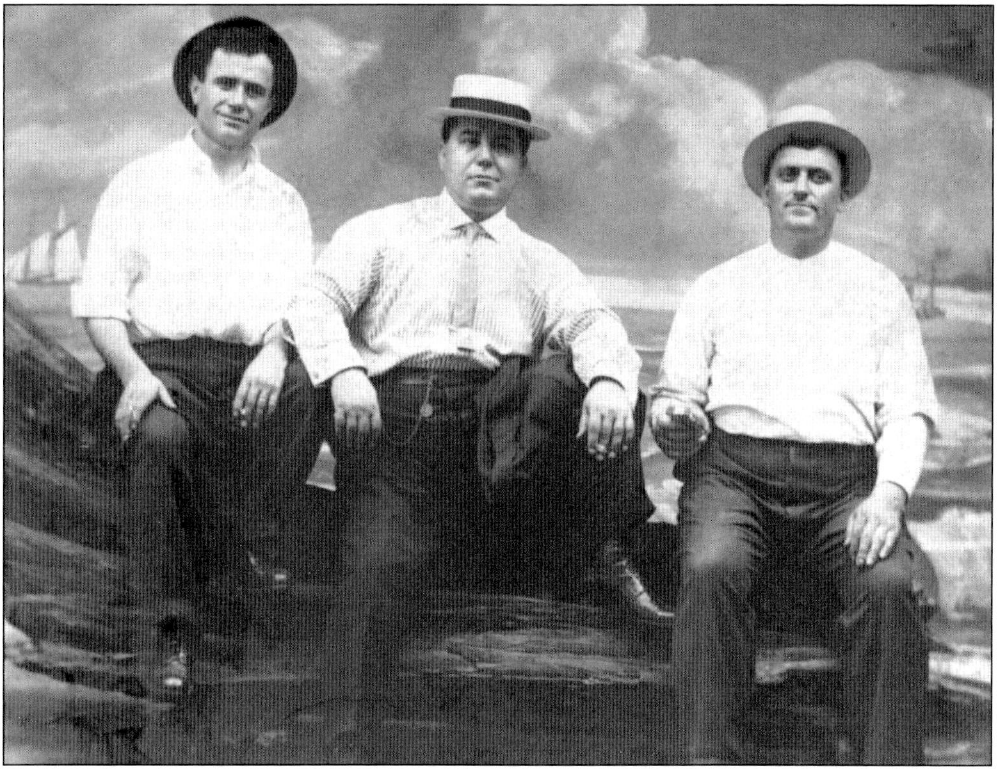

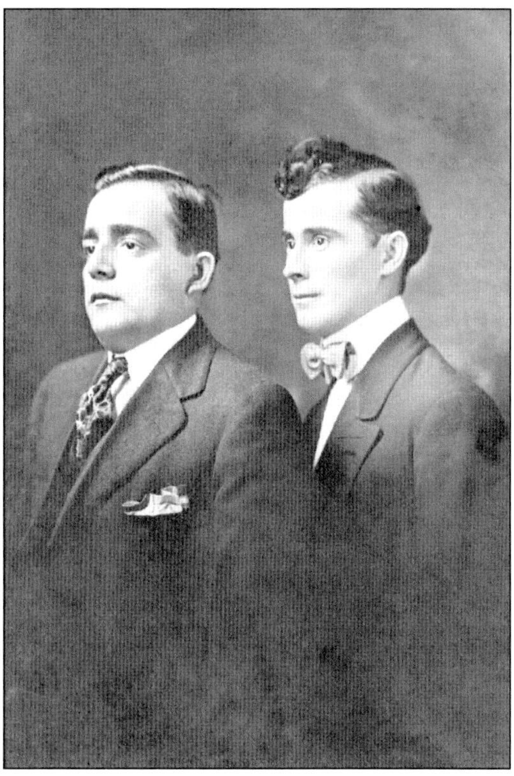

From left to right, George N. Picramenos (Peet), Christos Malavansos, and George Malavansos are posing on the ever-present driftwood at Galveston, across from the Buccaneer Hotel, in 1915. "Galveston was the town! It only cost a dollar to go on the Interurban; you caught it at Texas and Milam Streets," said Fotini "Fofo" Catsinas DeClaris. Chris Malavansos was the second president of the parish council in 1919, and George N. Picramenos was the seventh president of the parish council in 1924. (Courtesy of HMRC.)

Evangelos Mytelinaeos (Mytilen) and Peter Mousouliotes (Moss) went into business for a short time. Then, Mousouliotes opened his own restaurant on Lamar Street in 1916–1917. The ELPIS minutes of August 28, 1919, report that E. Mytelinaeos was elected treasurer at a general meeting in the church. He was later elected president of the parish council from 1925 to 1933. (Courtesy of HMRC.)

Here is a portrait of Gus and Lela Malakos (Malos), owners of the Houstonian Restaurant between Main and Travis Streets in 1917–1918. Gus and Lela were Tina Colias's (Batmanis) godparents and distantly related to the family of Thomas and Angeliki Panos. Upon their death, they bequeathed the Malos fund for the needy at Annunciation. (Courtesy of HMRC.)

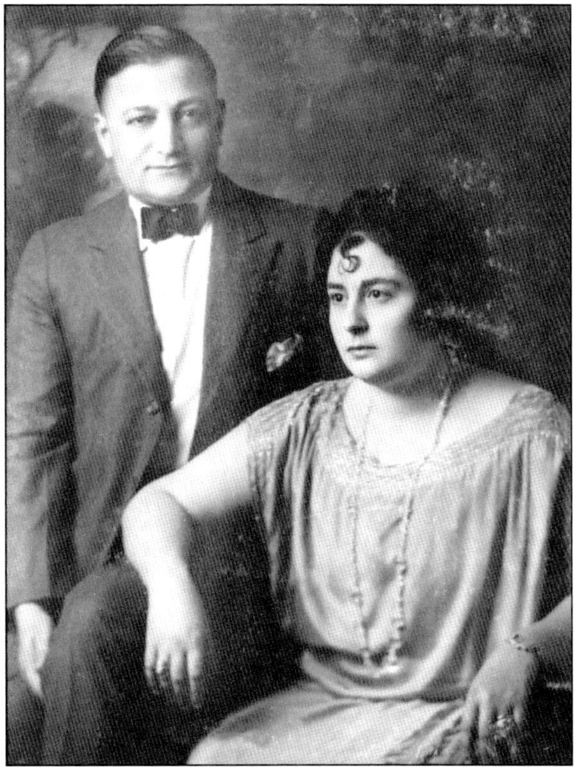

Arriving in America from Greece in 1919, Stavros Panousieris (Panos) found a job at a shine stand outside the Rice Hotel, where he buffed the boots of celebrities, such as Roy Rogers and Jesse Jones. After operating his own stand in an alley, Panos opened the Palace Boot Shop downtown on Fannin Street, later moving to the location near Houston's courthouse district. (Courtesy of the Annunciation Greek Orthodox Cathedral [AGOC] archives.)

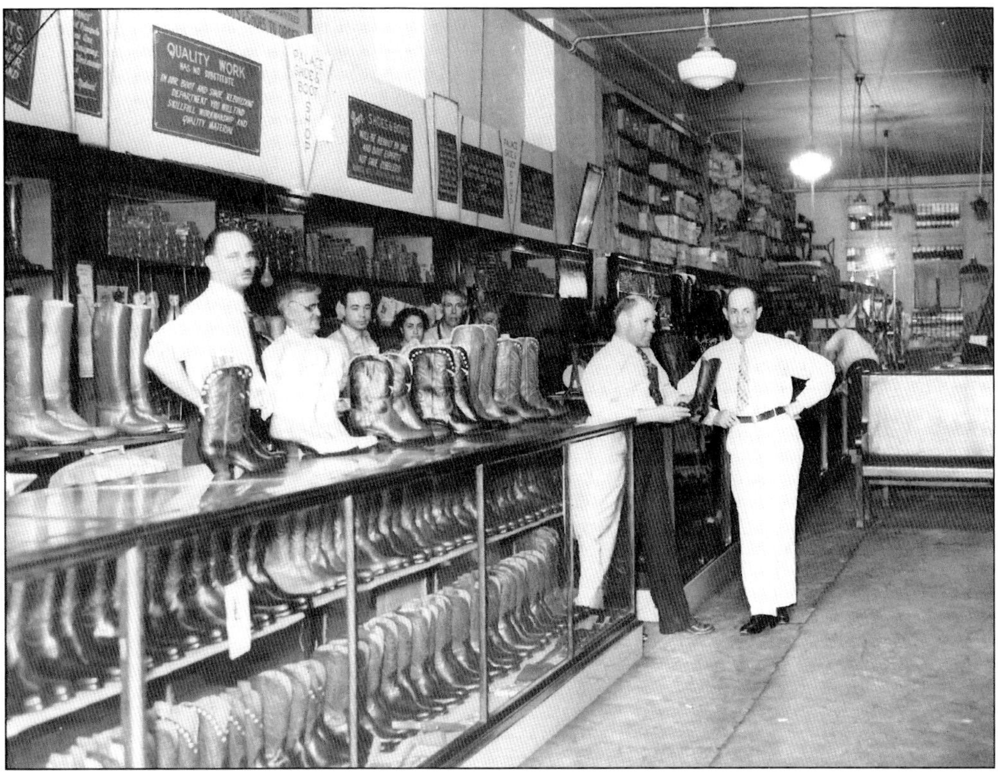

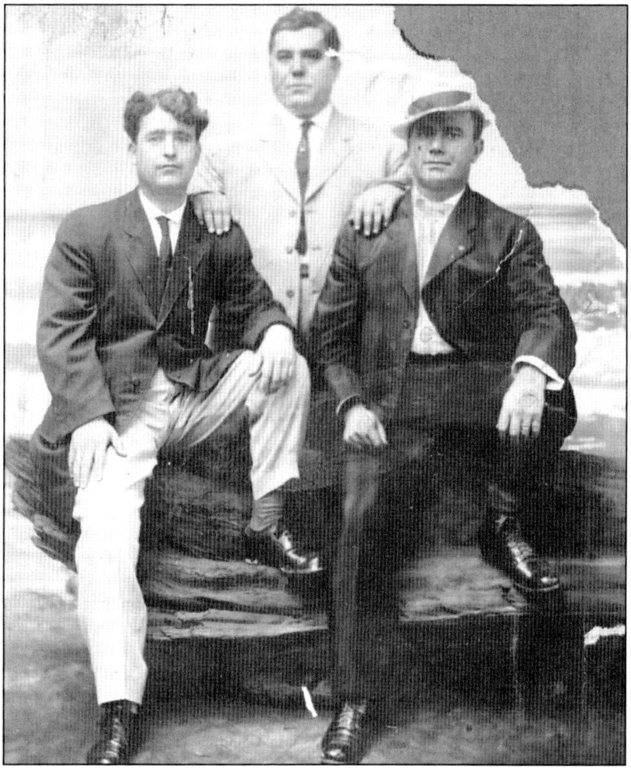

From left to right are John Papazoglakis (Papas), Chris Malavansos, and George Picramenos (Peet) at Murdock's in Galveston in 1919. Chris Malavansos owned Chris [sic] Palace, and George Picramenos owned the Royal Café, both in Houston. All three men served as president of the parish council: Chris Malavansos was the second president in 1919, George N. Picramenos was the seventh president in 1924, and John Papazoglakis was the twelfth from 1929 to 1939. (Courtesy of HMRC.)

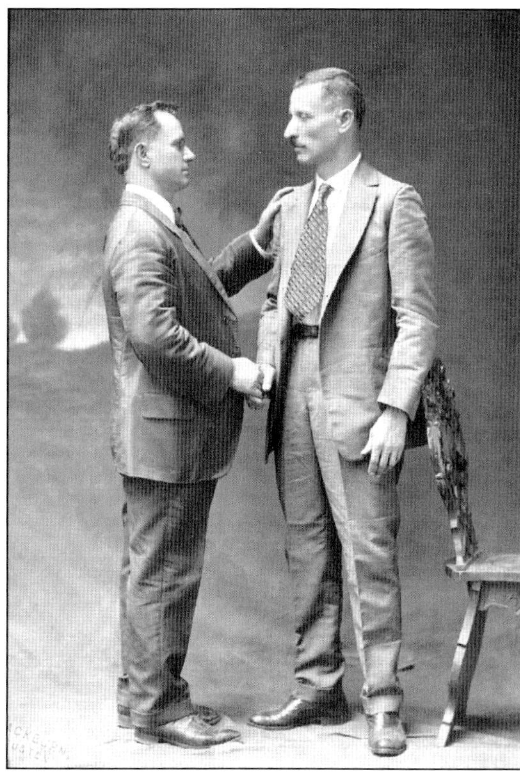

From left to right are George Picramenos (Peet) and a close friend. George considered Texas to be a progressive state. He invested heavily in oil and real estate and persuaded many of the old Greeks to buy land, which became profitable in 1920. George Picramenos was elected president of the parish council in 1924. (Courtesy of HMRC.)

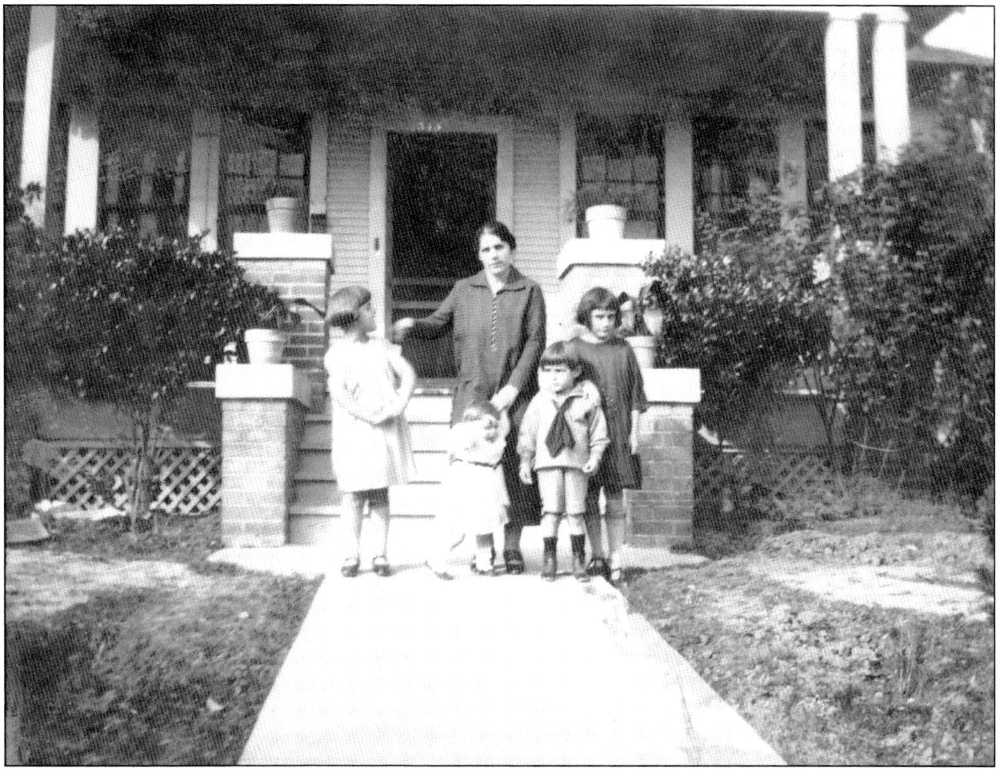

Posing in front of George N. Petheriotes's house at 4515 McKinney Street in the east end in the early 1920s are Sophia Petheriotes with her children (from left to right) Katherine, Angelo, and James; Mary Peet is on the right in the dark dress. The Petheriotes family bought that house when it was new and never moved. George owned the Elite Café. (Courtesy of HMRC.)

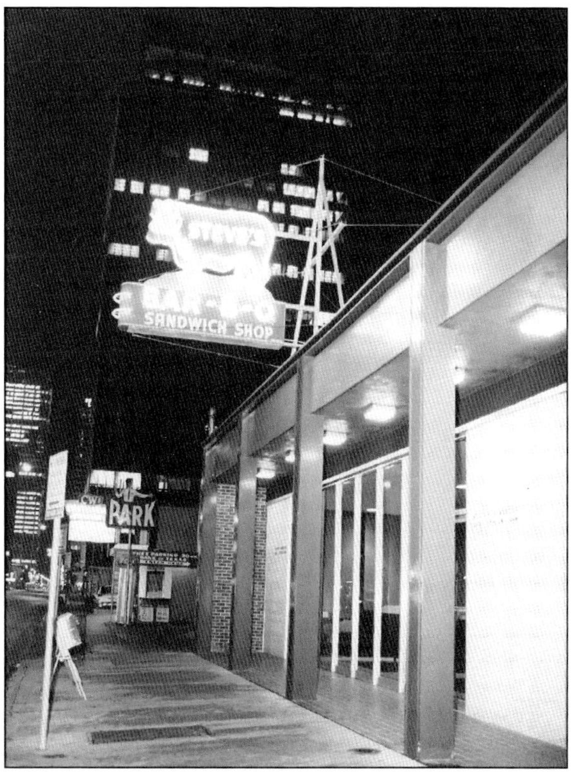

Stavros (Steve) Caloudas left Chios at the age of 17. When he arrived in New York in 1920, he left behind a widowed mother and two sisters. He worked menial jobs to bring his family to America. By the 1960s, Caloudas built a chain of cafés. He established seven Steve's Bar-B-Q Sandwich Shops in downtown Houston and was known as the "baron of barbecue." (Courtesy of Steve Caloudas Jr.)

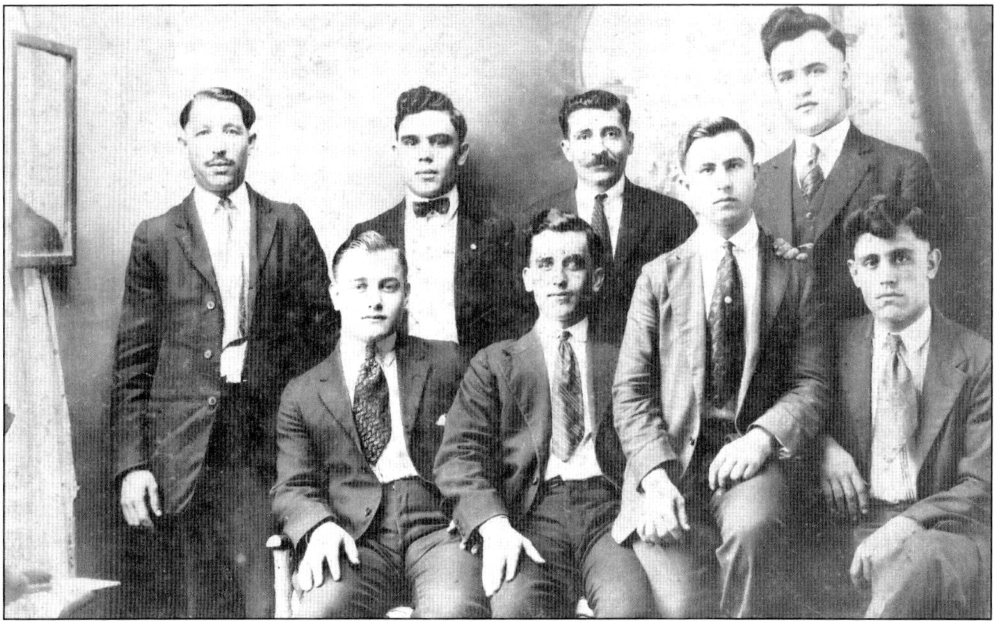

Here is a gathering of friends from the island of Patmos, Greece, in Houston in 1922. The photograph was taken to send back to parents and relatives in Patmos. Pictured are, from left to right, (first row) James Coronis, ? Tsochalis, Anastasi Mickelis, and Pete Voinis; (second row) Anastasi Keffalas, unidentified, Theodore Voinis, and Nicholas Voinis. (Courtesy of HMRC.)

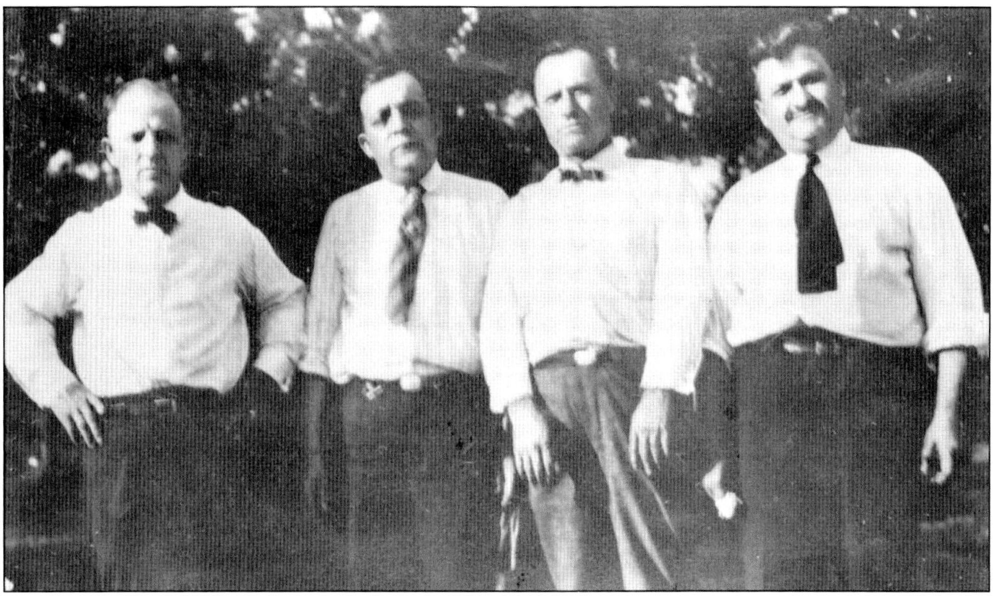

From left to right are George Petheriotes, married to Sophia Mytelinaeos (Mytelin); Evangelos (Angelo) Mytelinaeos, never married; George Picramenos (Peet), married to Constantina Mytelinaeos; and John Kousakis, married to Anastacia Mytelinaeos. They are brothers-in-law enjoying the Greek community picnic in 1922–1923. George Petheriotes was fifth president of the parish council (1921–1922); George N. Picramenos was the seventh president of the parish council (1924); and Evangelos Mytelinaeos was the eighth president of the parish council (1925–1933). (Courtesy of HMRC.)

From left to right, the Papazoglakis family members are, in 1923–1924, mother Georgia, father John, and children Freida, Evangeline, Thalia, and Louis. The children shortened their name to Papas. John Papazoglakis was the president of the parish council from 1929 to 1939. Thalia served on the parish council, and her husband, Andrew Vassiliades, was president (1955). Thalia was also active in the Daughters of Penelope and was named National Penelope of the Year. (Courtesy of HMRC.)

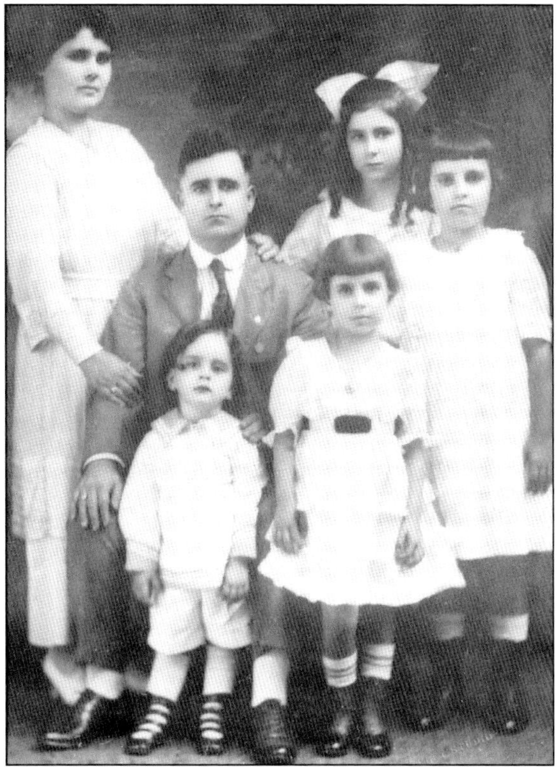

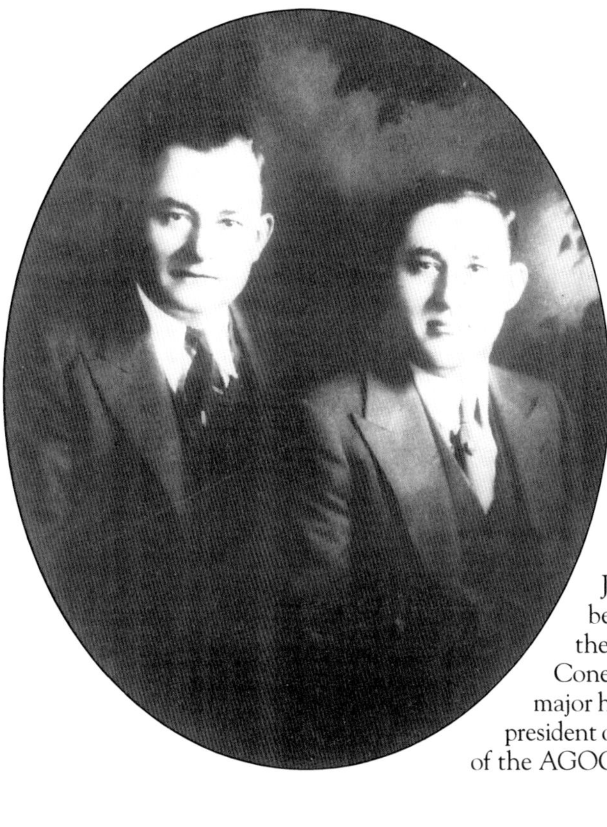

James Coney Island Inc. is a chain of fast-food restaurants in Houston that specializes in Coney Island hot dogs. Two Greek immigrant brothers, James and Tom Papadakis, the former being the company's namesake, founded the company in 1923. The original James Coney Island restaurant was one of the first major hot dog vendors in Houston. James was president of the parish council in 1938. (Courtesy of the AGOC archives.)

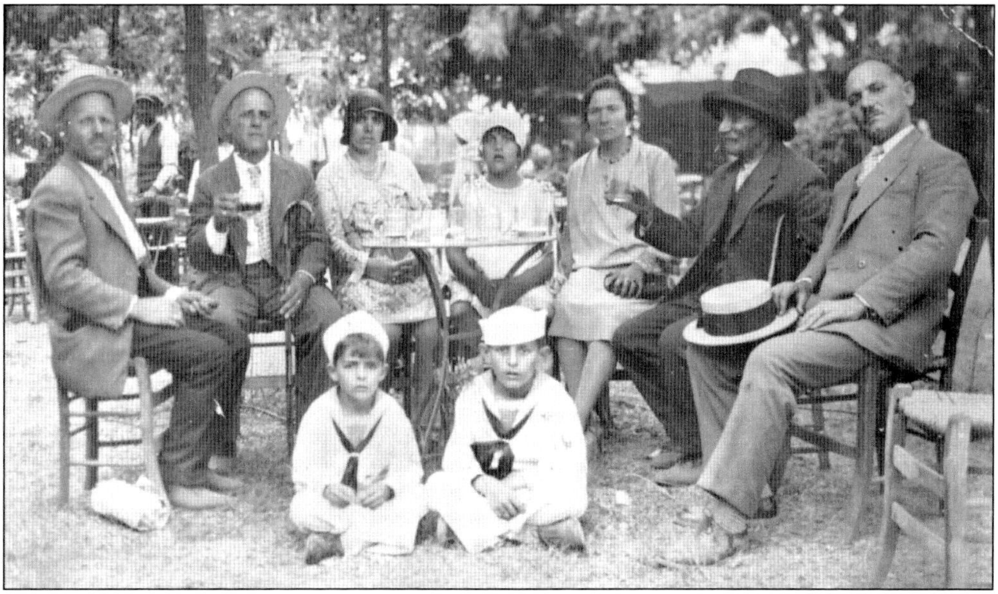

George Petheriotes married Sophia Mytelinaeos (Mytilen) around 1925. The family returned to their hometown of Tripoli, Greece, to visit his brothers and sister in 1929. George's brothers Paul and Chris had immigrated to Houston but, after a few years, returned to live in Greece. George was the only family member to remain in the United States. (Courtesy of HMRC.)

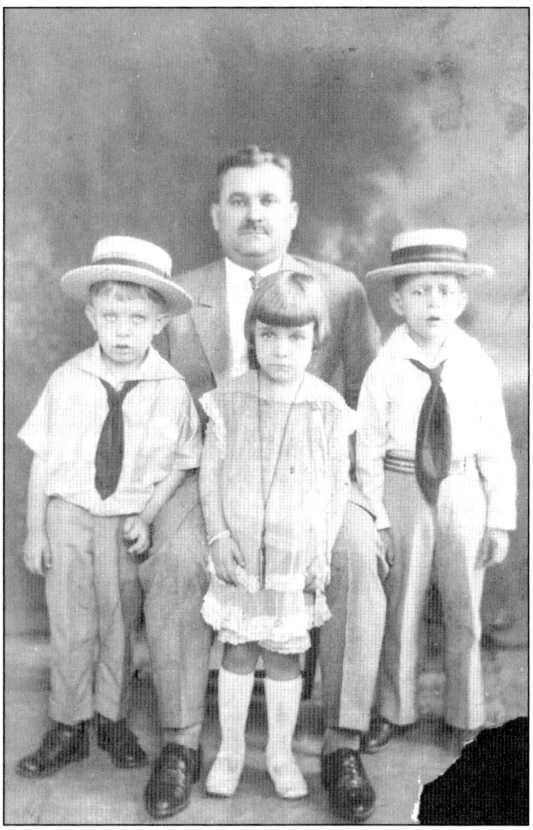

John Kousakis, who married Anastacia Mytelinaeos (Mytelin), is pictured with his children Peter and Matina (Bournias) and nephew Willie Peet in 1926. In the ELPIS minutes of March 21, 1917, John Kousakis was elected as one of the members of the parish council. (Courtesy of HMRC.)

The children of George Picramenos (Peet) and his wife, Constantina (Mytelinaeos), are pictured here from left to right in 1926–1927: Nick, James, Bessie, and Mary. The children all played instruments. The girls played the piano, and the boys played the violin and the mandolin. "Our dad made us play together all the time," one of the children said. Nick Peet was one of the founders of the first choir at Annunciation in 1937. Bessie Peet was the first woman to be elected to the parish council in 1977. (Courtesy of HMRC.)

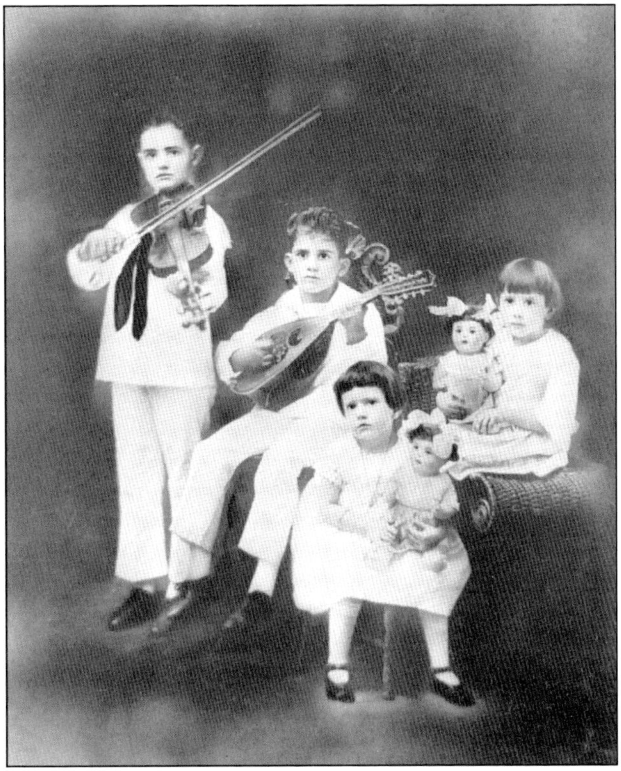

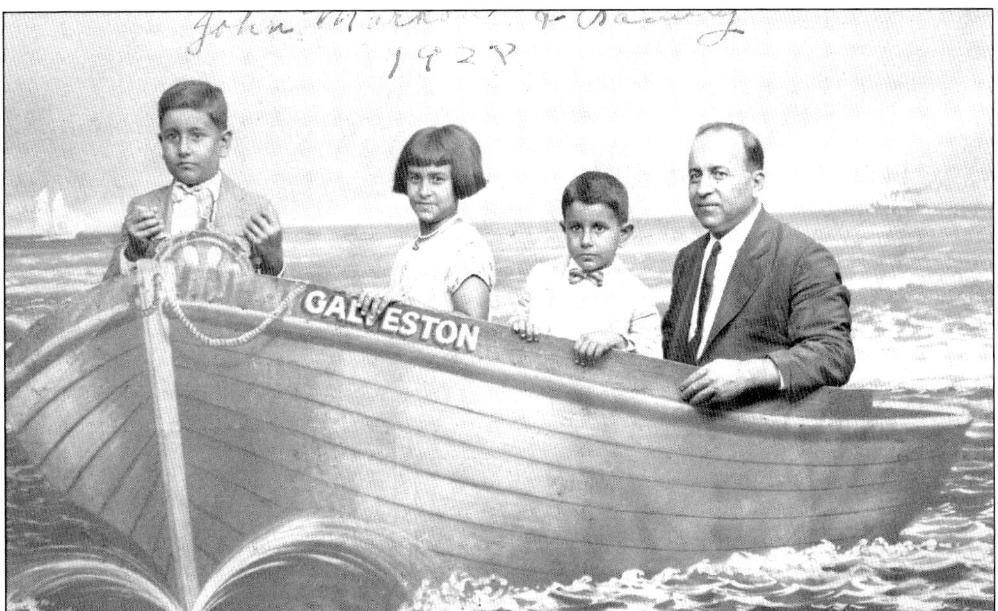

John Markou is shown with children (from left to right) Mark, Anastasia (Caridas), and Paul in 1928. Markou was the husband of Irene Coronis, who died in childbirth before this photograph was taken. The children were sent to Patmos, Greece, where the two boys died. The daughter, Anastasia, was also taken very ill but recovered and eventually returned to Houston. (Courtesy of HMRC.)

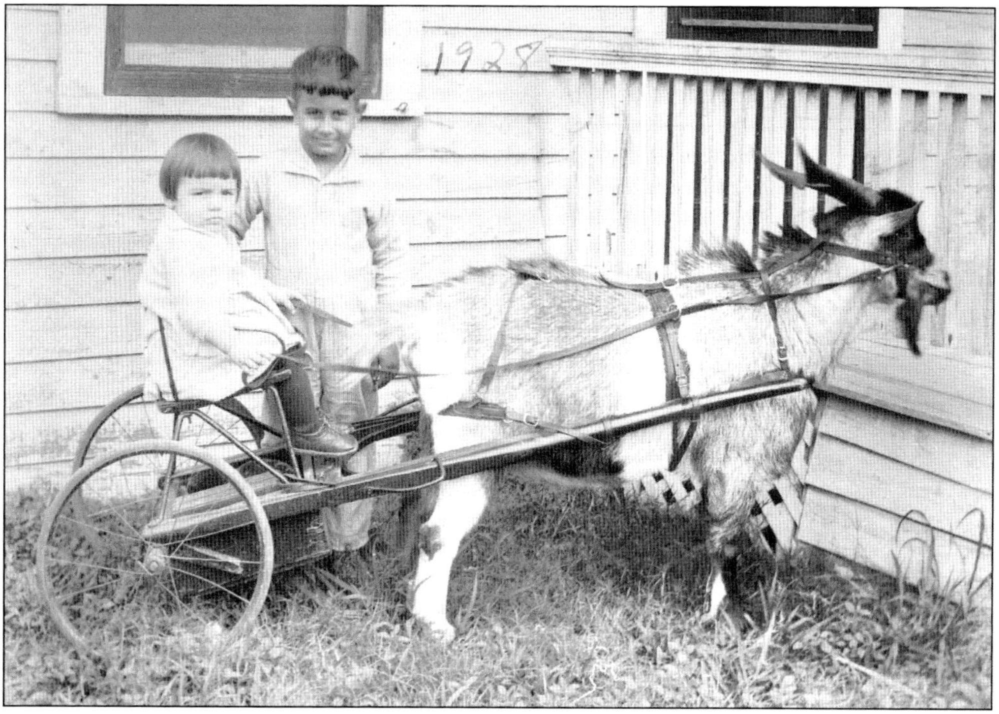

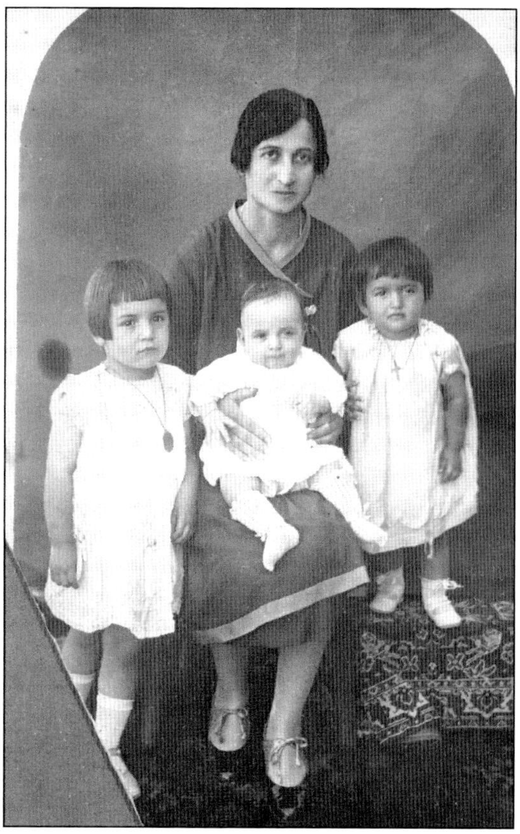

First cousins Irene Voinis (Chilivetis) and Paul Coronis are outside the modest rental home of Nick and Amalia Voinis on Alamo Street in Houston in 1928. Many Patmian families also resided in that area, preserving their customs and traditions and welcoming immigrants to the neighborhood. This fellowship helped the new arrivals ease into the American way of life. (Courtesy of HMRC.)

Amalia Coronis Voinis and her two children, Irene and Katherine, visited relatives in Patmos in 1929, leaving her husband, Nick, behind. However, she did not know she was pregnant at the time and could not return home. When the Depression followed after George was born, it was hard to raise money for their trip. Eventually, in 1933, Paul Coronis, Amalia's father, escorted the family back to Houston. (Courtesy of HMRC.)

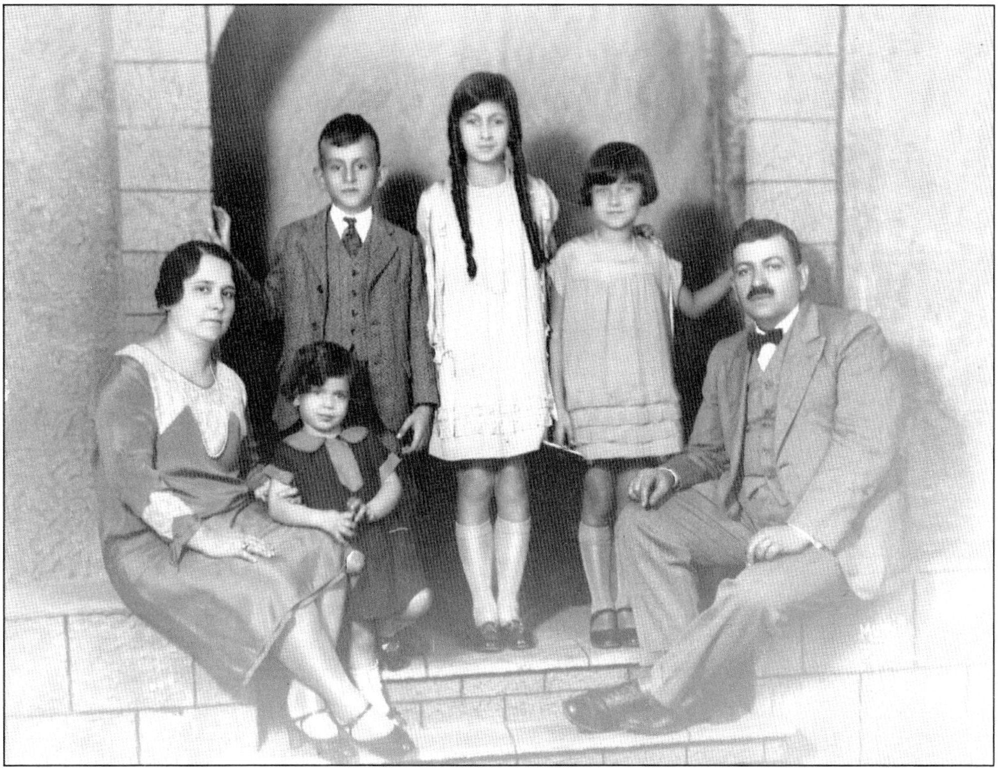

This portrait of the Catsinas family was taken at Murrillo Studio in the 1930s. From left to right are Catherine Pantelaki Catsinas, mother and housewife; Margaret Catsinas Kochauf, opera singer in Europe; Nicholas James Catsinas; Fofo Catsinas DeClaris; Anastasia Catsinas York, secretary; and Dimitrios Nicholas Catsinas, who had a produce stand at the old farmers' market at city hall. Fofo Catsinas DeClaris was the administrative assistant to several priests at Annunciation Greek Orthodox Cathedral from 1967 until the early 1990s. (Courtesy of HMRC.)

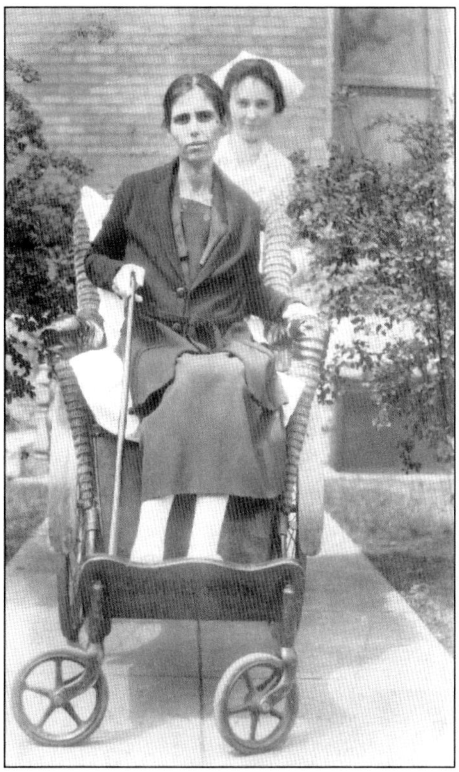

From about the 1930s, when this photograph was taken, Kaliope Picramenos (Peet) was always in poor health. The family lived on Stiles Street, near Harrisburg. Kaliope had a private nurse whom the family could afford because her father owned a successful restaurant in downtown Houston that specialized in Coney Island hot dogs. (Courtesy of HMRC.)

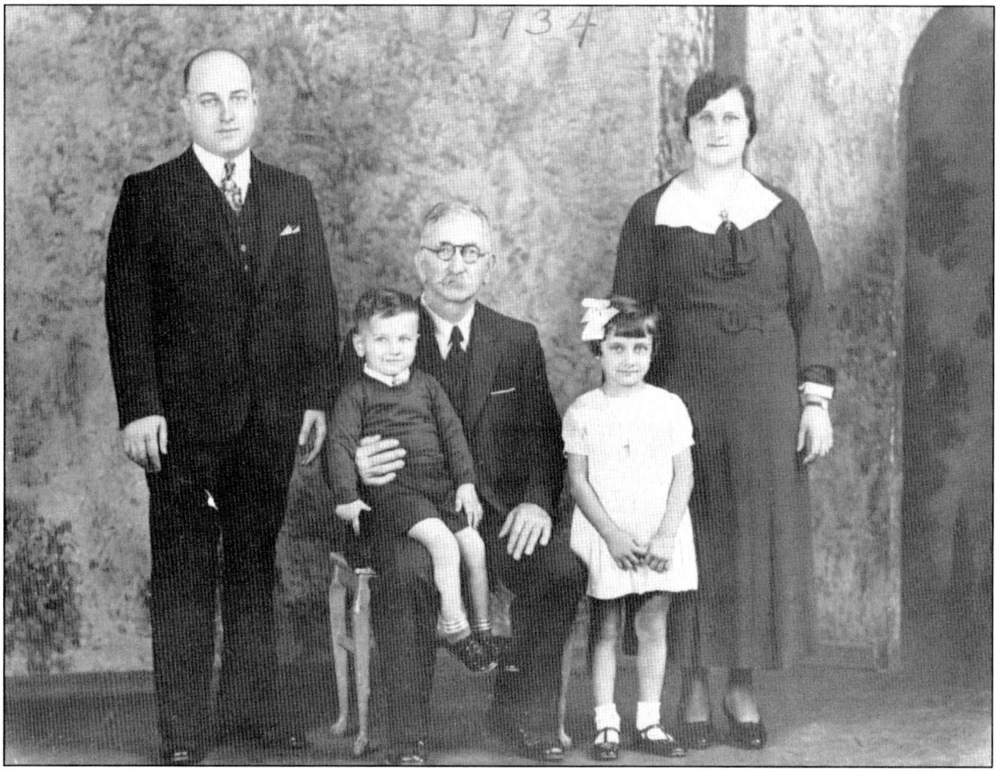

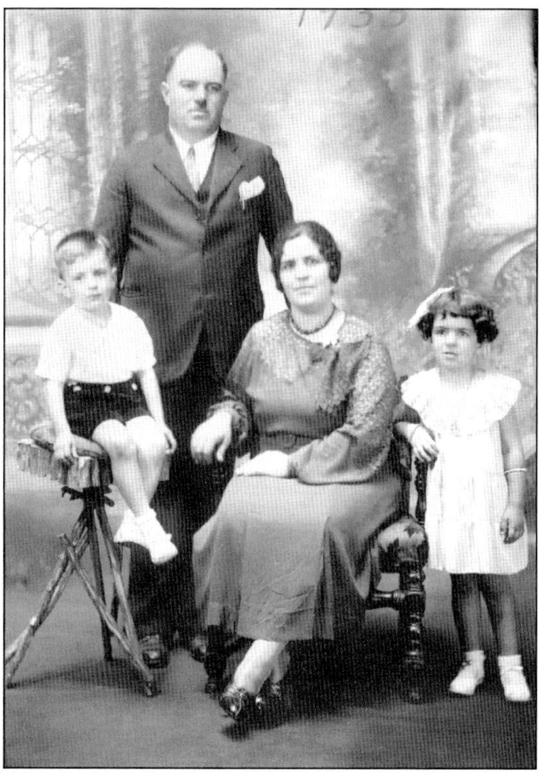

James Coronis (left) is seen with his father, Paul; his wife, Helen; and daughter Mary (Chilivetis) and son Paul, named after the grandfather (*papou*), which was customary. This family portrait was made in 1935, before the grandfather returned to Patmos. (Courtesy of HMRC.)

Alexander Koumondouros family members, pictured in 1935, are wife, Christine Christodouli; son John, and daughter Katherine (Economides). Another son George was born in 1936. The family moved to Houston in 1947, where Alexander was a restaurateur. He died at the age of 57 of heart disease. (Courtesy of Katherine Economides.)

From left to right are George Voinis, Arthur Fotinos (with hat), and his children John and Irene in 1937. Arthur Fotinos and Nick Voinis (not pictured) were partners in the Lone Star Café. (Courtesy of HMRC.)

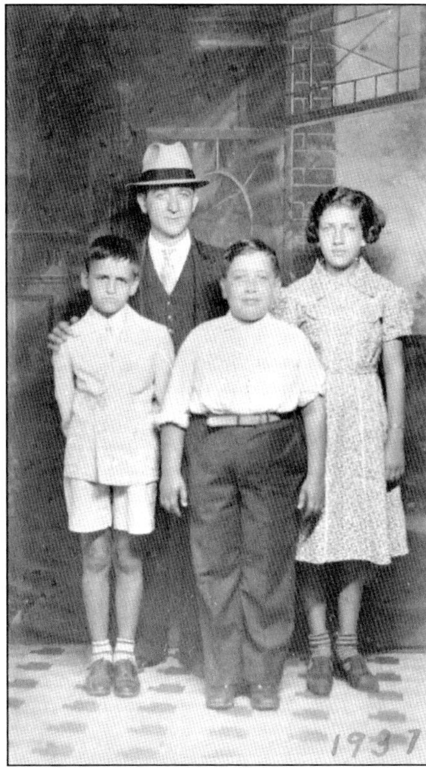

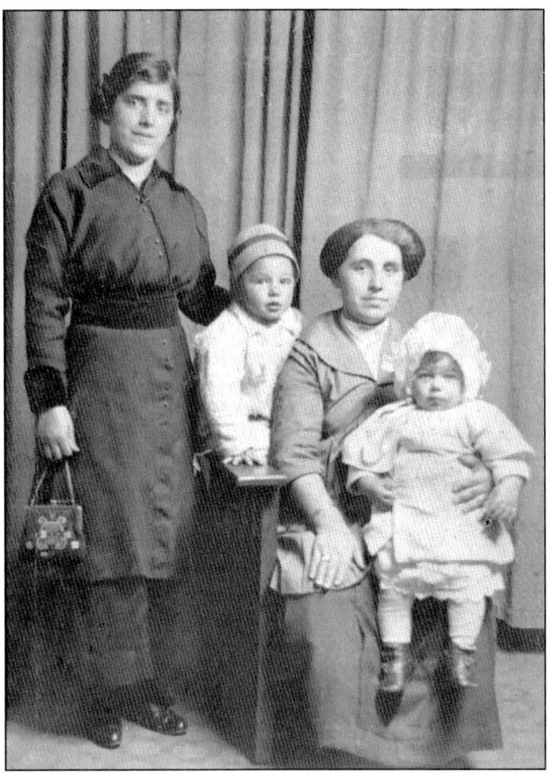

Here is a portrait of, from left to right, Sophia Petheriotes, Harry Verges, Faye Verges, and Bessie Verges. Sophia Mytelinaeos married George Petheriotes, and Faye Mytelinaeos married George Verges. They were sisters. Harry and Bessie were Faye's children. (Courtesy of HMRC.)

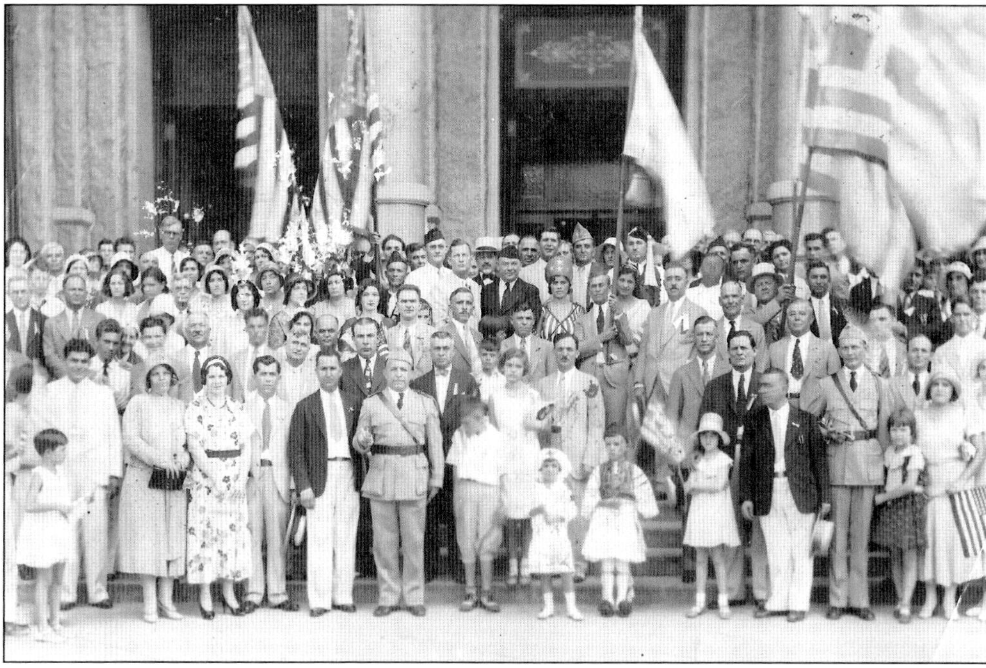

Houstonian Paul G. Pavlides, pictured to the left of the officer in the front row, is attending a gathering in Athens in 1940. Paul served as president of the parish council in 1936. (Courtesy of George Gazis.)

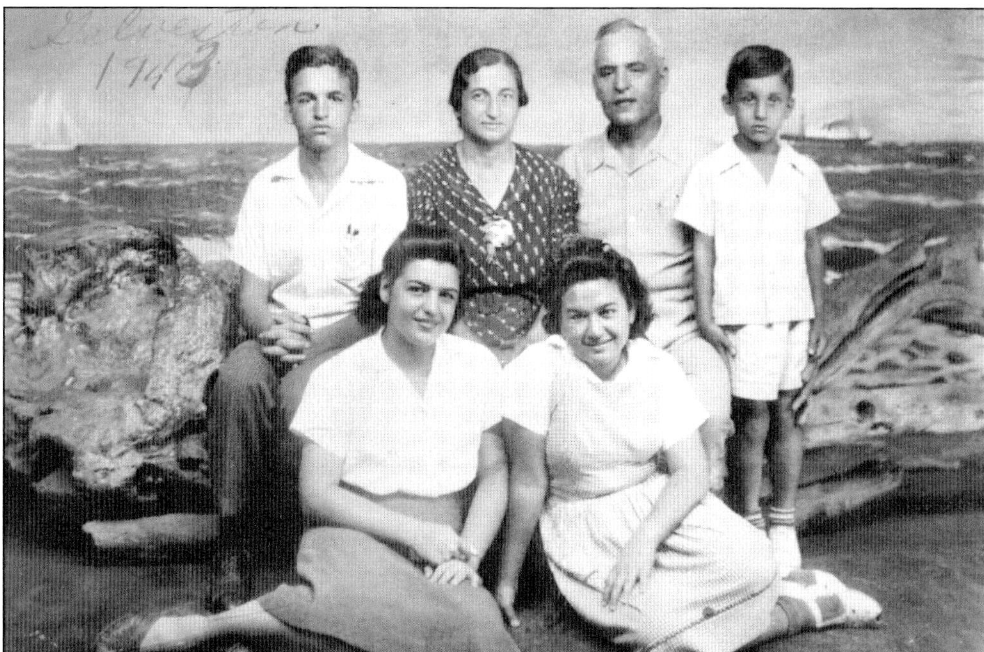

The Voinis family is seen at Murdock's in Galveston in 1943. From left to right are (first row) Irene Voinis (Chilivetis) and Katherine Voinis (Cramer); (second row) George Voinis, Amalia Voinis, Nick George Voinis, and Steve Paul Voinis. Nick Voinis was one of the first Patmians to own an automobile. (Courtesy of HMRC.)

The Gazelas family is shown in Lesvos, Greece, in 1946. George Gazelas (not pictured) served in France in World War I and was awarded American citizenship for his children and himself. His wife, Chrysanthe Gazelas, taught herself to read and write in order to get her citizenship papers. Pictured are, from left to right, (first row) Aristedis "Harry," Titika (Liollio), and Toula (Kaldanis); (second row) Chrysanthe holding Irene (Cassis). (Courtesy of Irene Cassis.)

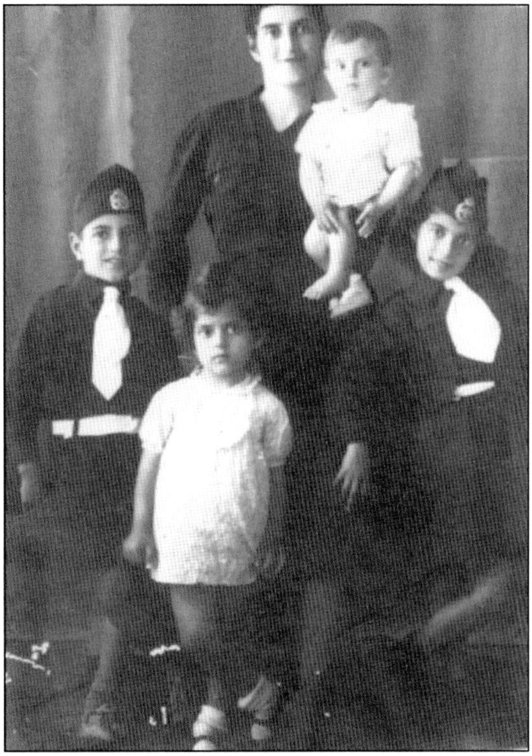

On April 6–8, 1947, graduates of the University of Texas, College of Pharmacy in Austin, are seen in front of the Lilly Research Laboratories. These graduates were guests of Eli Lilly and Company. Manuel Gazis, a graduate of this program, is seated in the first row, ninth from the left. James Bellos later graduated from University of Texas, College of Pharmacy in 1951. (Courtesy of George Gazis.)

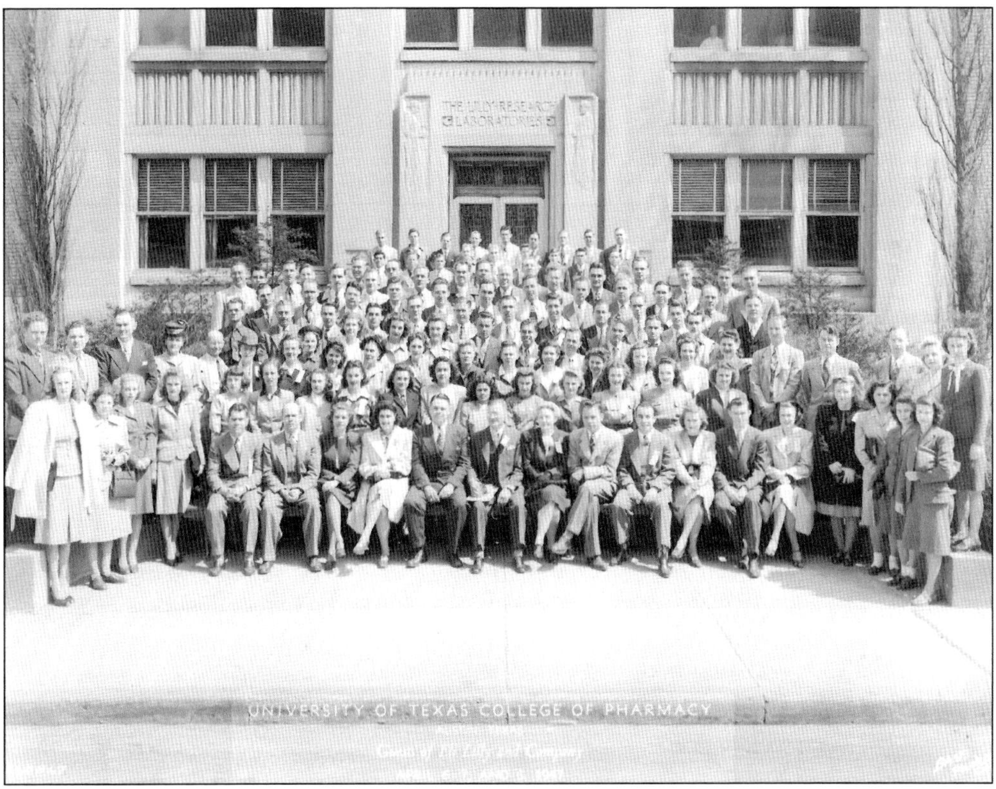

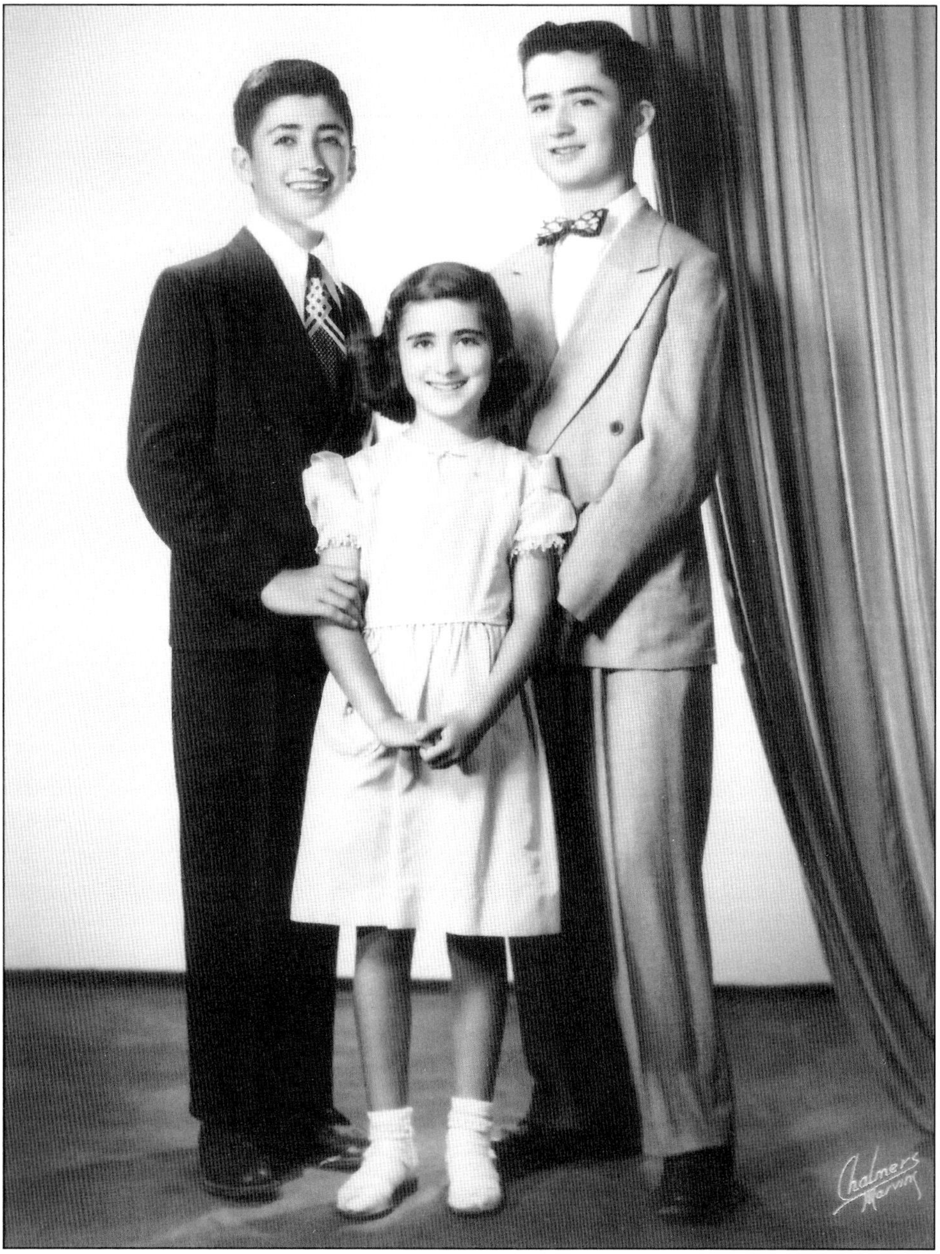

From left to right, George, Georgia, and Anastasios Papasarandopoulos witnessed their mother Evyenia's execution by Greek communist guerillas on July 20, 1944; their father, Aristeide, was executed two months later. "My father made the ultimate sacrifice to preserve the integrity of Greece by joining and fighting in the Resistance during the Civil War of Greece. After our parents' deaths, our infant brother Vasili died of starvation. Maternal absence and Germany's occupation of Greece during World War II were the factors that caused this tragedy," said Georgia. Under the Displaced Greek Orphans Act, the Papasarandopoulos children arrived in the United States in 1951. After passing through Ellis Island, they traveled to Ogden, Utah, where their uncle and sponsor, William G. Sarandos, lived. Finally, in September 1951, they were welcomed to Houston by Steve T. Boozalis, their father's cousin, and his family. (Courtesy of Georgia Poutous.)

In 1947, Frank A. Demeris (pictured) brought his children Kosta (Gus) and Georgia to the United States to escape civil unrest following the German occupation in Greece. Gus started working at Steve's Bar-B-Q Sandwich Shop in downtown Houston. Within a year, he brought his mother and brothers, Nick and Jimmy, to Houston. Gus and his father founded the G&N Café, which became Demeris Barbecue, the third largest catering company in Houston. (Courtesy of the AGOC archives.)

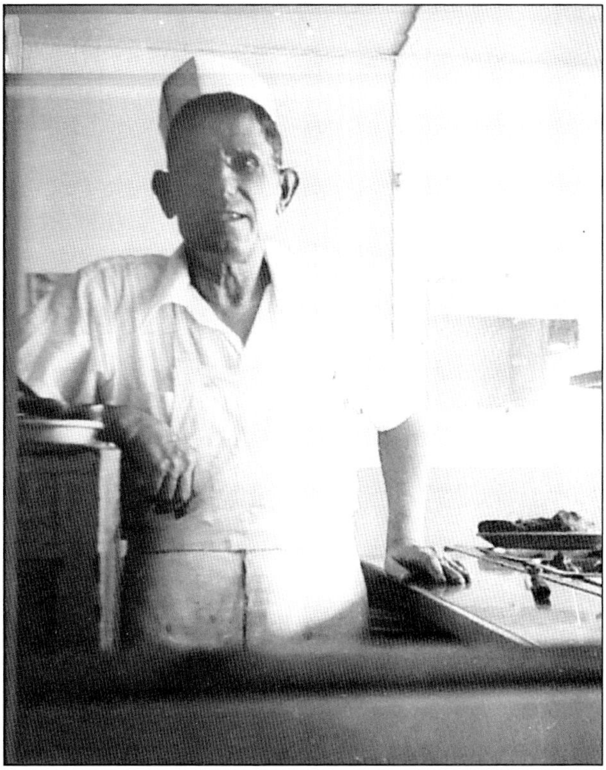

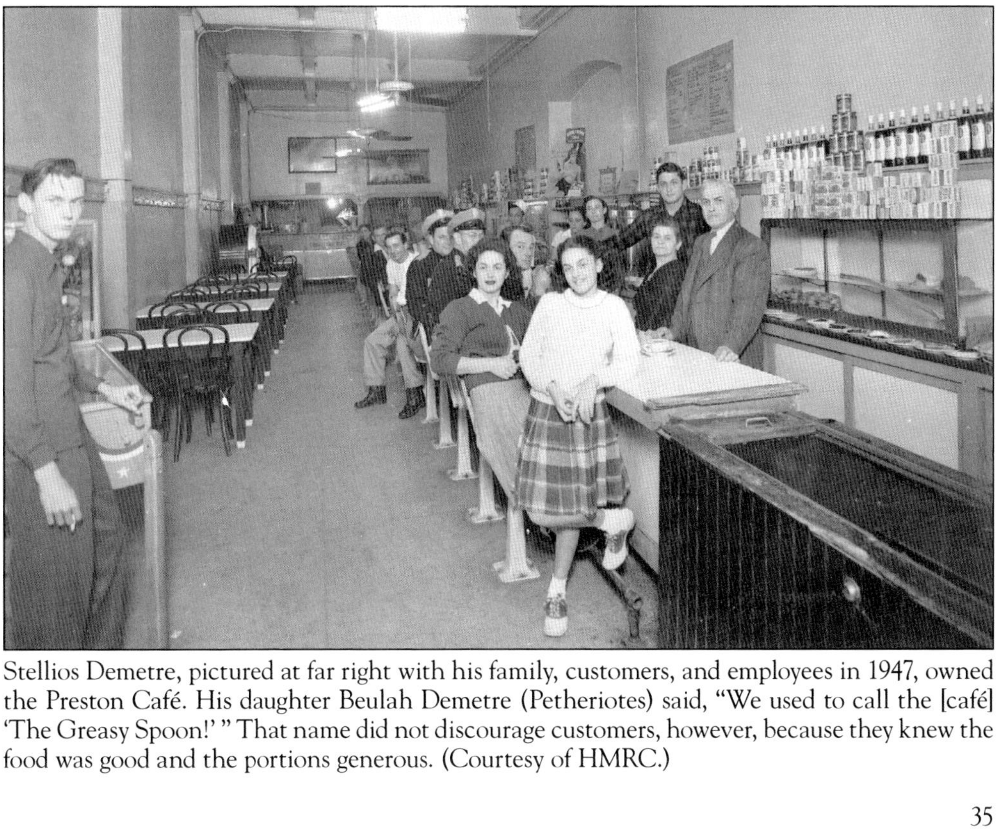

Stellios Demetre, pictured at far right with his family, customers, and employees in 1947, owned the Preston Café. His daughter Beulah Demetre (Petheriotes) said, "We used to call the [café] 'The Greasy Spoon!' " That name did not discourage customers, however, because they knew the food was good and the portions generous. (Courtesy of HMRC.)

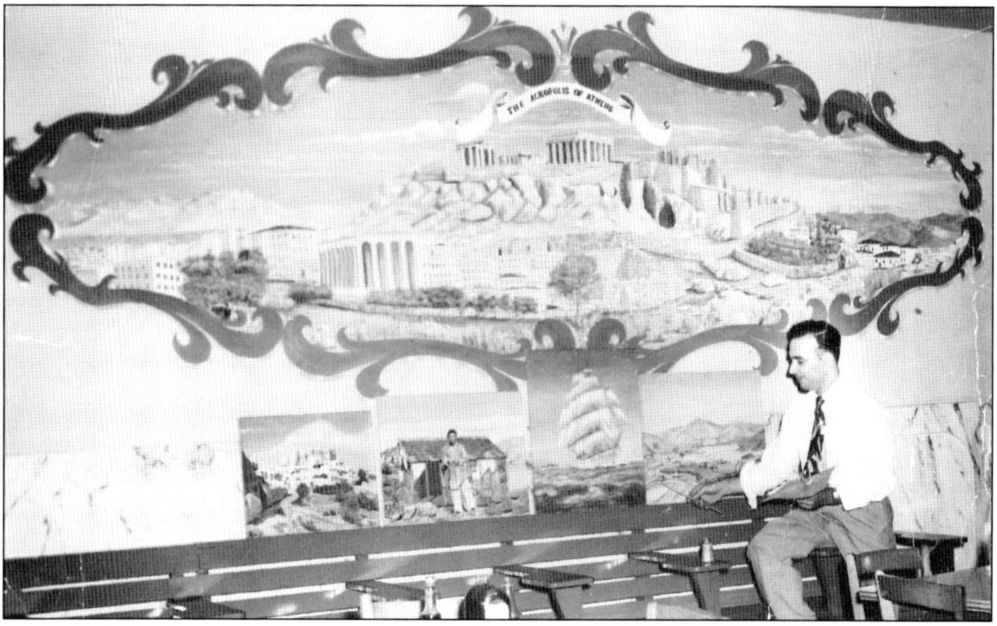

Nick Mickelis, from Patmos, Greece, arrived with $2.50 in his pocket and a note pinned to his jacket that read, "Houston," in 1948. Working in his brother's restaurant, he saved enough to buy a barbecue restaurant. Nick painted murals on the walls because he could not afford canvas. Nick and his wife, Pat, bought Cleburne Cafeteria. Pictured is Nick Mickelis admiring his mural of the Acropolis. (Courtesy of the AGOC archives.)

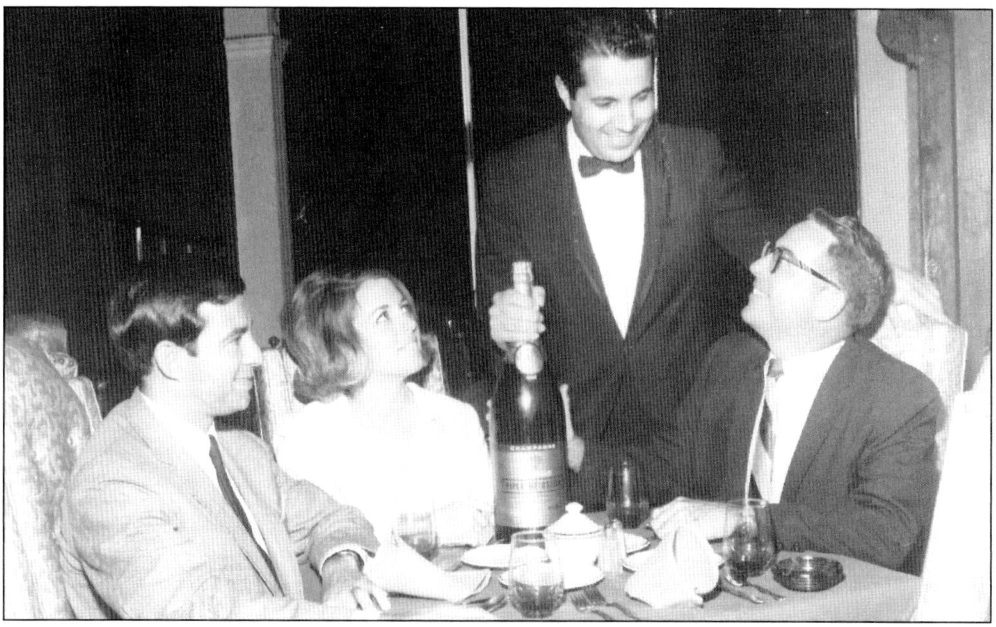

Spiros "Leo" Kalantzakis (standing) came from Patmos in 1955. By 1960, he began to acquire restaurants. At one time, he owned 24 restaurants and clubs. In 1965, he opened The Parthenon, the first Greek restaurant in Houston, and brought a band from Greece every six months that presented a live show seven days a week. Kalantzakis helped popularize the era of the supper club in Houston. (Courtesy of Leo Kalantzakis.)

Three

The Church Is Planted

While the immigrants were taking pains to establish themselves in their new homes, they desired their own church where they could worship as Orthodox Christians. They wanted to bring their children to church to solidify their small community. Since they had no church in Houston, they arranged for out-of-town priests to perform the liturgy and celebrate weddings, baptisms, and important holidays. These services were held in a rented hall downtown, the Royal Café's poolroom, or in other churches, such as the Christ Episcopal Church. In addition, families often traveled to Galveston to receive the sacraments at SS. Constantine and Helen Serbian Orthodox Church, which served Serbians, Russians, and Greeks.

After a liturgy held at Christ Episcopal Church on February 23, 1910, where a visiting priest from New Orleans officiated, a consensus was reached that the community would build its own church. In 1914, the Panhellenic Benevolent Brotherhood was founded. This organization, whose Greek letters spelled ELPIS, meaning "hope," became the nucleus of the church. They invited everyone who wished to build a church to become a part of this endeavor and even advertised for contributions in the *National Herald* and *Atlantis* newspapers.

On February 12, 1917, a committee was appointed to obtain a permit from the city for the erection of the church at 509 Walker Street. The committee also had to procure liturgical utensils, a liturgical gospel, and icons to adorn the church. Gus Makris was commissioned to paint the icons for the icon screen. These icons still hold cherished places in the Yoakum Boulevard church today. The parishioners voted to name the church Evangelismos of the Theotokos, and the Rev. Christos Hadjipapas celebrated inaugural services of the new church on February 10, 1918.

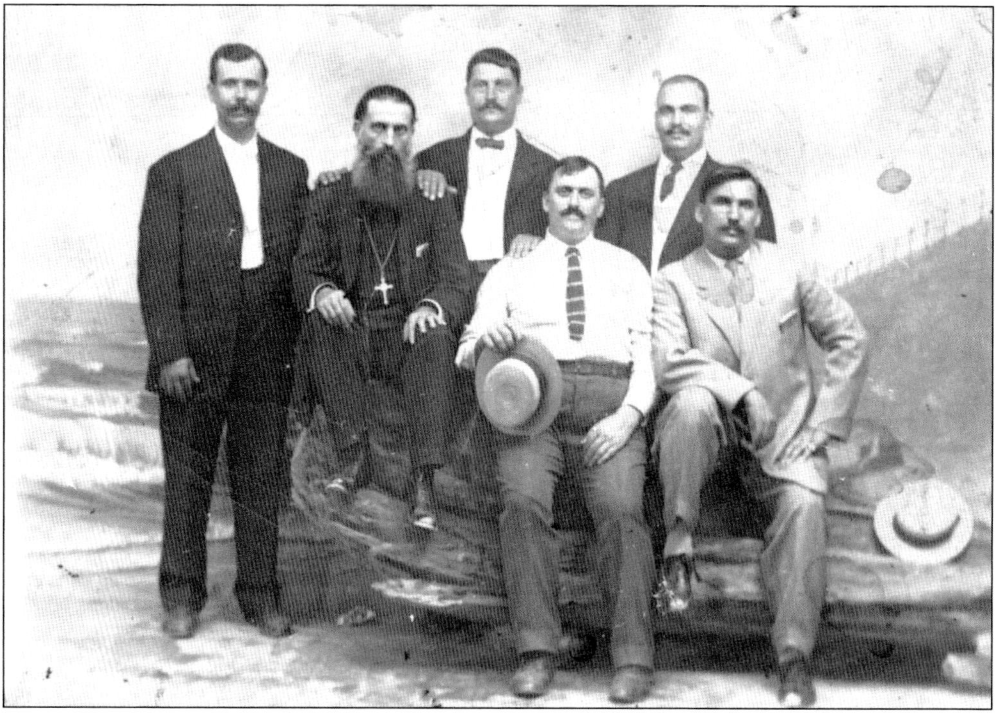

Second from the left is Archimandrite Theoclitos (Triantafilides) of SS. Constantine and Helen Serbian Orthodox Church, Galveston, where Greeks from Houston went to worship in 1895. Tsar Nicholas II helped the Orthodox Christians build this church, and the congregation again appealed to him to send a priest. He sent them their first priest, Father Theoclitos, in 1896. Serbs, Greeks, and Russians worshipped there, but the services were conducted in Greek. By 1933, the Greek community decided to have its own church. (Courtesy of HMRC.)

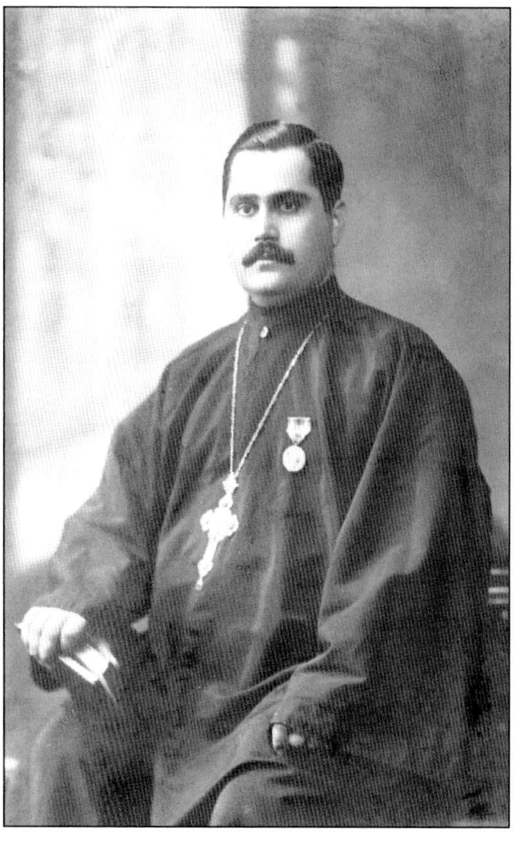

While the church was being built, ELPIS advertised for a priest in the Greek newspapers. Rev. Fr. Ioannis Papadopoulos was the first priest hired. However, six months later, he was dismissed because he would not separate himself from political problems between King Constantine and Eleftherios Venizelos. After a series of priests, Fr. Anastasios Vlamides, pictured here, served Annunciation Church from 1924 to 1929. (Courtesy of HMRC.)

By 1910, a total of 30 Greek families resided in Houston. Without a church, they arranged for visiting priests to perform worship services at other locations. They also rode an electric streetcar to SS. Constantine and Helen Serbian Orthodox Church in Galveston, which served other Orthodox Christians, though Fr. Theoclitos (Triantafilides) conducted the services in Greek. On February 23, 1910, the families formally moved to establish their own church and, in 1917, purchased the Walker Street property. (Courtesy of the AGOC archives.)

STATE OF TEXAS, * KNOW ALL MEN BY THESE PRESENTS
COUNTY OF HARRIS. *

That whereas, Frederick Bockel, has conveyed to me as trustee, part of Lot No. 12 in Block No. 88, fronting fifty feet on Walker street and running back One hundred feet in depth in the City of Houston, S. S. B. B. in Harris County, Texas; and,

Whereas Two Thousand Seven Hundred and Four & 50/100 ($2704.50) Dollars, of the purchase price for said property was paid by George Malavansos;

NOW, THEREFORE, I hereby acknowledge and declare that I hold said property in trust for the purpose of securing the payment to the said George Malavansos, on demand of said sum of money with interest thereon at the rate of Eight per cent per annum from January 19th, 1917.

WITNESS my hand this 31st day of January 1917.

Chris Malavansos
Trustee.

STATE OF TEXAS
COUNTY OF HARRIS.

Before me L. D. Morse, a Notary Public in and for Harris County, Texas, on this day personally appeared Chris Malavansos, known to me to be, the person whose name is subscribed to the foregoing instrument, and acknowledged to me that he executed the same for the purpose and consideration therein expressed.

Given under my hand and seal of office this 31st day of January 1917.

L. D. Morse
NOTARY PUBLIC, HARRIS COUNTY, TEXAS.

August 4th, 1917

Hon. Mayor and City Commissioners
Houston, Texas

Sirs:

We, the official board of the Panhellenic Benevolent Brotherhood Elpis of Houston, Texas, an organization of Greek citizens, numbering 250-300 Greeks, male and female, purpose building a Greek Orthodox Church to create a better citizenship among persons of our nationality in this community.

We are able financially at this time to build only wooden structure to cost approximately $2,800. However, our treasury is $2,300 at this time and it is our intention as soon as practicable to erect a structure that will be a credit to this city of substantial material to cost from $10,000 to $75,000, but at this time we are unable financially to carry out this, plus our first congregation will comprise 30 families, with two to five children in each, and it is our earnest desire to secure your permission to build this much needed church in order that we may train the children for the duties of citizenship and in order to solidify the better element of our present citizenship. We ask your permission to erect the frame structure mentioned and assure you that your cooperation and helpful consideration will be very highly appreciated.

Respectfully,
Panhellenic Benevolent Brotherhood Elpis
of Houston, Texas
V. J. Boozalis, Secretary

The appointed committee obtained a permit from the city to build a church on February 17, 1917. The petition read, "It is our earnest desire to build this much need [sic] church in order that we may train the children for the duties of citizenship." After obtaining the necessary funds, ELPIS engaged a contractor to begin the work just as the United States entered World War I. (Courtesy of the AGOC archives.)

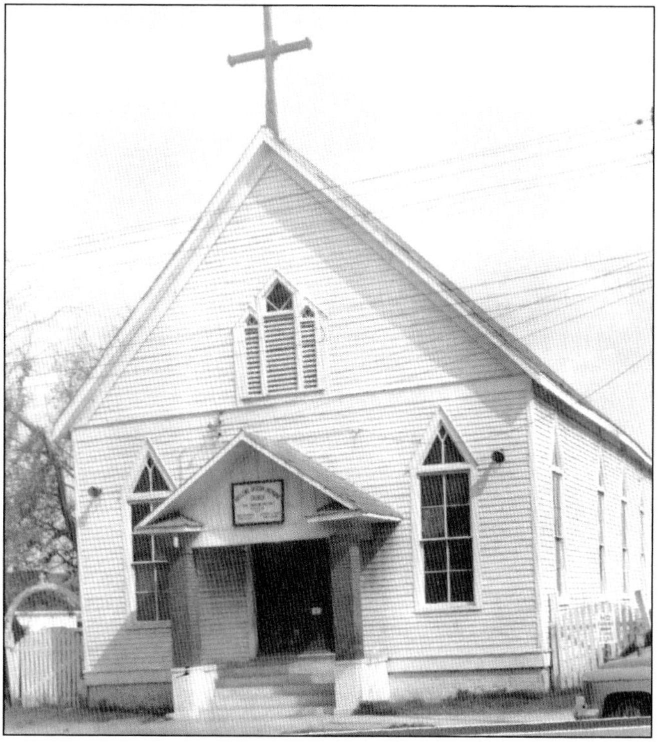

The Evangelismos of the Theotokos was an unimpressive frame structure; however, inside were Byzantine icons, and the altar was covered with two cloths, symbolizing Christ's shroud and the glory of God's throne. The Bible and the Communion chalice rested on the altar; the church's relics, inside the altar, remind people that the church was built on the blood of the martyrs. (Courtesy of HMRC.)

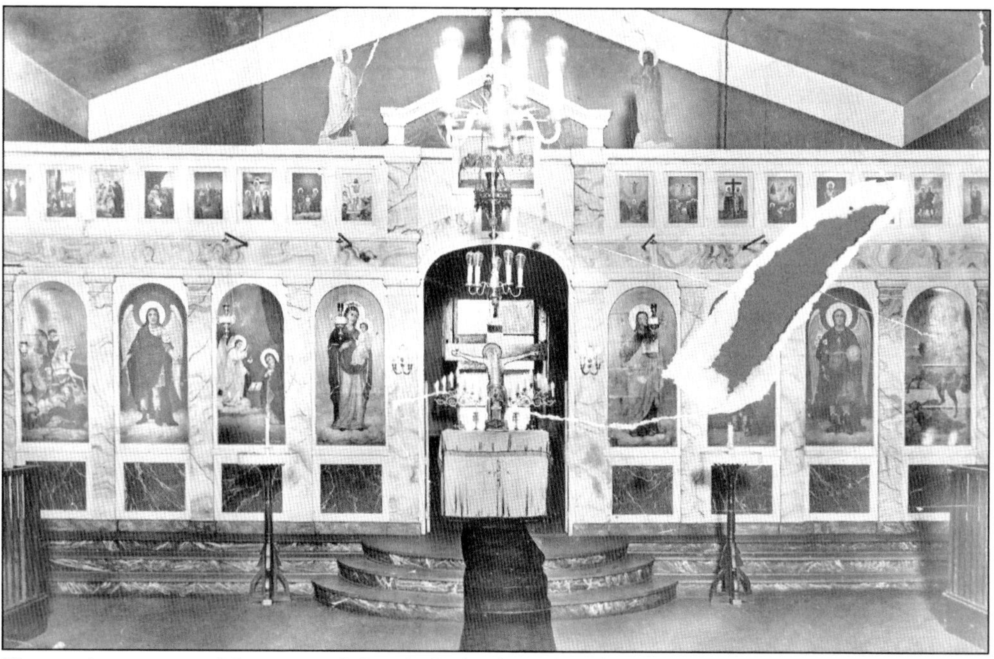

Here is the interior of the original Greek Orthodox Church at 509 Walker Street, constucted in 1917–1918. Gus Makris, the great uncle of Nick J. Papas, painted the icons. As tradition dictates, the second icon to the left of the royal doors depicted the Evangelismos (Annunciation) of the Theotokos, the church's namesake. The icons were later moved to the new church location on Yoakum Boulevard when the sanctuary was built. (Courtesy of HMRC.)

The first parish council was elected on March 21, 1917. The minutes of the ELPIS recorded the following members: Theodoros Dameris, president; Theodoros Picramenos, vice president; Dimitris Katsinas, treasurer; Vasilios T. Boozalis, secretary; Alexis Alexopoulos, collector of money; John Panzarakis; John Papazoglakis; George Petheriotes; Christos Malavansos; John Kousakis; George Pahis; and George N. Spiliotopoulos. The auditing committee included Evangelos Mytelinaeos, Dimitrios Angelopoulos, and George N. Picramenos. (Courtesy of the AGOC archives.)

The minutes of the ELPIS record the proud day, March 21, 1917, when the first parish council was elected in the presence of their first priest, the Reverend Ioannis Papadopoulos.

The First Parish Council

Theodoros Dameris, President
Theodoros Picramenos, Vice President
Dimitris Katsinas, Treasurer
Vasilios T. Boozalis, Secretary
Alexis Alexopoulos, Collector of Money
John Panzarakis
John Papazoglakis
George Petheriotes
Christos Malavansos
John Kousakis
George Pahis
George N. Spiliotopoulos

Auditing Committee

Evangelos Mytelinaeos
Dimitrios Angelopoulos
George N. Picramenos

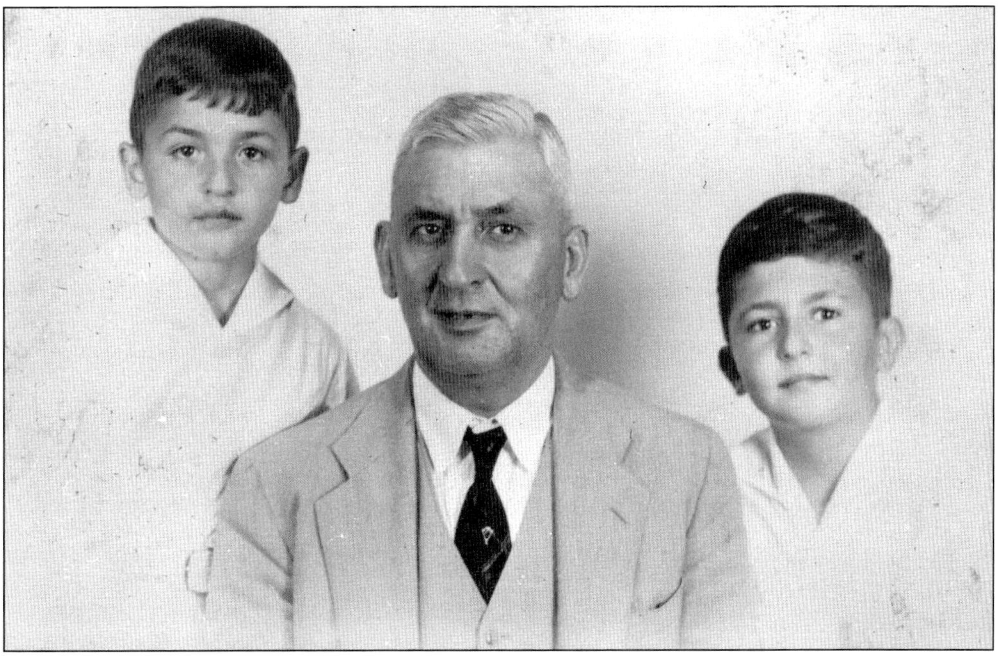

Theodore N. Dameris was the first elected president of the Parish Council of Annunciation Church on March 21, 1917. He is seen with sons Athanasios "Thano" (left) and Nick T. Dameris (right). Nick served as treasurer on the parish council from 1968 to 1970 and as vice president in 1977. He and Gregory Catsinas were cochairmen of the 50th anniversary celebration committee in 1967. Thano later served as president of the parish council in 1981. (Courtesy of HMRC.)

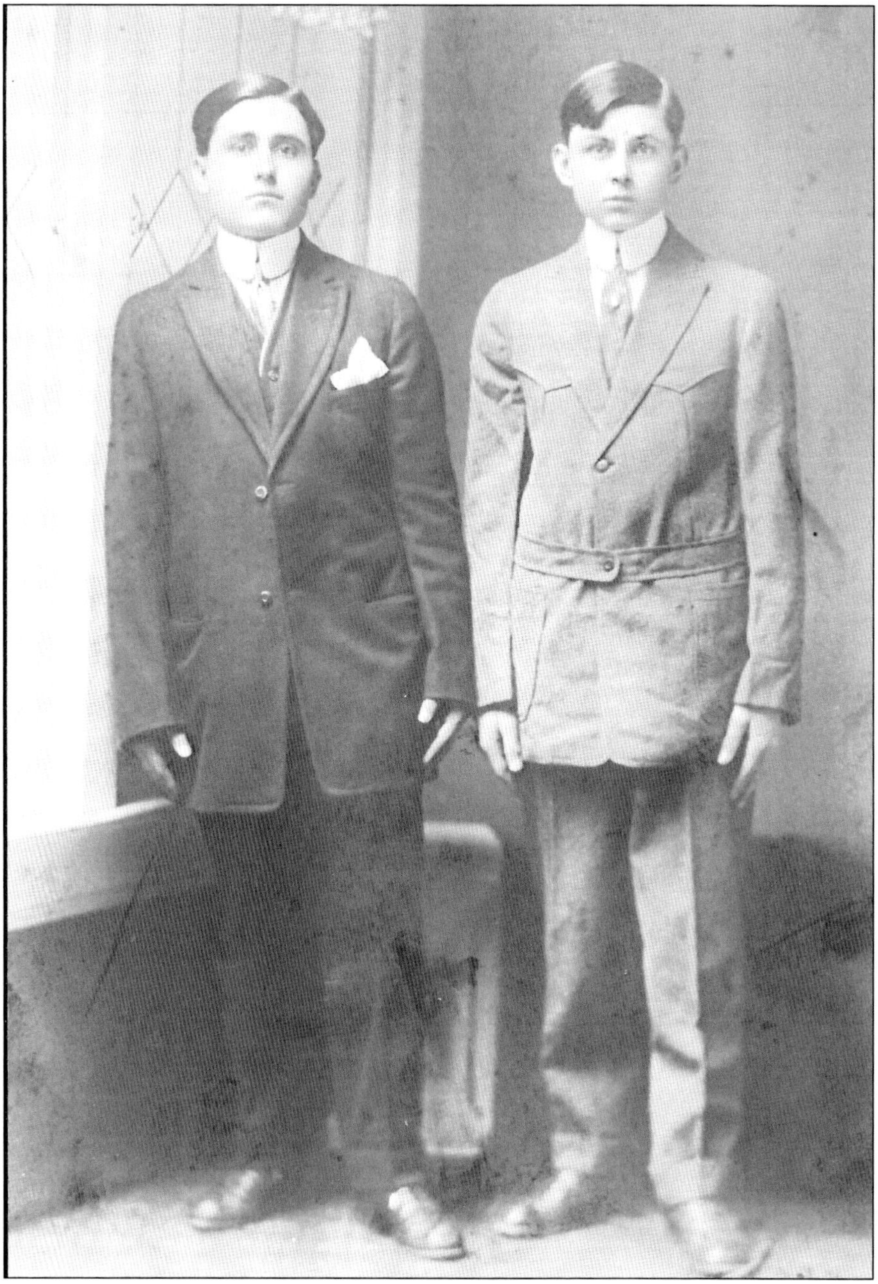

Stavros (left) and Victor (right) Boozalis came to the United States from Vasilitsi, Greece. Stavros came in 1909 at the age of 15 and settled in Tennessee, working, attending night school to earn his high school diploma, and sending money home to his family. In 1912, he moved to Houston to work in his uncle's restaurant. Victor came to Houston in 1916, where he found Greek immigrants that "were either illiterate or semiliterate, squabbling all the time. They were united for only one purpose—to build a church for the children." Both brothers were involved in establishing the church on Walker Street in 1917. Victor Boozalis took John Papazoglakis's place on the parish council as secretary when Papazoglakis quit because of a dispute regarding where the new church was to be built. (Courtesy of Constantina Boozalis.)

Cleopatra Roupakioti, pictured with Peter Mousouliotes (Moss), was the caretaker of the church building on Walker Street in the late 1920s. Her responsibilities included cleaning the church and making candles for the services. She was a faithful woman, and this responsibility was a labor of love. (Courtesy of HMRC.)

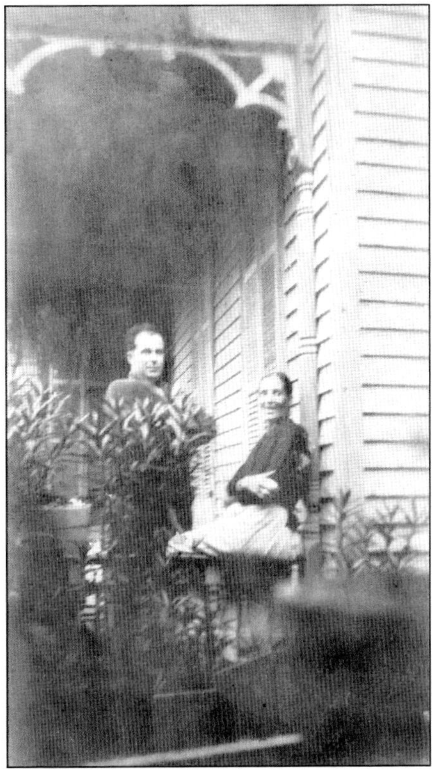

Nick G. Peet and John Zgourides, an experienced chanter, formed the first choir on December 15, 1937; Virginia Gianakis (Howell) was the organist; Fr. Chris Nanopoulos was the priest. Choir members were between 17 and 18 years old. Conceived to enhance church services, the choir was initially opposed because choirs were not used in Greece. Eventually, the choir program was successfully implemented. (Courtesy of HMRC.)

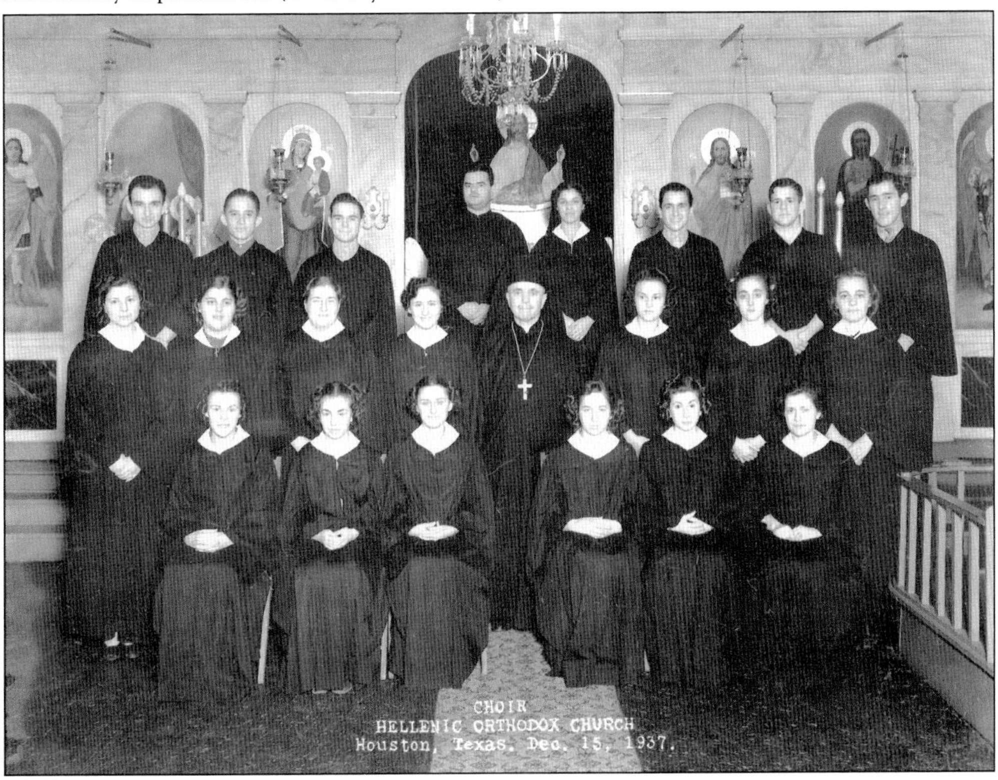

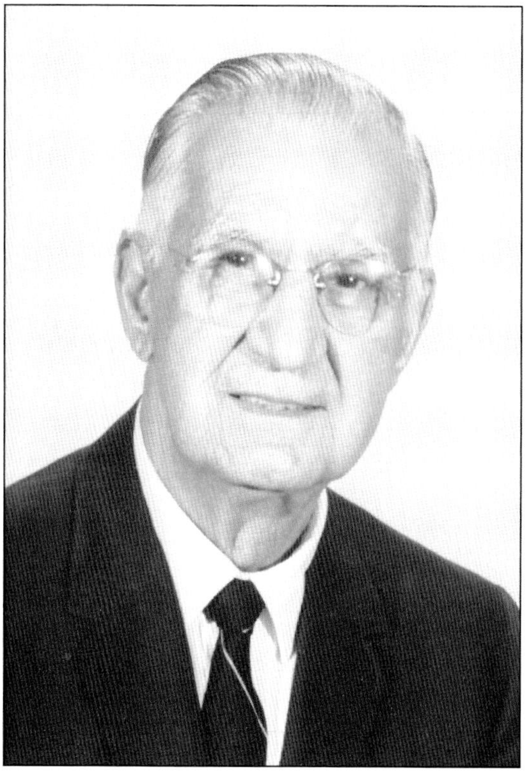

John C. Zgourides was the chanter at the Walker Street church from 1929 until his death in 1970. He left Thasos, Greece, to join his brother George and his cousins John and Gus Economides in Galveston in 1912. John was the chanter at SS. Constantine and Helen Serbian Orthodox Church under Archimandrite Theoclitos (Triantafilides). He married Anastacia Picramenos (Peet) in 1928, and they moved to Houston, where he became a restaurateur and owned the Farmers' Market Lunch Room with George Spillios. (Courtesy of Gus Zgourides.)

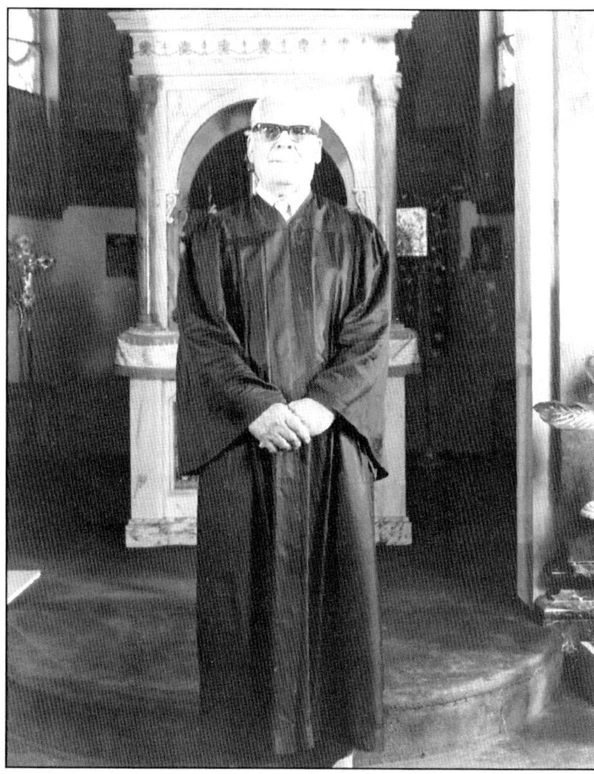

At 19 years old, George Michael Grivon emigrated from Karpathos, Greece, in 1920 and came to Houston in 1946. He served as chanter at Annunciation for 52 years. In 1996, at the age of 95, Grivon was honored by His Eminence Archbishop Iakovos and the National Forum of Greek Orthodox Musicians "in grateful appreciation for his more than 60 years of service in several Orthodox Churches throughout the United States." (Courtesy of the Grivon children.)

Four

The Church Blossoms

The completion of the Walker Street church was a joyful event. Now, with their own priest to care for their spiritual needs, the community began to settle into a comfortable pattern. Individuals gave their financial resources, and their time and talents as well. The men were the administrators of the church while the women were in charge of keeping it clean and collecting money. The community even produced the candles used in the services.

As American customs became more familiar to the Greeks, a natural blending of lifestyles began to evolve. Nevertheless, although they desired to become good Americans, they did not wish to abandon their heritage and included traditions from Greece in celebrations of name days, holidays, weddings, and baptisms. The immigrants believed the only way to retain their religion and culture was through the preservation of their language. One of the primary duties of the priests was to teach Greek to the children, but as the parish grew and the priests became busier, Greek school teachers were hired. These teachers were as vital to the parish as the priests. Only qualified people with strong academic credentials were accepted for this important role. They taught language and grammar, reading, writing, history, mythology, geography, and religion, including prayers such as the Nicene Creed and the Lord's Prayer.

The new church also undertook some revolutionary changes to the worship experience. Conceived to enhance the services, the first choir was formed in 1938. Because choirs were not used in Greece, there was some opposition at first, but the choir program was implemented successfully. From this small beginning, the choir grew into an inspiring and didactic aspect of worship. Fr. Seraphim Haginas (1946–1954) ended the practice of the segregation of men and women in the church and instituted adult religious education classes. The Greek language was still seen as a priority in the perpetuation of the Orthodox faith and in transmitting the Greek heritage to the young. Liturgies, sermons, Sunday school lessons, and adult religious education, as well as board and general assembly meetings, were all conducted in Greek.

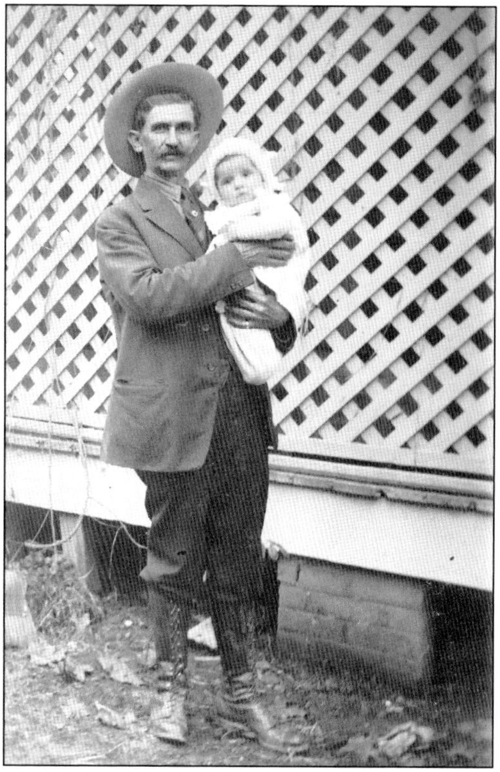

Vasili Economides, known as William Thomas "Ham," came to Houston from Sparta in 1888 and lived here until he died in 1933. Ham worked for Peter Menutes at several of his saloons. He was called "Uncle Ham" because he loved ham so much. Ham came from the same area of Sparta as Peter and lived with the Menutes family on and off for several years. (Courtesy of HMRC.)

Theo and Kaliope Picramenos (Peet) and their daughter Anastacia are seen at Murdoch's, a pier and bathhouse in Galveston, in 1910. Day trips to Galveston for church services and beach outings were very popular among Houston's Greeks. Theo served as president of the parish council in 1926. (Courtesy of HMRC.)

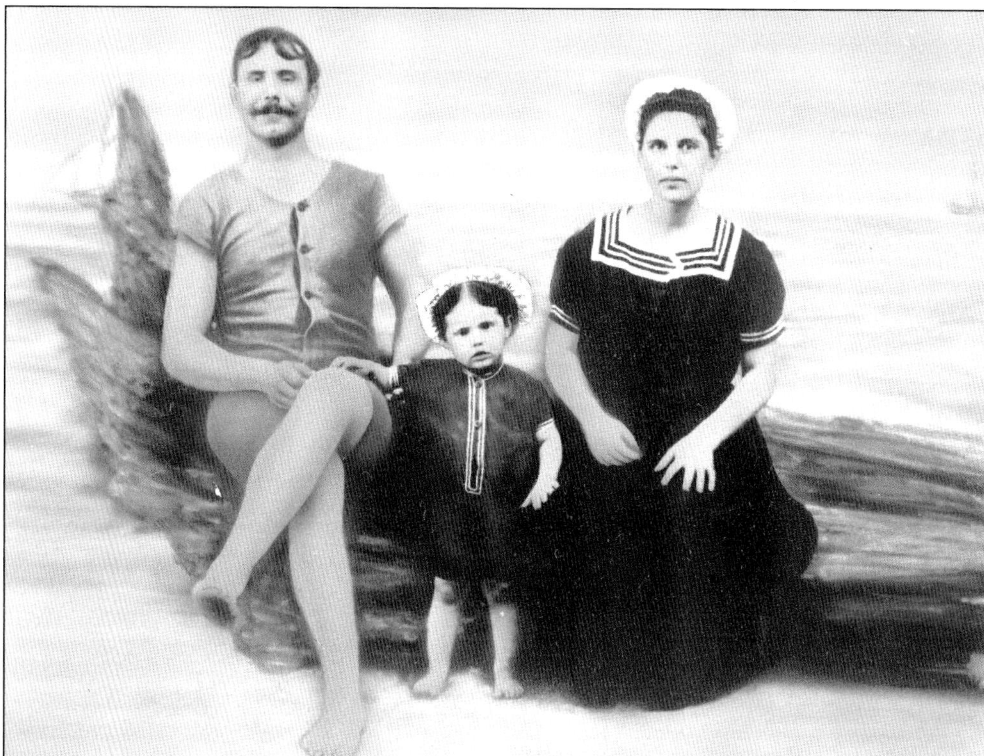

Here is a wedding portrait of George N. and Constantina Picramenos (Peet) in 1915–1916. George was a restaurateur; he co-owned the Blue Front and Palace Café with Angelo Mytelinaeos (Mytilen) and was one of the owners of the Royal Café. He served as president of the parish council of Annunciation Church in 1924. (Courtesy of HMRC.)

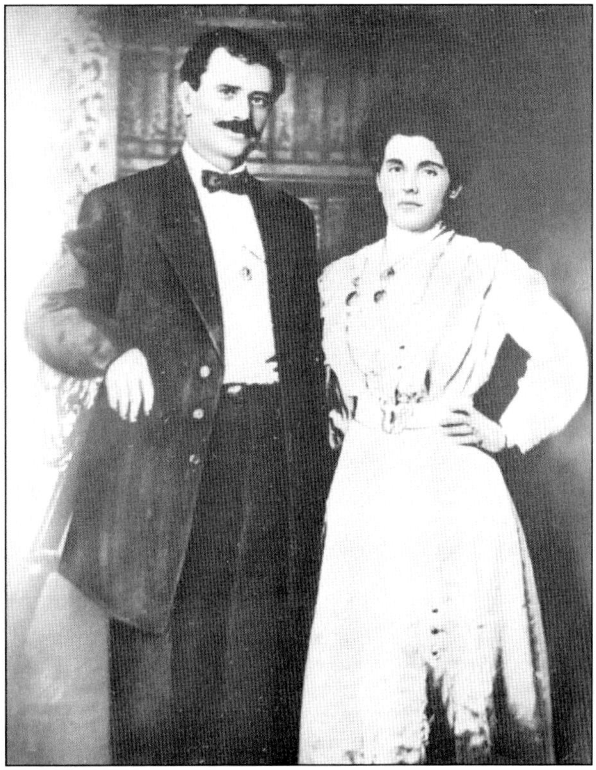

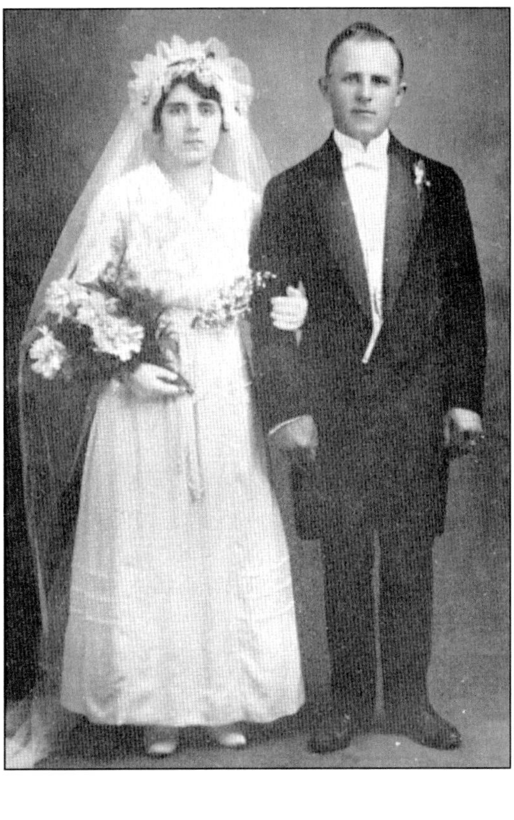

This wedding portrait is of George Petheriotes and Sophia Mytelinaeos (Mytilen) in 1916. Marriages were arranged through relatives and friends. According to the family's wealth and position, dowries, a Greek tradition, could be small or large. A prospective groom also had to show that he had good prospects as a husband and provider and that he was of good moral character. (Courtesy of HMRC.)

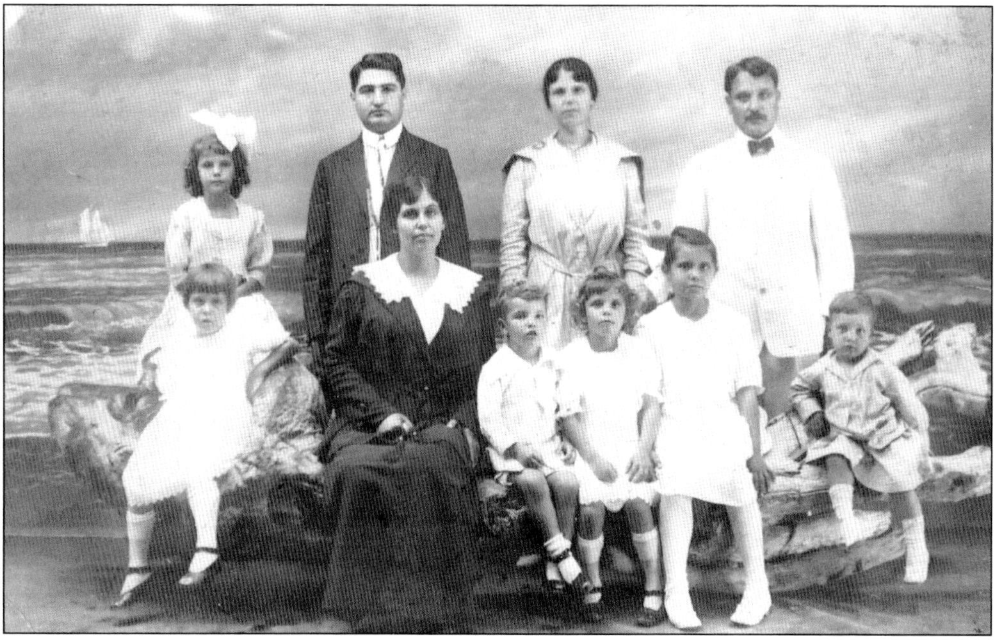

Pictured in Galveston in 1917, Giannukos family members are, from left to right, (first row) Georgia Giannukos (Platos), Kaliope Peet, Sam and Fofo Giannukos (Sfiris), Anastacia Picramenos (Zgourides), and John Giannukos; (second row) Helen Giannukos (Govatos), Sam, Dionysia, and Nick Giannukos in 1917. (Courtesy of HMRC.)

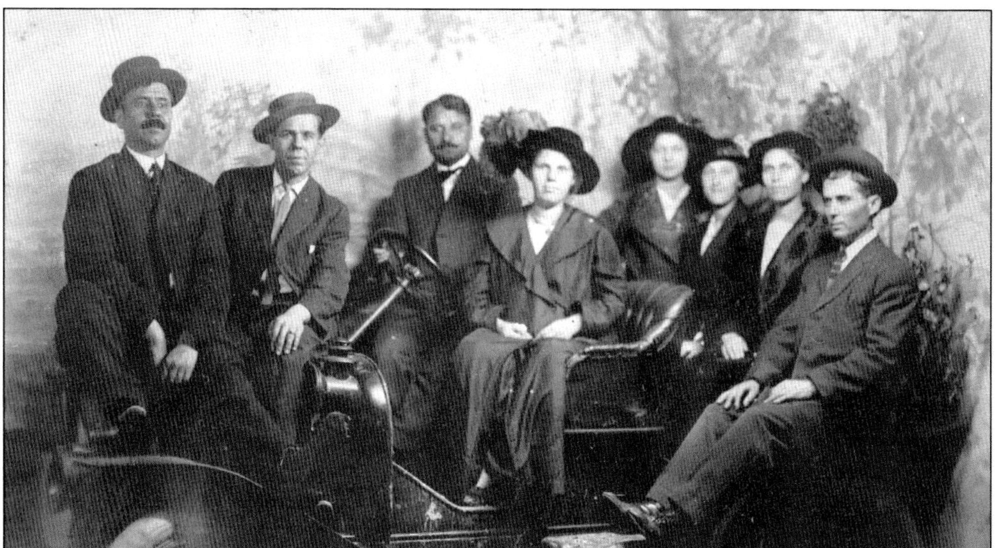

From left to right are Theo Picramenos (Peet), his brother George N. Picramenos (Peet), Nick and Dionysia Giannukos, Blanche (an American who worked for Theo Picramenos), Elizabeth Picramenos (Peet), Kaliope Picramenos (Peet), and George Tsikinis around 1919. (Courtesy of HMRC.)

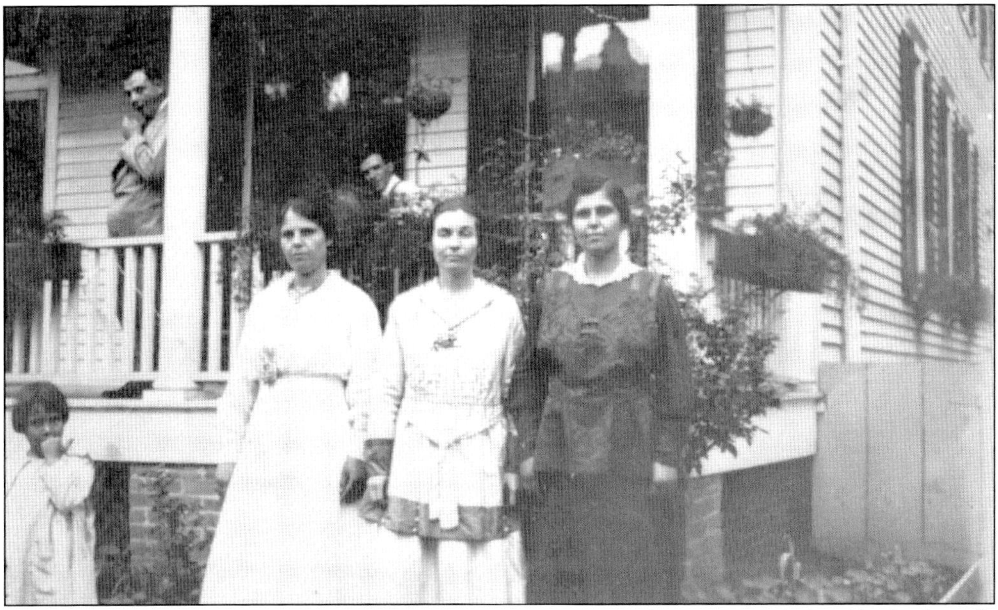

At the home of Nick Angelos about 1919 are, from left to right, Irene Cafcalas (the little girl), who later married Roy Hofheinz, mayor of the city of Houston in the 1950s; Dionysia Giannukos; Ethyl Cafcalas; and Kaliope Picramenos. (Courtesy of HMRC.)

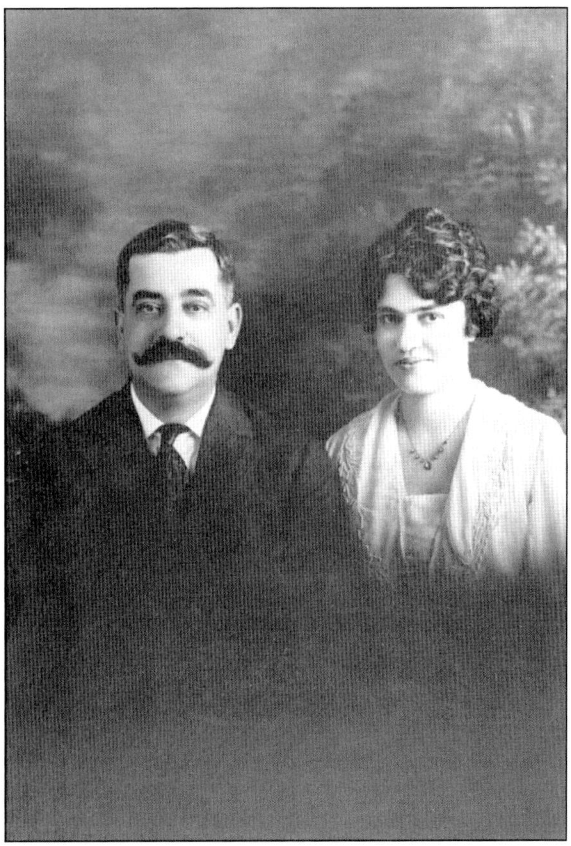

Peter Menutes and Maria Lardis Menutes are pictured in early 1919. She is in her wedding dress. They had already been married a couple of years, and their son Edward had already been born, but this was the first time she was able to persuade her husband to have their photograph made as a wedding portrait. (Courtesy of HMRC.)

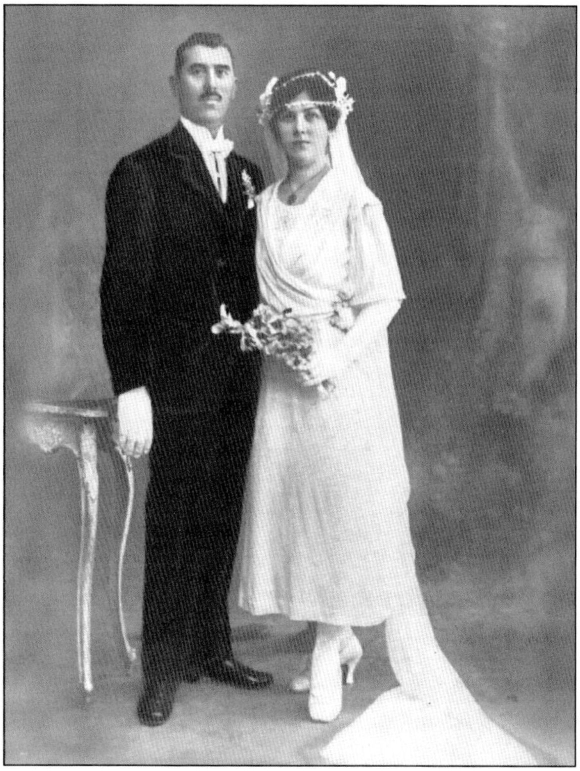

Anastasios Pete Poulos and Chrissi Kalaboukidou settled in Galveston from Constantinople in 1920. Anastasios ran the soda fountain and café at Murdoch's. They had six children: Pete, Raleigh, John, Katherine, Mary, and Ann. The family moved to Houston after their three sons returned from World War II. Mary has served as president of Philoptochos (2005–2009) and on the parish council. Ann has worked for the dean of the cathedral since 1994. (Courtesy of Ann and Mary Poulos.)

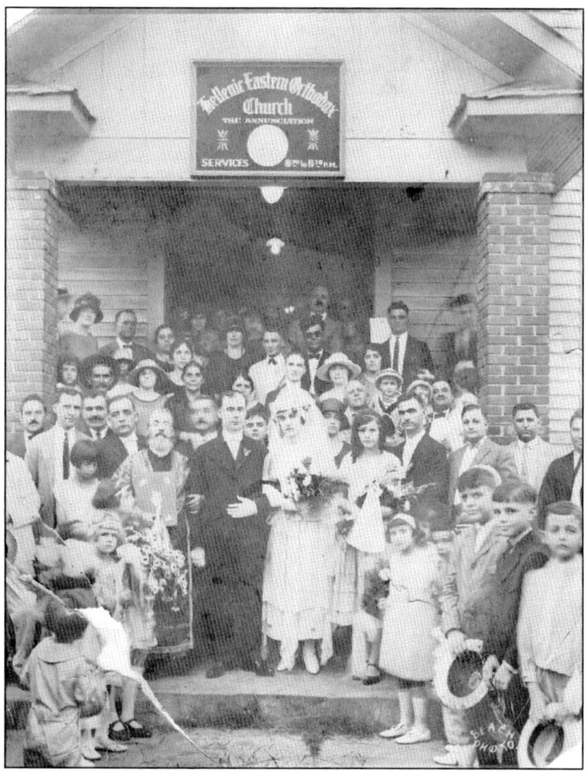

The wedding of Peter Mousouliotes (Moss) and Julia Lardis occurred at the Annunciation Church on Walker Street on June 22, 1924. Julia immigrated to Houston in 1920. Peter came here around 1916 and went to work for his first cousin Angelo Mytelinaeos (Mytelin). Four years later, Peter opened the Plaza Café and invested in real estate. He was active in the establishment of the Walker Street and Yoakum Boulevard churches. (Courtesy of Phillip Moss.)

Here is a 1924 portrait of Louis Comet and Stella Galanos Comet. Stella's mother, Lefkothea Galanos, is between them. When Stella was widowed, she later married Stelios Demetre. (Courtesy of HMRC.)

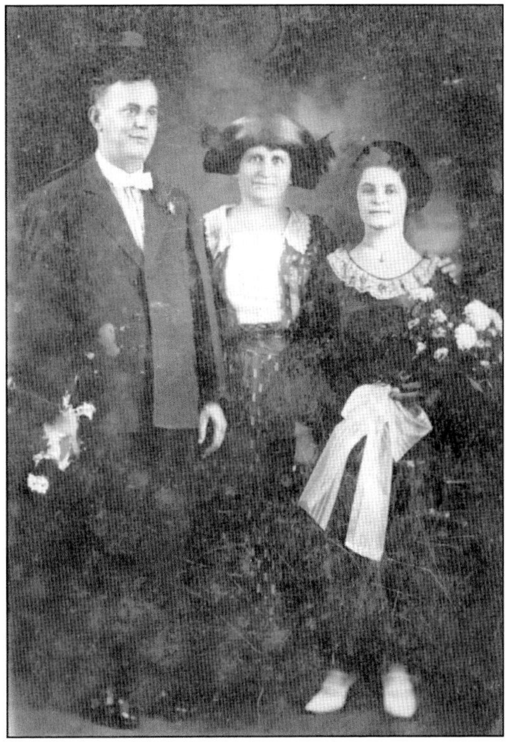

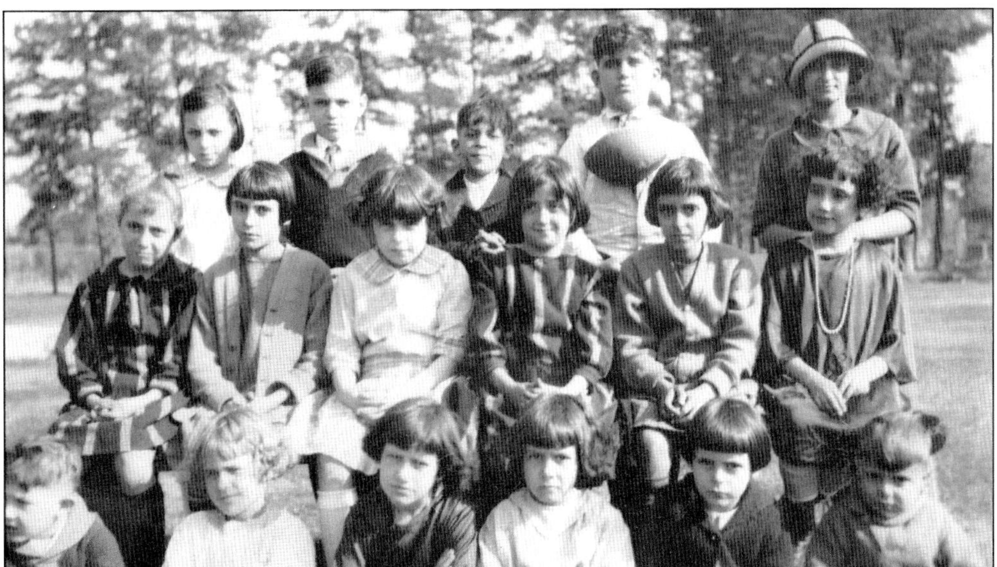

The Greek school was founded in 1918 to preserve the Greek language and traditions. Children attended classes five afternoons a week for two hours. The teachers were all well educated and included Kyriaki Economidi (1918); Mrs. E.T. Mavrakis (1918–1928); John Emmanuel George, who was attending Rice Institute at the time he taught (1928–1932); Dimitrios Sakellarides (1932–1934); and Catherine Demeris (1945–1957). Mrs. E.T. Mavrakis is pictured with her Greek school students during recess in an empty lot on McKinney near her home in 1925. (Courtesy of HMRC.)

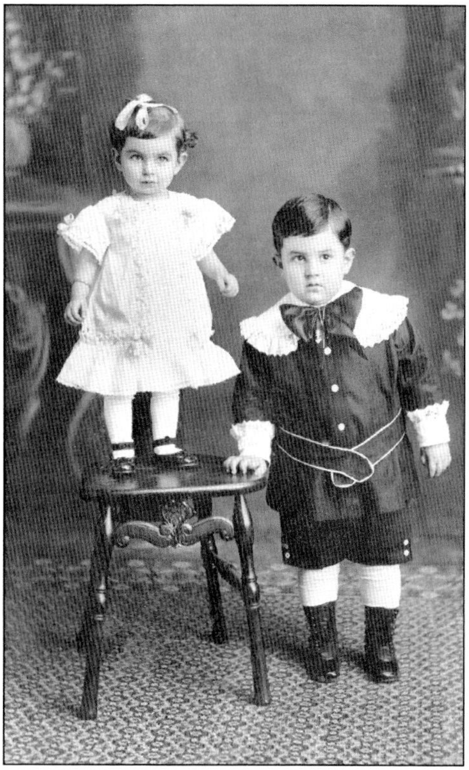

This portrait is of Nellie and Stanley Bournias. George and Constantina Picramenos (Peet) baptized Stanley. The Bournias family lived in Brenham, Texas, and came to Houston for church services on special holidays such as their name days. It was a very long trip in the 1920s. (Courtesy of HMRC.)

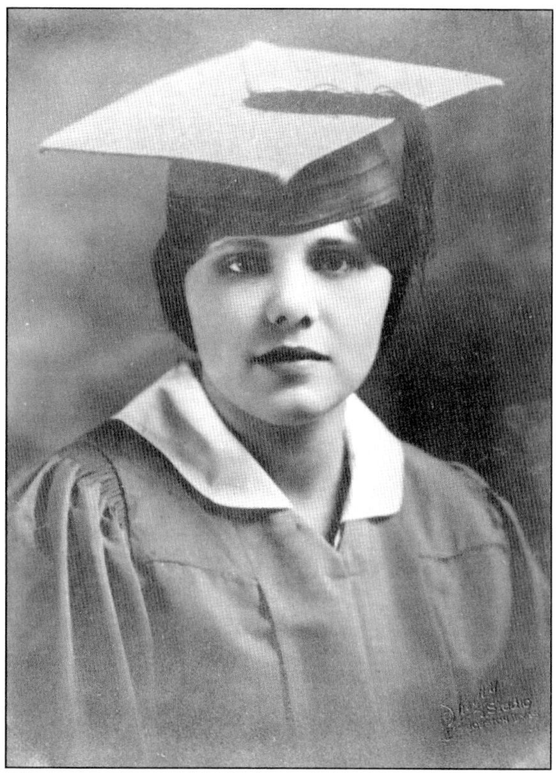

Anastacia Picramenos (Zgourides) was the first Greek girl in Houston to graduate from high school. In June 1926, she graduated from Central High School, which later became Sam Houston High School. (Courtesy of HMRC.)

Here is a wedding portrait of Anastacia Picramenos (Peet) and John Zgourides in 1928. The groom had immigrated to Galveston from Thasos, Greece, in 1912. The sacrament took place at the Annunciation Church in Houston. The reception was at DOKY Hall. It was said that "the wedding was a real event in the community," and everyone from Galveston as well as the Houston church was invited. John served as a chanter in the Galveston and Houston churches. (Courtesy of HMRC.)

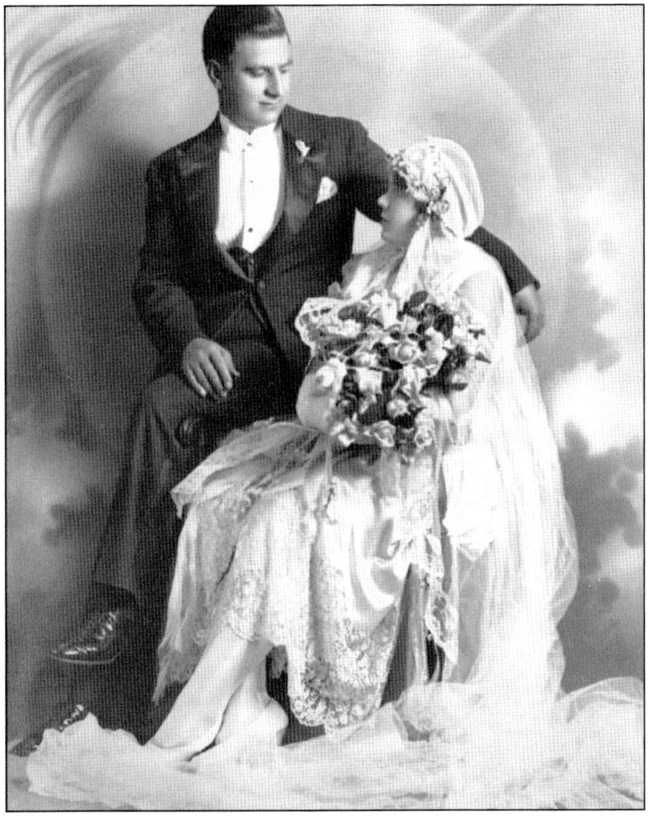

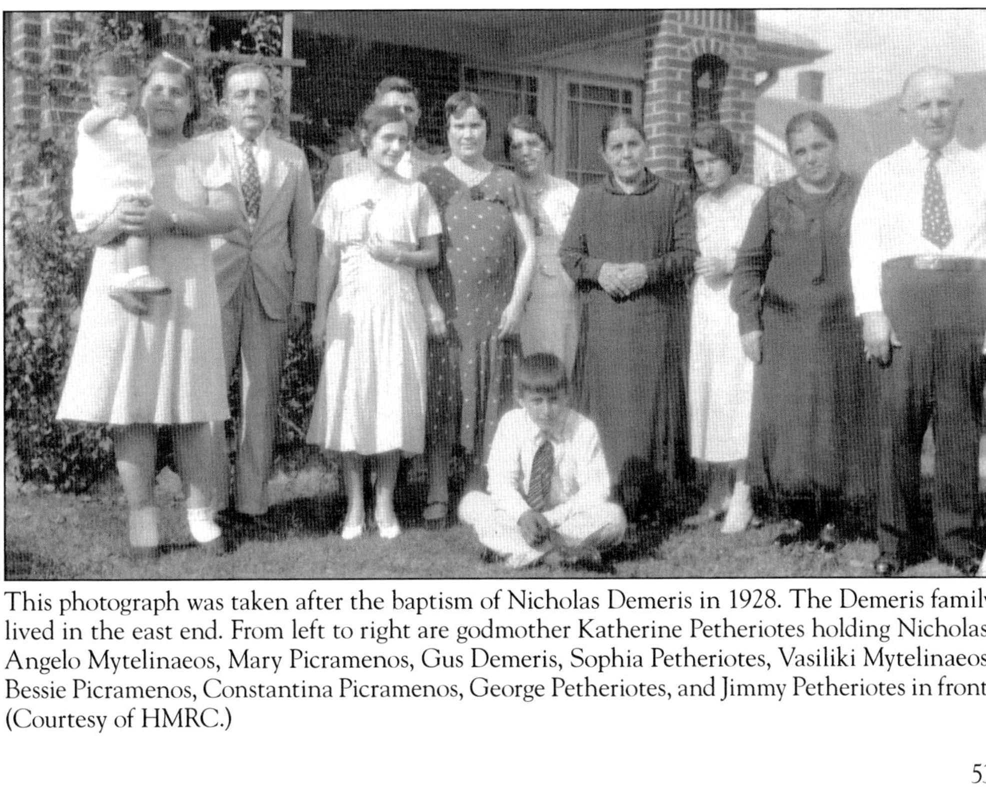

This photograph was taken after the baptism of Nicholas Demeris in 1928. The Demeris family lived in the east end. From left to right are godmother Katherine Petheriotes holding Nicholas, Angelo Mytelinaeos, Mary Picramenos, Gus Demeris, Sophia Petheriotes, Vasiliki Mytelinaeos, Bessie Picramenos, Constantina Picramenos, George Petheriotes, and Jimmy Petheriotes in front. (Courtesy of HMRC.)

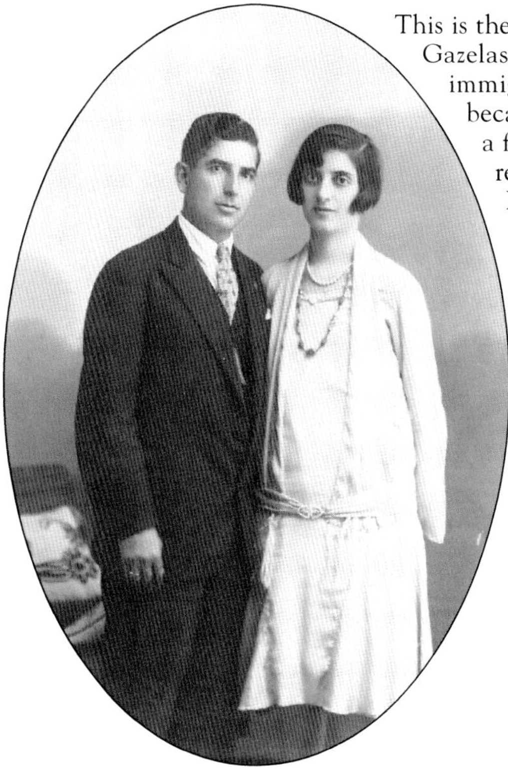

This is the wedding portrait of Chrysanthe and George Gazelas. Married in 1929 in Lesvos, Greece, they immigrated to Charleston, South Carolina, and became the proprietors of a grocery store. After a few years, nostalgic for their homeland, they returned to Greece. In 1946, they immigrated to Houston. (Courtesy of Irene Cassis.)

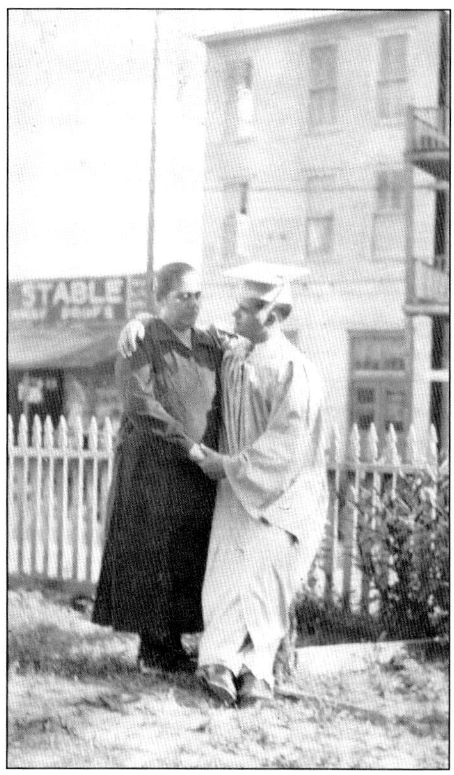

Constantina Picramenos (Peet) is seen with her eldest child, Nick, who was the first in their family to graduate from Sam Houston High School at 309 Preston Street in the early 1930s. (Courtesy of HMRC.)

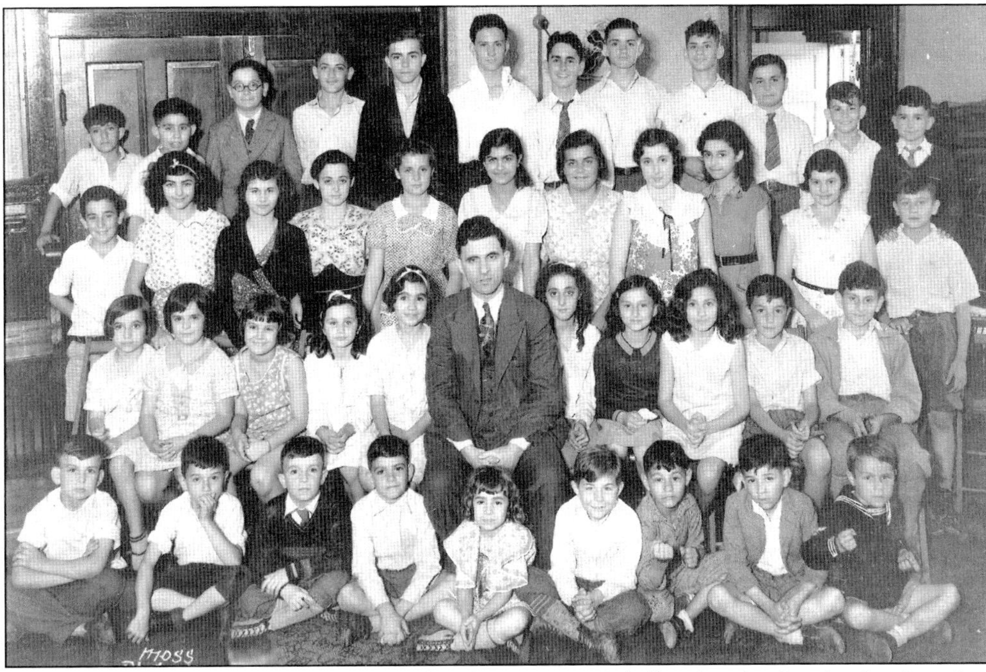

The Greek school class of 1931 is pictured with Dimitrios Sakellarides, the Greek school teacher, in back of the church on Walker Street. Dimitrios was the son of Fr. Nicholas D. Sakellarides, who served Annunciation Greek Orthodox Church (1931–1933). When Father Nicholas was reassigned to another parish, Dimitrios left as well. (Courtesy of HMRC.)

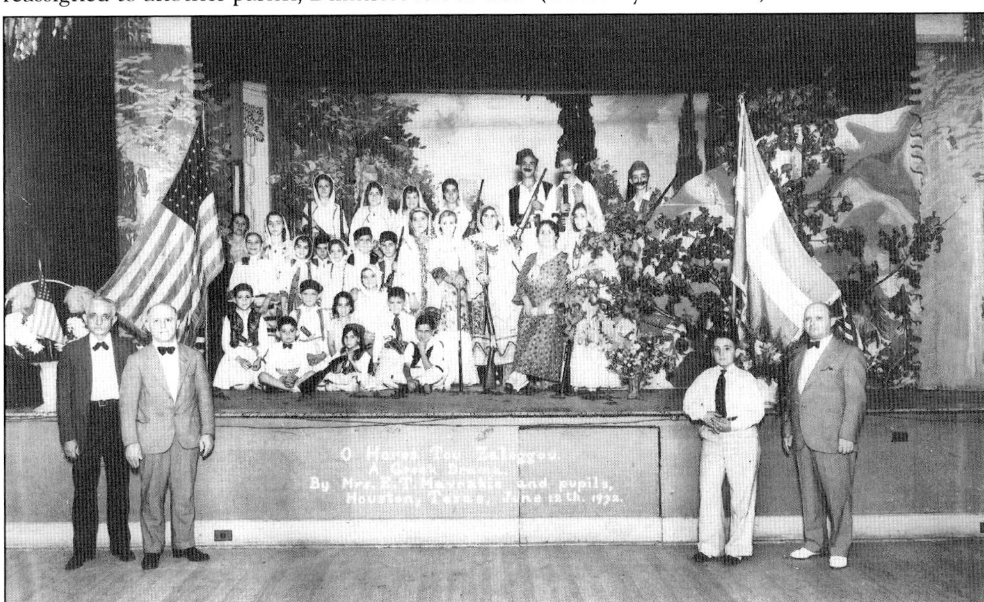

Mrs. E.T. Mavrakis's Greek school students presented "O Horos Tou Zaloggou" on June 12, 1932. Mavrakis converted one large room in her home at 305 McKinney into a classroom. She was such a dedicated teacher that she would pick up students who could not make it to class and bring them to her home. She returned to Greece with her husband prior to World War II. (Courtesy of the AGOC archives.)

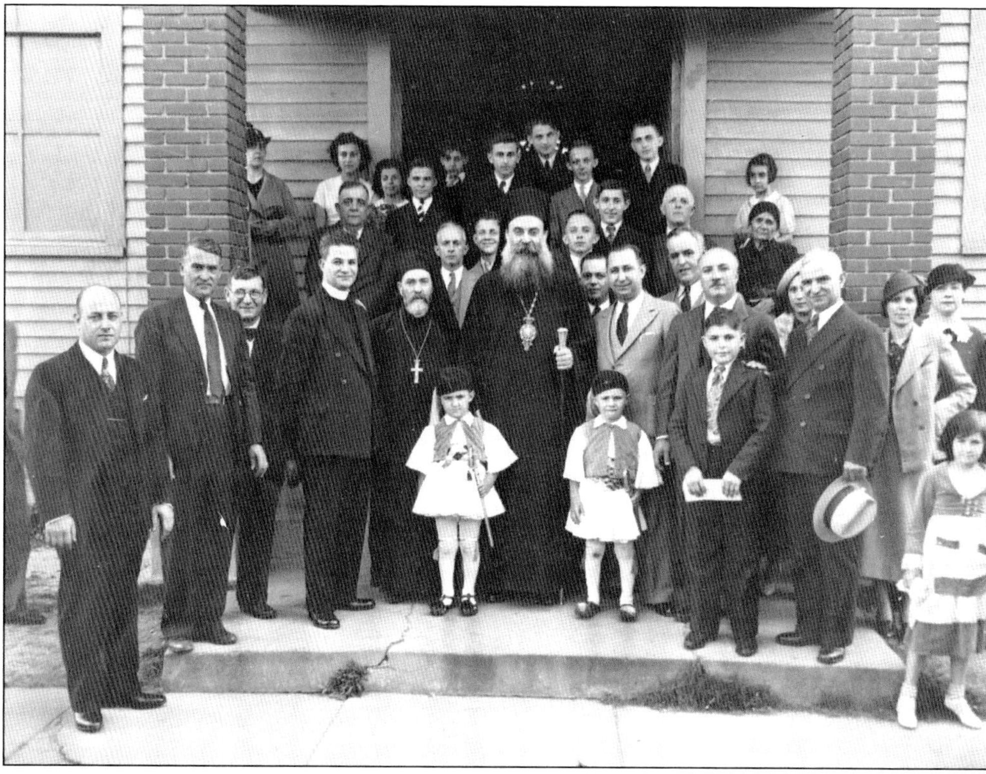

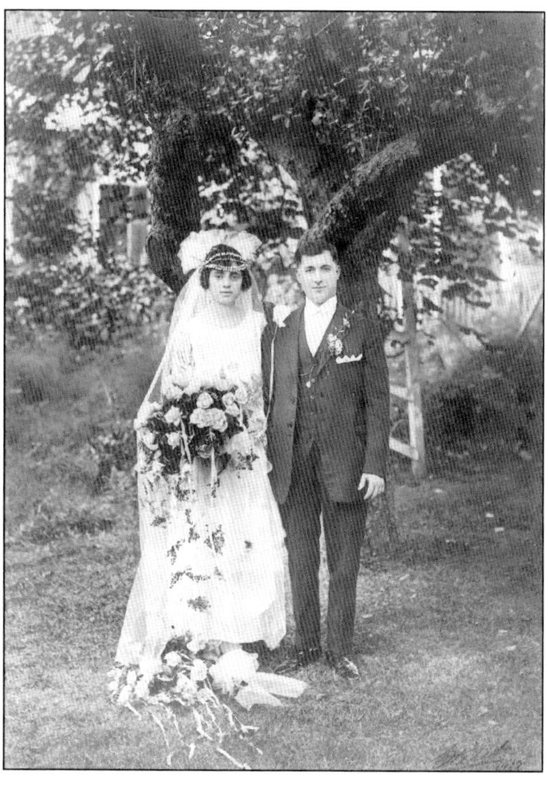

His Eminence Archbishop Athenogoras of the Greek Orthodox Archdiocese of North and South America from 1930 to 1948 is pictured in the center of a group on the steps of Annunciation Church at 509 Walker Street, Houston, in 1934. His Eminence later became the patriarch of Constantinople from 1948 to 1972. (Courtesy of HMRC.)

Mercena Tropoli, from Lesvos, Greece, was promised to Sam Tragakis from Connecticut in 1936. They settled there until Sam developed heart problems. They sought medical care in Houston from Dr. Michael DeBakey, but Sam died a few years later. The young widow went to work as a seamstress to support her family, and later married Steve Panos, proprietor of the Palace Boot Shop. (Courtesy of John Cokins.)

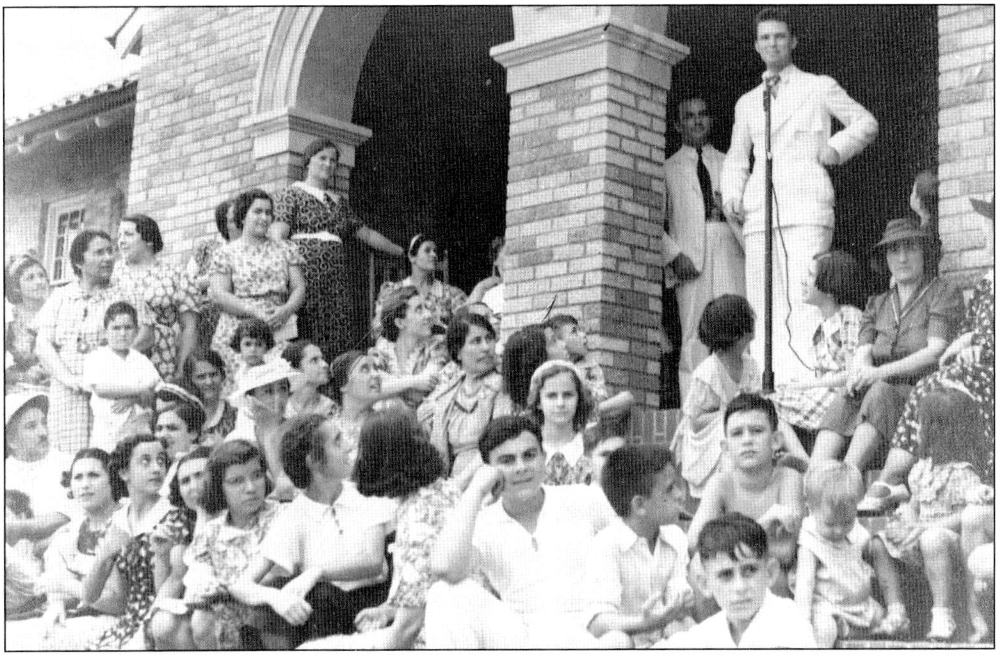

Pictured is a community picnic in Clear Lake, Texas, sponsored by the Patmian Society in July 1937. Although the Patmian Society also had picnics for themselves, the entire church community was invited. Chris Dixie, a young lawyer from Dallas, gave a speech at this event to inspire the young people in Houston to also seek a higher education since few young Greeks were college-educated at that time. (Courtesy of HMRC.)

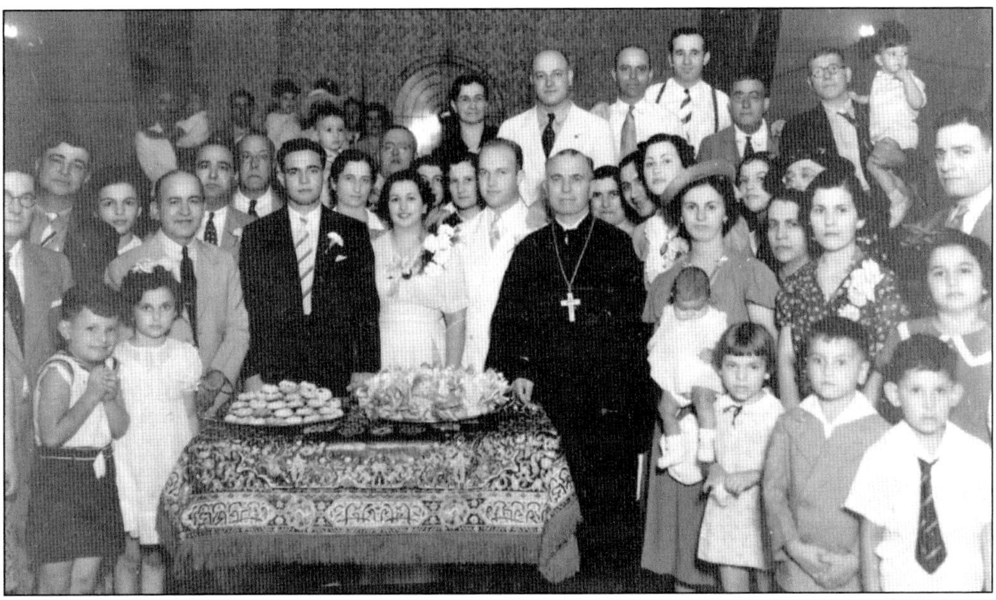

The engagement blessing and party of Anastasia Markou and George Caridas occurred at a local hall in 1938. Most of the guests were from Patmos, Greece. The wedding was officiated by Fr. Chris Nanopoulos, who served Annunciation Church from 1937 to 1946. Though the betrothal is now part of the wedding ceremony, at the time, the exchange of rings and the crowning (*stefana*) were two separate ceremonies. (Courtesy of HMRC.)

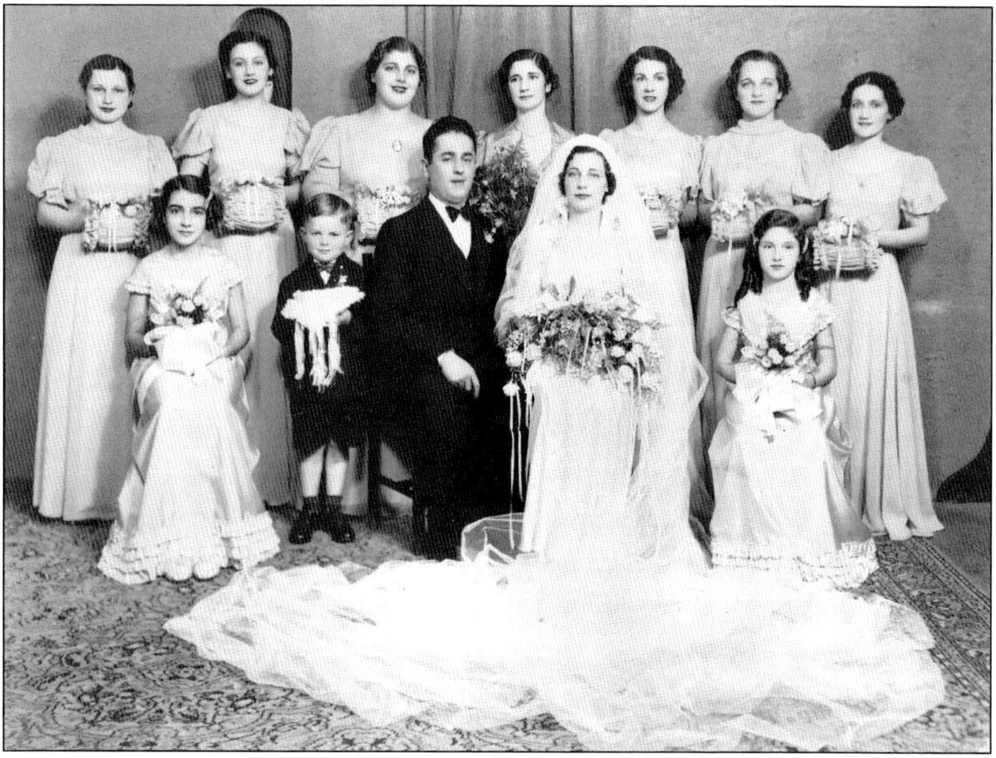

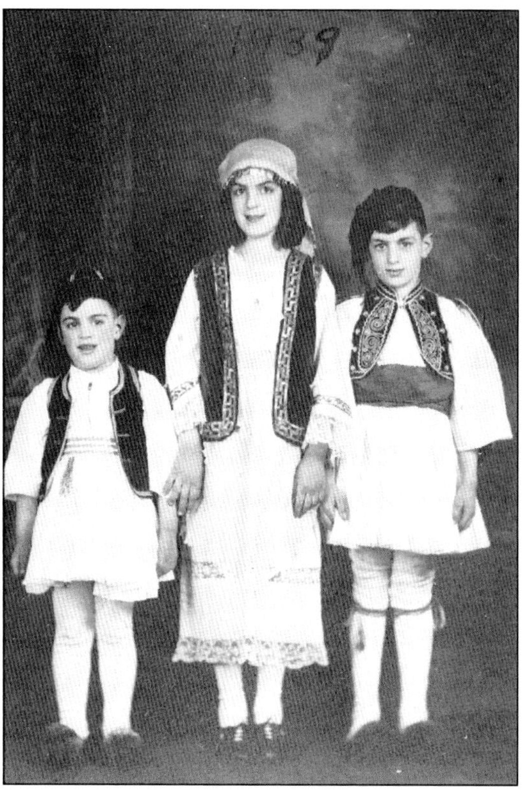

Here is the wedding party of Bessie Verges and John Retsios in Corpus Christie, Texas, in 1938. Soon after their wedding, they moved to Houston, where John had a hamburger stand on Cushman Street. Bessie went to work for the Harris County Tax Office to support herself and her son, Alfred, after John died of a heart attack in his mid-thirties. (Courtesy of HMRC.)

From left to right, George, Katherine, and John Koumonduros are dressed in traditional Greek costumes in celebration of Greek Independence Day on March 25, 1939. Immigrants and Greek Americans commemorated this historical event in honor of their culture and heritage. The feast of the Annunciation of the Theotokos also falls on March 25, affording the community another opportunity to celebrate. Their parents, Christine Voinis (Koumonduros) and Alex Koumonduros, emigrated from Greece in 1930. (Courtesy of HMRC.)

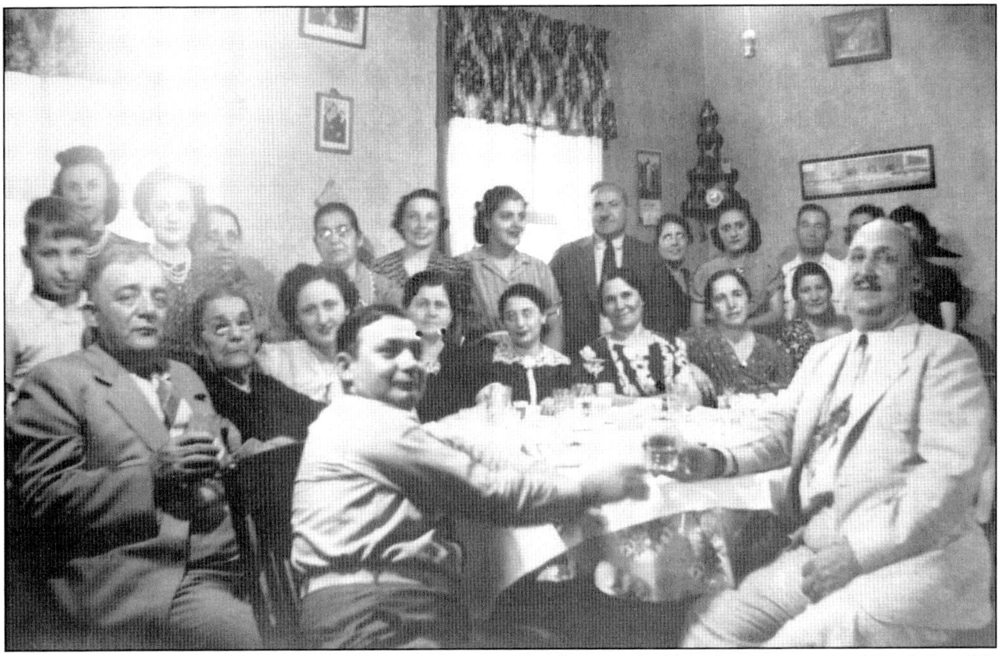

The engagement party for Nick Peet and Catherine Chiakos was held at the Picramenos (Peet) family's house at 309 Preston Street. Nick and Catherine got to know each other from singing in the choir together and enjoying that fellowship in 1939. They married in January 1940. (Courtesy of HMRC.)

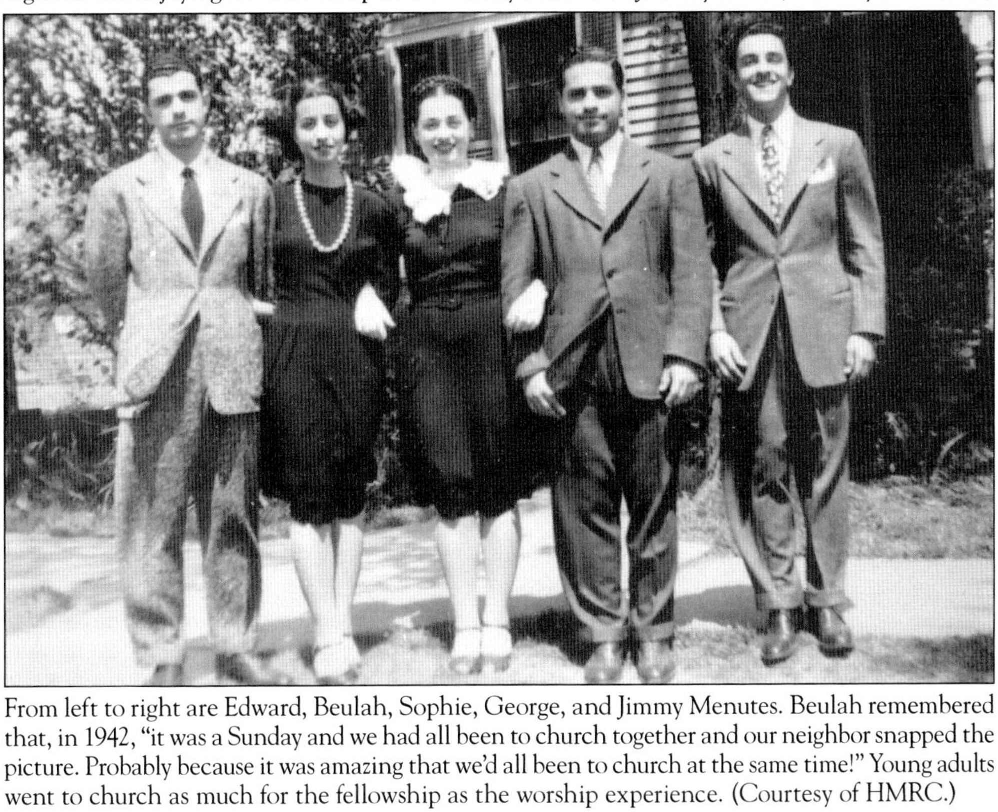

From left to right are Edward, Beulah, Sophie, George, and Jimmy Menutes. Beulah remembered that, in 1942, "it was a Sunday and we had all been to church together and our neighbor snapped the picture. Probably because it was amazing that we'd all been to church at the same time!" Young adults went to church as much for the fellowship as the worship experience. (Courtesy of HMRC.)

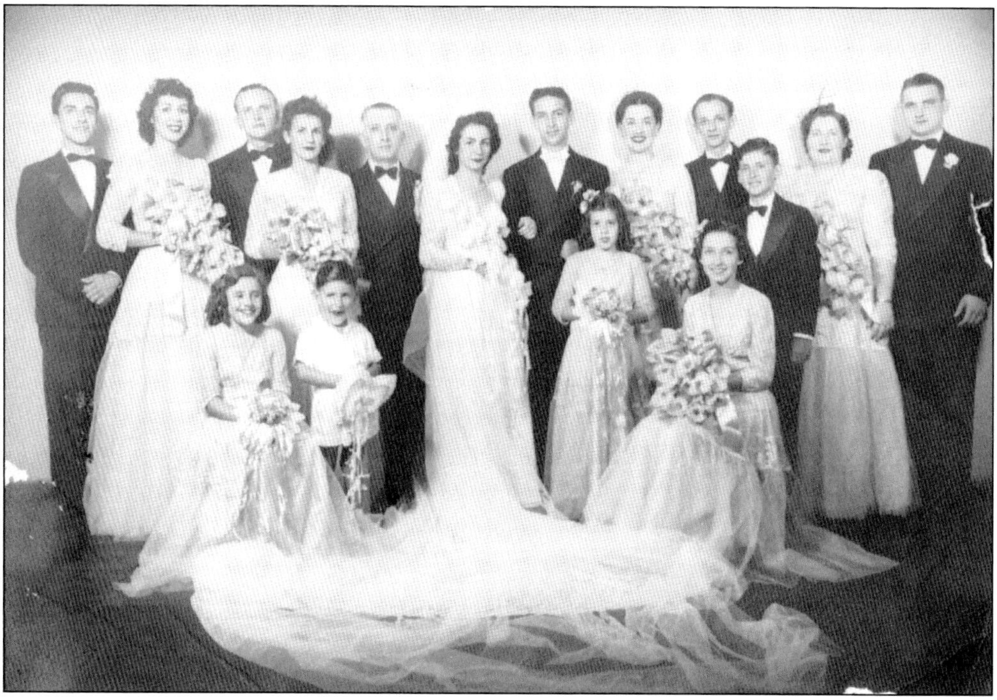

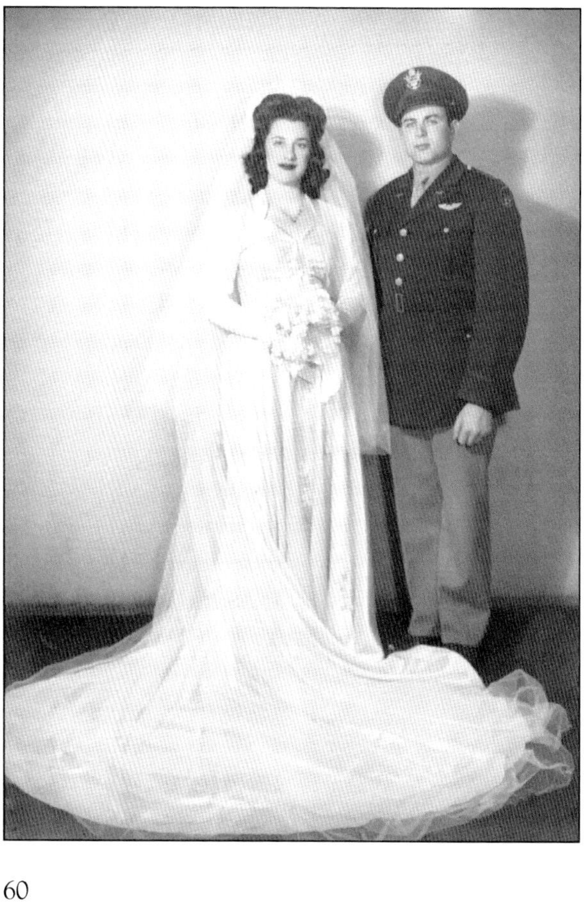

This is the wedding party portrait of Paul Kamas and Theresa Damiris on June 7, 1942. From left to right are (first row) unidentified, George Caloudas, Effie Panos (standing), and sister of the groom Pauline Kamas Verges; (second row) Jimmy Menutes, Mickey Pappas, two unidentified, father of the groom Sam Kamas, bride Theresa Damiris, groom Paul Kamas, Sophie Menutes Hadjes, ? Jelson, sister of the bride Mary Damiris, and Angelo Verges. (Courtesy of Argo Georgandis.)

This wedding portrait is of Sophie Menutes and Willard Hadjes on February 10, 1944. Their wedding reception took place at the Menutes home, located at 411 Dallas Street. Sophie was the daughter of Peter Menutes and Maria Lardis Menutes. They met in church while he was home on leave during World War II. (Courtesy of Argo Georgandis.)

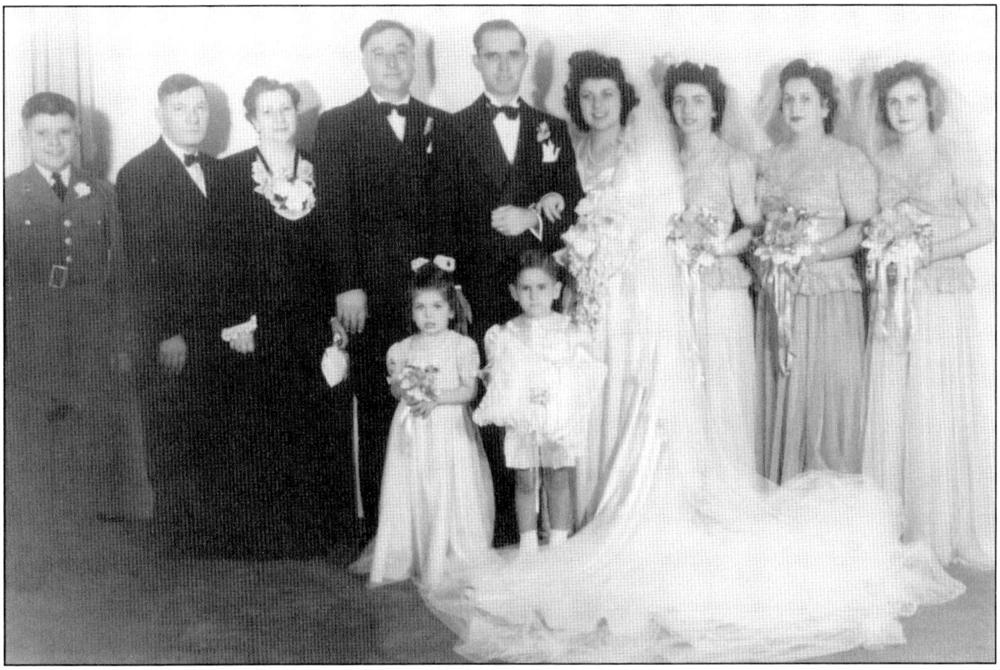

Here is the 1945 wedding party portrait of Dimitri "Captain Mimi" Couvielos and Calliope Lewis. From left to right are Michael Lewis, John Lewis, Koula Kritikos Lewis, Gus Kritikos, Dimitri Couvielos, Calliope Lewis Couvielos, Ouraneia Fokakis, Anastacia Carides, and Stella Makris. The children in front are unidentified. (Courtesy of Carol Lewis Senkel.)

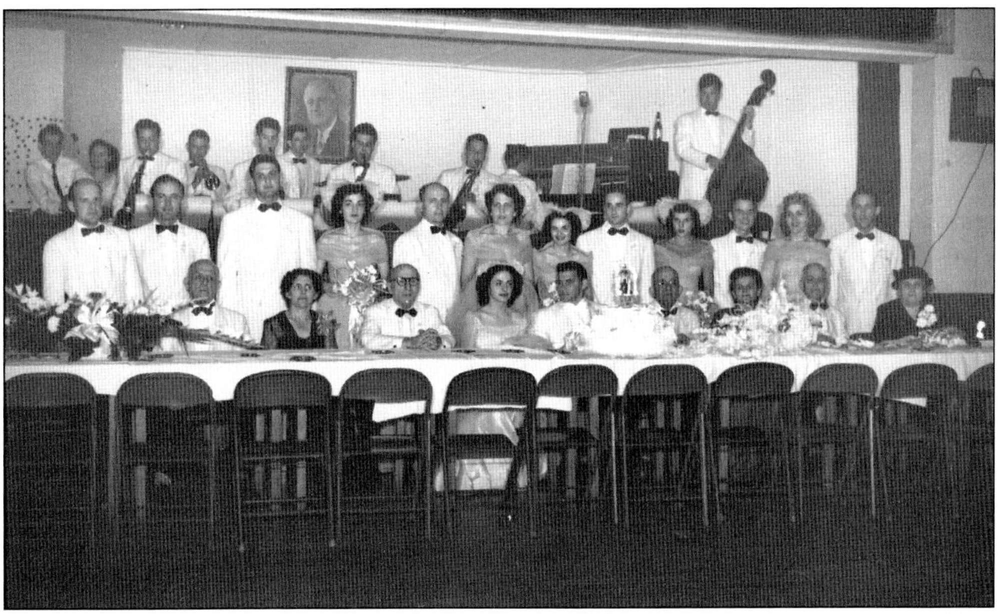

The wedding celebration of Angelo Petheriotes and Beulah Demetre occurred on June 12, 1949. Following the wedding ceremony, the wedding party went to Ship Ahoy for dinner, and the reception followed at the American Legion Hall. Buddy Brock and his band played American music, and records were played for Greek dancing. By the late 1940s, American traditions and Greek traditions were assimilated into the wedding celebrations. (Courtesy of HMRC.)

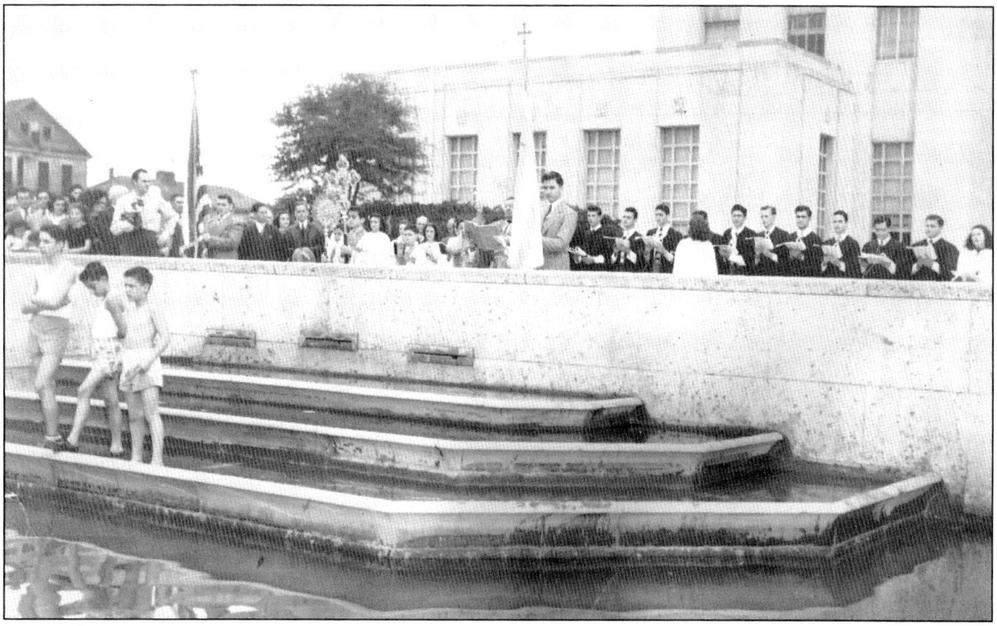

Here, the community is celebrating Epiphany on January 6 in front of city hall in the 1940s. This feast was celebrated with a Divine Liturgy and a blessing of the water. A cross was thrown into the reflection pool in front of city hall; young men dove in, vying to retrieve it. The victor returned the cross to the priest to receive a special blessing. (Courtesy of HMRC.)

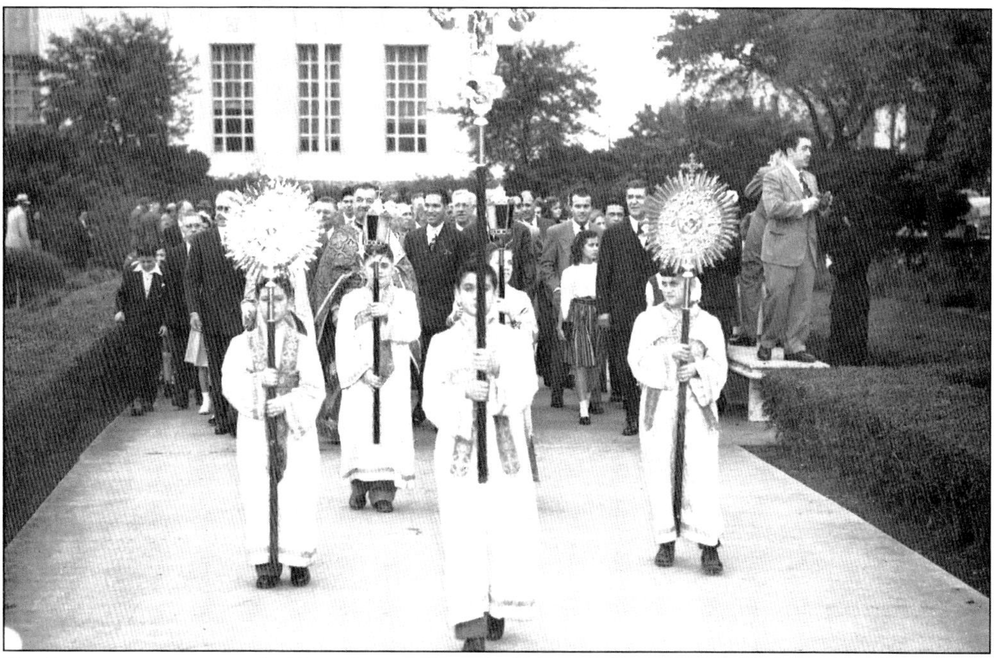

Epiphany services were held in front of city hall across from the church on Walker Street. Pictured in 1948 are, from left to right, altar boys Angelo Safos, Alfred Retsios, Angelo Vasos, and Anthony Kouzounis. In the back row are George P. Kelley, president of the parish council; Fr. Seraphim Haginas; and Councilmen James Peet, Nicholas Plainos, and John Fotinos. (Courtesy of HMRC.)

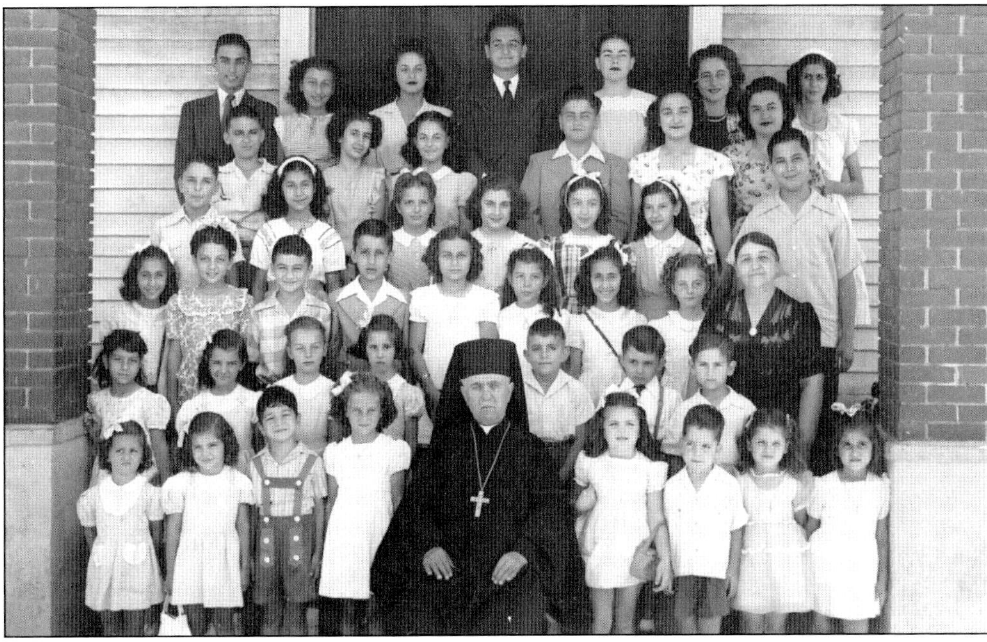

Fr. Chris Nanopoulos (1937–1946) is pictured with the Greek school students in the 1940s. The Greek school teacher was Catherine Demeris (third row). In the beginning, the priest's duties included teaching Greek to the children. However, as the priest's duties increased, Greek school teachers were hired. The first Greek school teacher was Mrs. Kyriaki Economidi, who was Fr. Michael Andreades's half sister. She taught in her home until the death of her husband in 1927. (Courtesy of HMRC.)

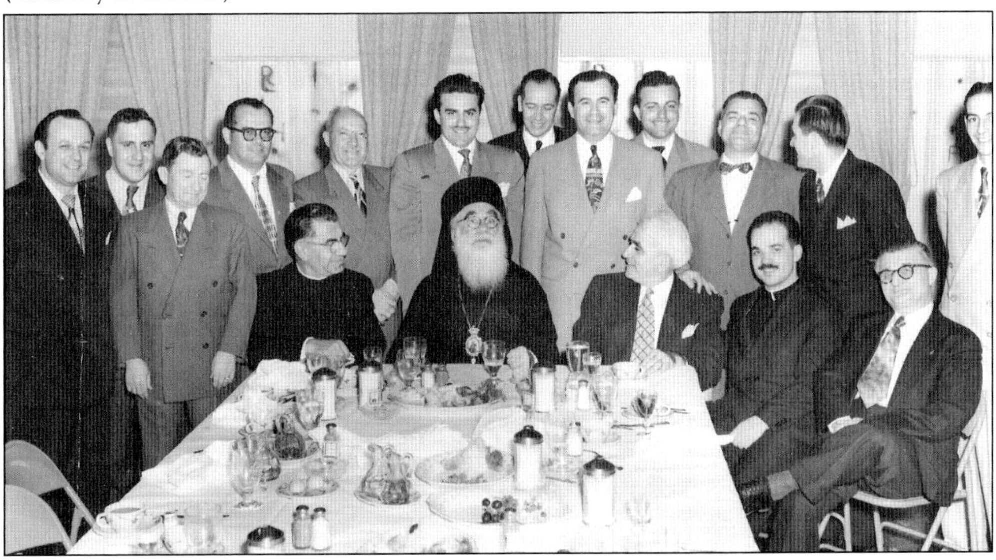

Here, His Eminence Archbishop Michael meets with the parish council at Ye Old College Inn to discuss raising funds for the church in the 1950s. Pictured are, from left to right, Paul Santire, Steve Pepps, Tom Arapolis, George Pappas, Bill Kousakis, Victor Pappas, Angelo Jelson, Jim Pappas, Nick Pappas, Nick Peet, Kosta Papavassiliou, Paul Kamas, Fr. Seraphim Haginas, His Eminence Archbishop Michael, George P. Kelly (parish council president, 1950–1952), unidentified, and Jimmy Prappas. (Courtesy of the AGOC archives.)

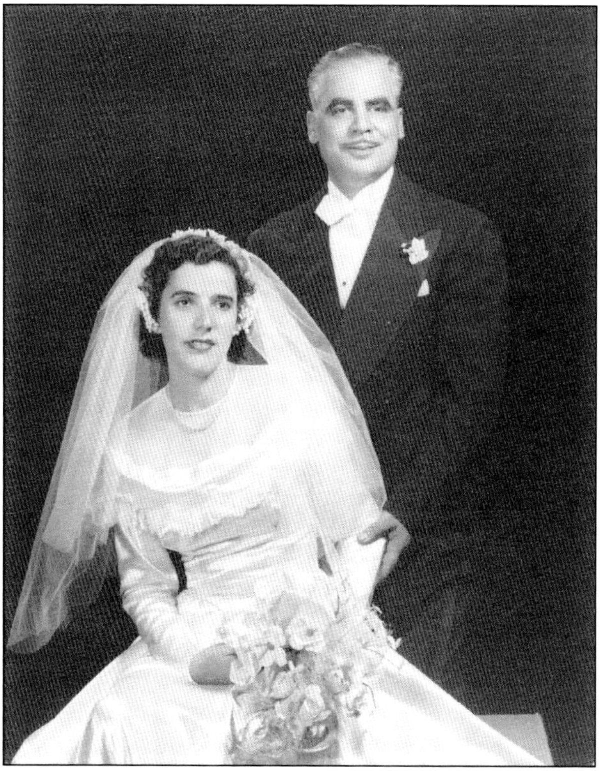

The wedding of Haido Dislianis and George Michael Grivon was on April 23, 1950. Chrisanthe Despos, a very close family friend, introduced George to Haido. Three weeks later, they were married in San Angelo, Texas, where the bride's uncle Pete Kehagas gave her away. (Courtesy of the Grivon children.)

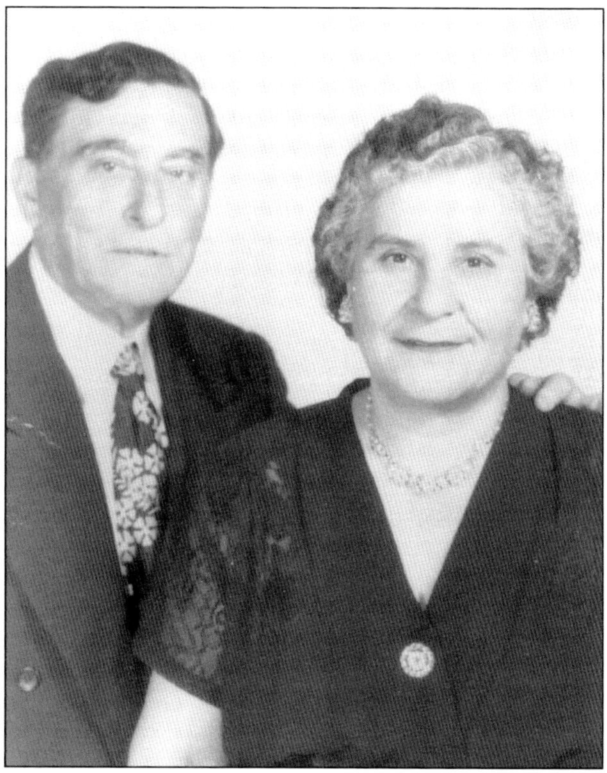

Peter and Giasemitsa Pomonis are pictured in 1955. Active members of the community, Peter and Giasemitsa attended church services faithfully as well as all the social events that the church sponsored. They were known for their love of dancing. Fr. Nicholas C. Triantafilou later named Giasemitsa Pomonis "Mother of the Community." (Courtesy of the AGOC archives.)

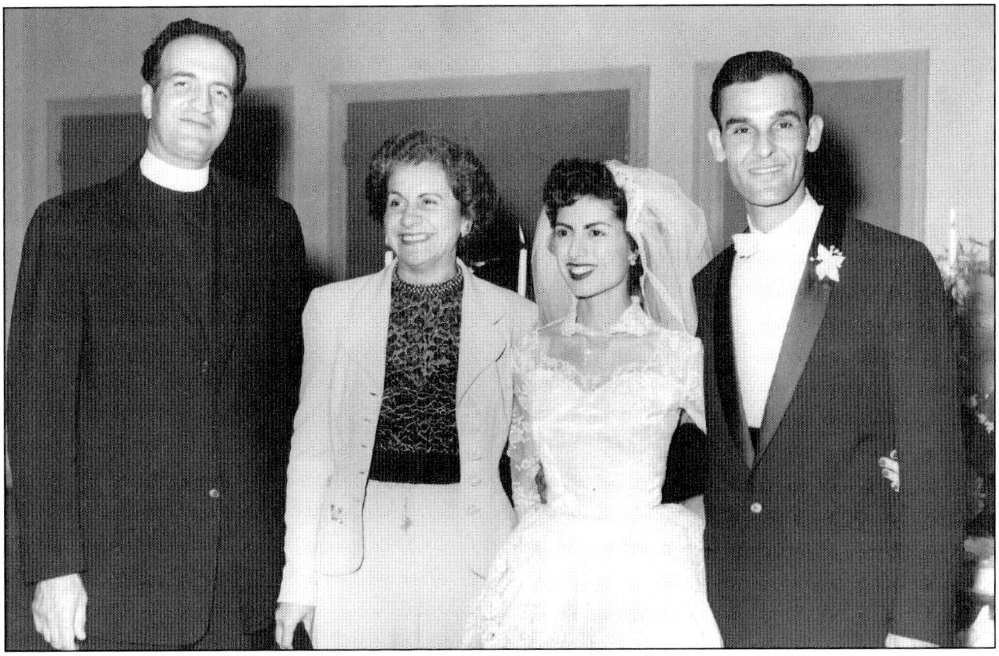

Pictured is the wedding of Toula Gazelas and Steve Kaldanis in 1955. From left to right are Fr. George Kalpaxis, Presbytera Athena Kalpaxis, Toula Kaldanis, and Steve Kaldanis. Father Kalpaxis served the church from 1954 to 1966. The groom was from Charleston, South Carolina, but moved to Houston when he met the bride. (Courtesy of Toula Kaldanis.)

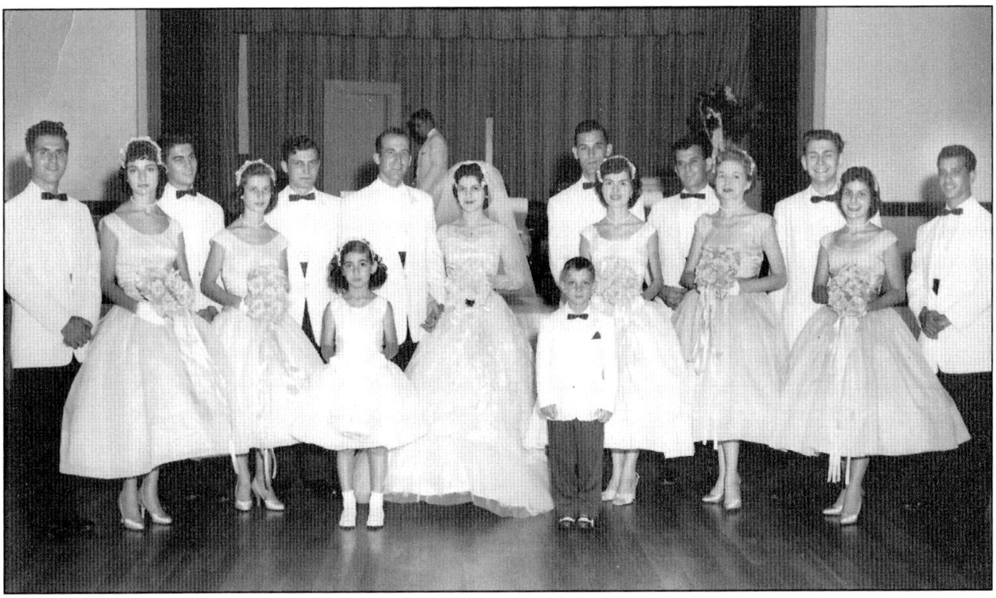

The wedding of Titika Gazelas and Steve Liollio occurred in 1957. From left to right are (first row) flower girl Meropy Pappas (Kariotes) and ring bearer Nick Gazelas; (second row) Sylvia Karahal Gazelas, Irene Gazelas (Cassis), groom Steve Liollio, bride Titika Gazelas, Toula Gazelas Kaldanis, Mary Noll, and Elaine Caloudas (Kouzounis); (third row) Harry Gazelas, Anthony Kouzounis, best man George Liollio, Steve Kaldanis, Jerry Marks, Artie Tropoli, and Mimi Mallios. (Courtesy of Toula Kaldanis.)

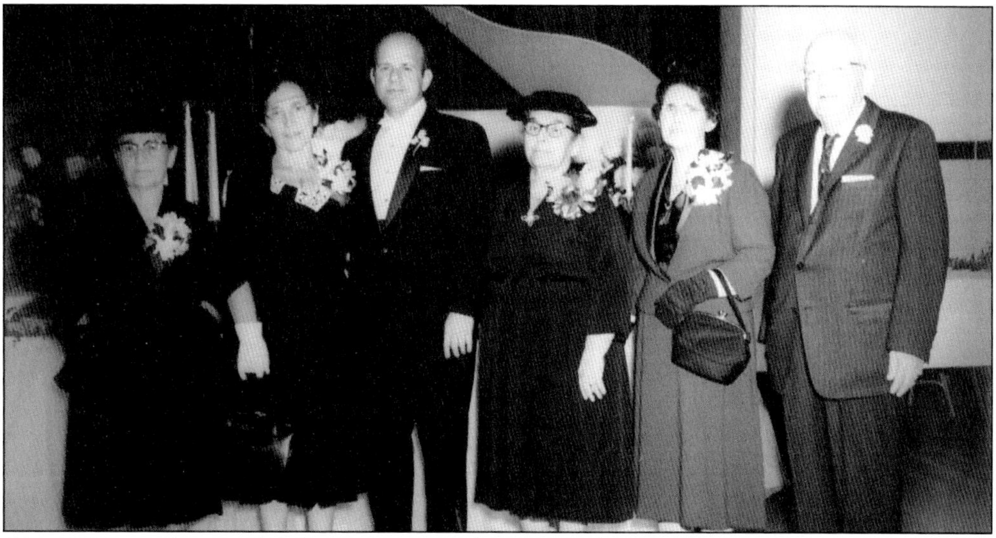

About 300 people attended the ceremony and reception for the wedding of Matina Pappas and William Peet, childhood friends, in the S.P. Martel Auditorium in October 1957. From left to right are Aphrodite (Mytilen) Verges, Tasia (Mytilen) Kousakis, groom William Peet, the groom's mother Constantina (Mytilen) Peet, Sophia (Mytilen) Petheriotes, and the groom's uncle Angelo Mytilen. (Courtesy of George Peet.)

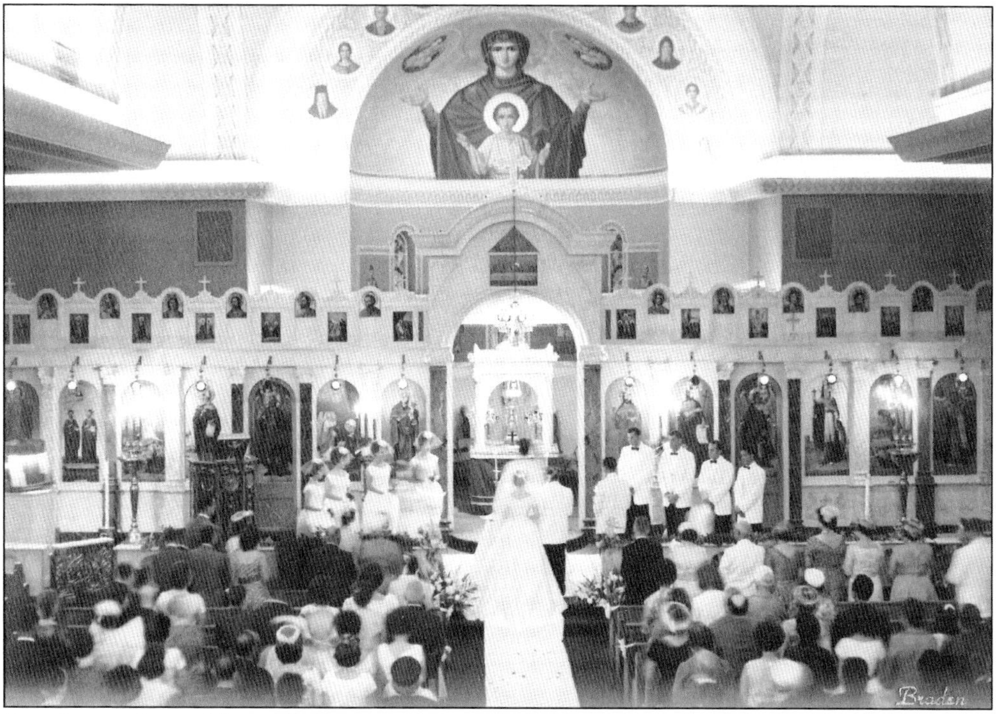

Seen here is the wedding of Diamantis J. Cassis and Irene Gazelas in the Annunciation Hellenic Eastern Orthodox Church in 1961. The groom immigrated from Galaxidi, Greece, in 1946 with his mother and joined his father in Shreveport, Louisiana. His father had left Greece 10 years earlier and established a restaurant. Diamantis moved to Houston when he married Irene. Irene's family also emigrated from Greece in 1946. (Courtesy of Irene Cassis.)

Five

The Great Wars

Just as construction on the new church at 509 Walker Street began, the United States entered World War I. Some of the men who enlisted in the US armed forces earned instant citizenship for themselves and their children. Angelo Pontikes and Leonidas Vlahos served in World War I, but Leonidas, who had recently turned 18, was killed just before the war ended.

Despite the difficulties of World War I, Houston continued to grow throughout the Roaring Twenties. Although times were hard after the stock market crash, the Greeks were familiar with adversity and sacrifice and, therefore, persevered. Because the Greek Orthodox Church was still small, its members took care of each other.

The Depression years faded, but in October 1940, Mussolini's forces invaded Greece. Greek American organizations quickly banded together to form the Greek War Relief Association. In Houston, the women sent shiploads of food and clothing to Greece and held many fundraising activities for the cause. The Greek military resistance against these invaders won the admiration of the free world because Greece resisted the Axis powers much longer than any other European country that was invaded. No longer were Greek Americans viewed as foreigners.

The Japanese attack on Pearl Harbor drove the United States into World War II. Now, with sons, husbands, and brothers in the war, the women also became regular workers at the Red Cross and YWCA, sewing and knitting for the American soldiers and selling war bonds. A banner was placed in the narthex of Annunciation listing all of the men who served with blue stars beside their names. When one was killed, a gold star replaced the blue one. Peter B. Phucas, 26, married less than a year to Vaso Chickenis, was killed in Normandy. She was three months pregnant when he left for the war. Others, like the Fress, Kanakis, and Verges families, also lost sons, husbands, and fathers. Jim Adams and Angelo Jelson were among the wounded. The courageous service of many Greek Americans further solidified and established their loyalty to the United States.

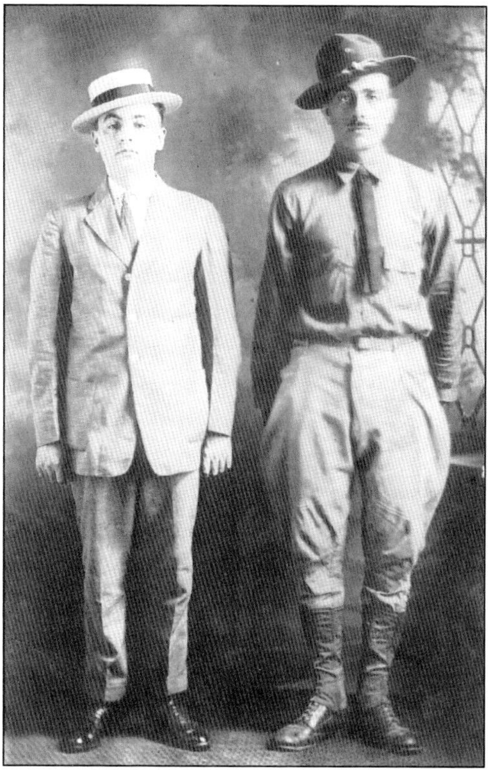

Pictured are cousins George Sacaris (left) and George Ainadjoglou (changed to Kostas). During the Balkan Wars, George Ainadjoglou left Turkey to avoid conscription in the Turkish army. In 1918, he came to the United States and enlisted in the US Army Air Force and was in the Ellington Field Flying Detachment. He was a cook for his unit. He obtained US citizenship during World War I. (Courtesy of Anastasia Poulos.)

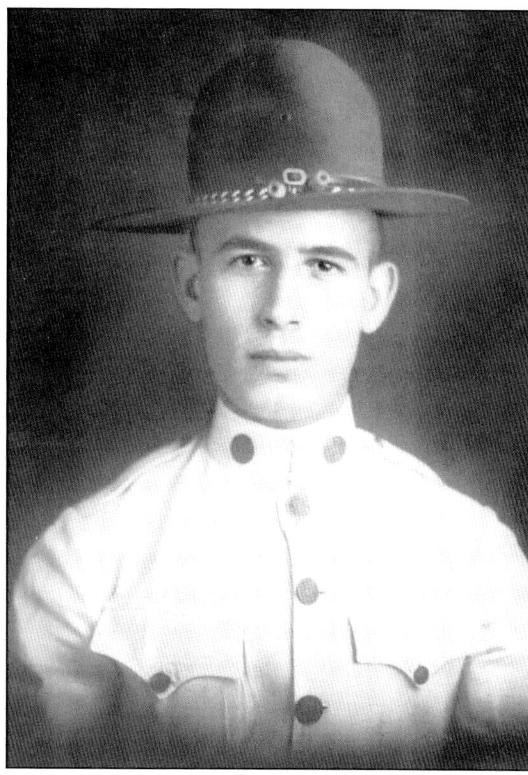

Pvt. Alexander J. Kanakis, a 20-year-old in 1918, enlisted in the US Army in World War I. He was stationed in Fort Sam Houston, in San Antonio, Texas. After the war, he returned to Houston and worked as a waiter at Kelley's Restaurant until he opened his own restaurant in the 1930s. He was an active member of the church and served as a chanter. (Courtesy of Gus Kanakis.)

Raleigh Poulos enlisted in the US Army and served in World War II in 1942. A sergeant, Raleigh was in the artillery battalion and served in four campaigns with Gen. George S. Patton's army in Europe. They landed in France three days after D-Day. Raleigh was injured in France and served until 1945. (Courtesy of Mary Poulos.)

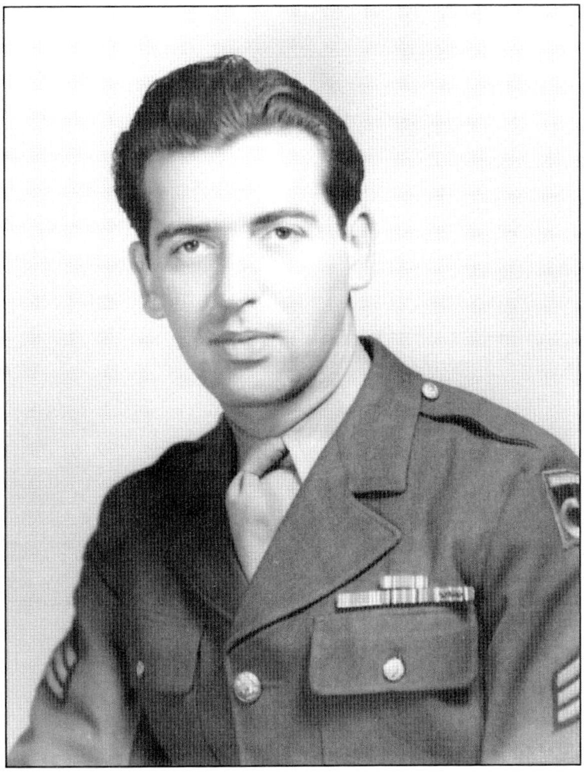

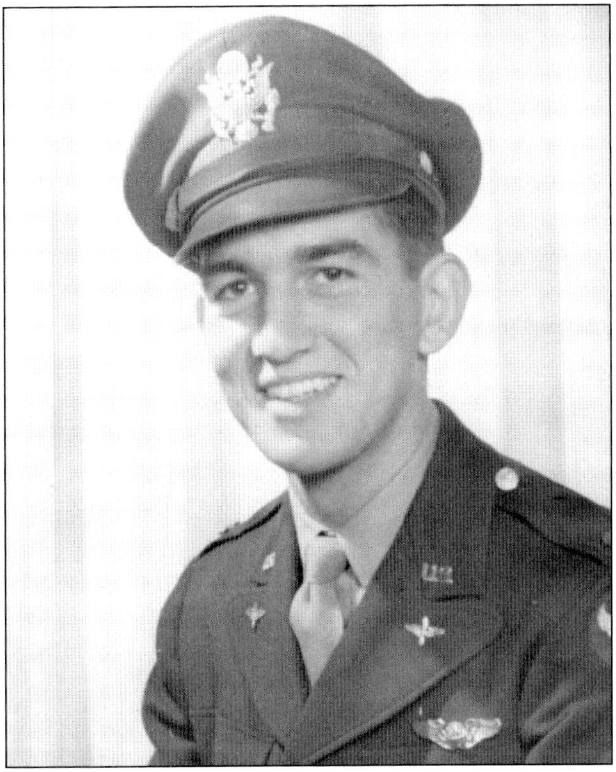

John Poulos enlisted in the Army Air Force during World War II, attaining the rank of first lieutenant in 1943. He served as navigator in the 13th AAF's famed "Snoopers" B-24 Liberator Squadron's history-making 18-hour raid of Batavia, Java. John was in the Air Force Reserves from 1945 to 1955 and was recalled during the Korean Conflict (1952–1955). John Poulos served as president of the parish council (1963–1964). (Courtesy of Mary Poulos.)

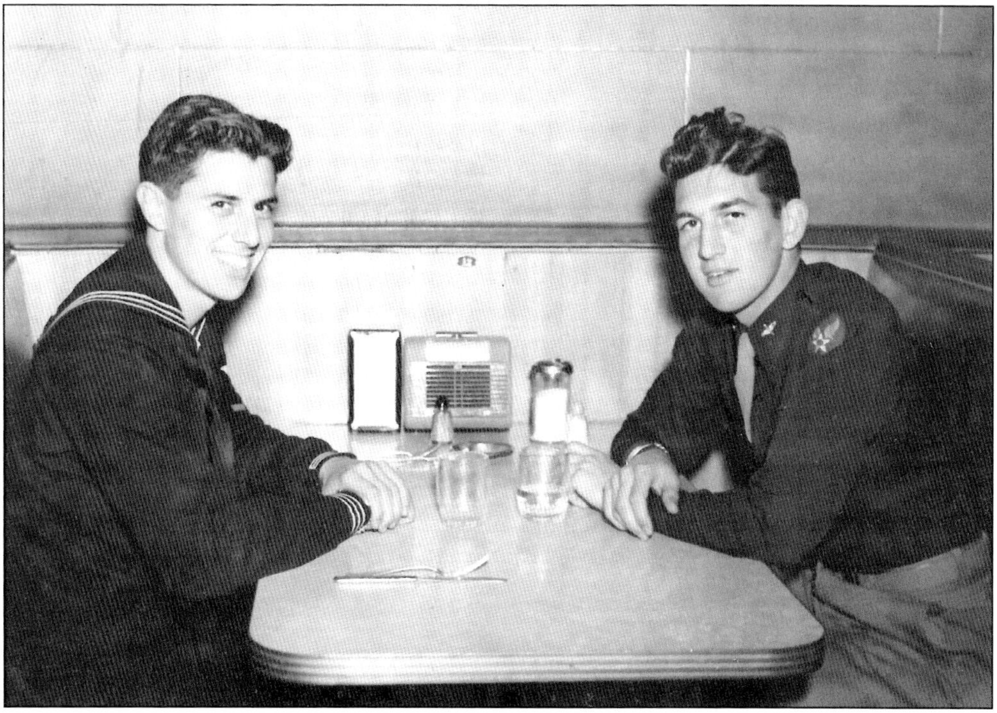

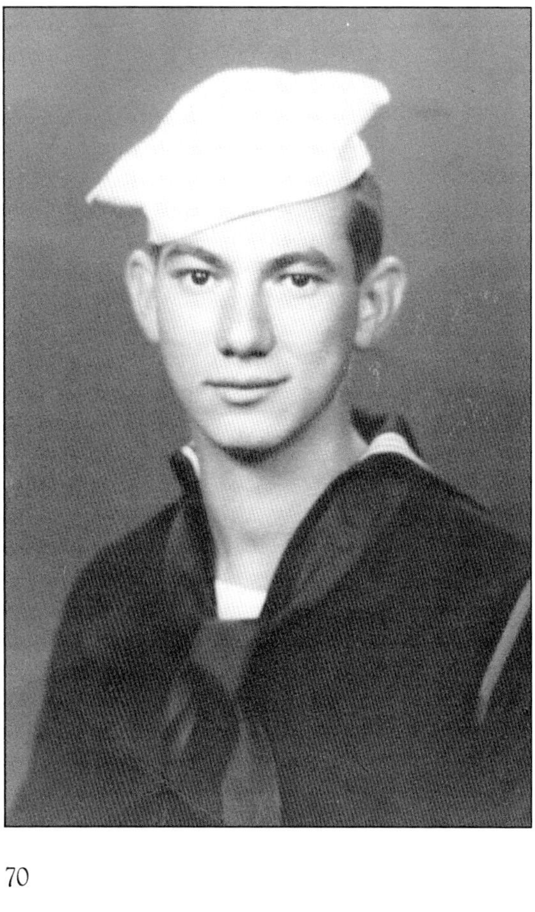

Pictured are brothers Pete A. Poulos (left) and John A. Poulos on leave in San Francisco in 1945. Pete enlisted in the US Navy in 1944 and served in World War II. He was on a patrol craft subchaser (PCS-1400), stationed in San Diego. They conducted training missions off the coast of Mexico, training sailors to use sonar to detect submarines. (Courtesy of Ann Poulos.)

In 1943, at the age of 18, Nick Lewis enlisted and served in the US Navy in the South Pacific during World War II. He served on a cruiser and patrolled the South Pacific. His family believes that his death due to lung cancer when he was 48 years old may have been caused by his exposure to an explosion on the ship he was serving on. (Courtesy of Carol Lewis Senkel.)

Sgt. Joseph A. Kanakis served in the US Army Air Force as a belly gunner in a B-17 bomber in World War II in 1943. He was stationed in Ganders, Newfoundland, and was reported missing in action on December 19, 1943, when his plane went down. Unable to recover his body, the crew, or the aircraft, the US Army Air Force declared Joseph A. Kanakis officially dead one year later. (Courtesy of Gus Kanakis.)

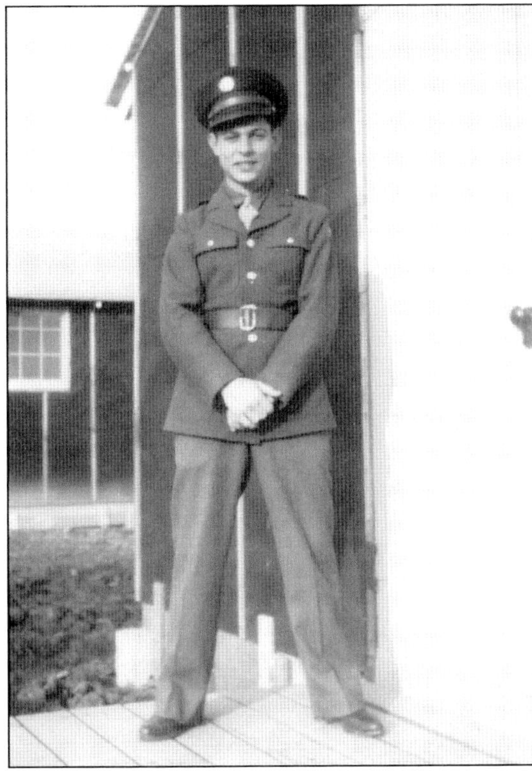

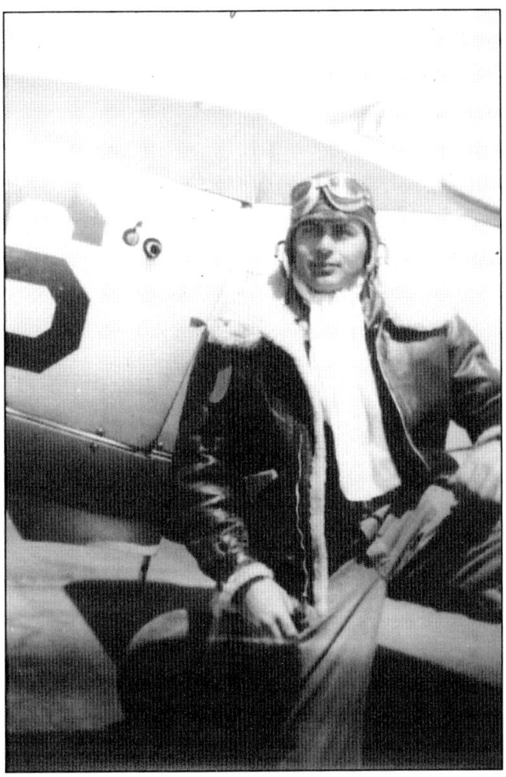

Capt. Willard Hadjes served in the US Army Air Force in World War II. Among the original B-17 crewmembers of the 398th Bomber Group, he flew in the first wave over Normandy on D-Day. On June 18, 1944, his plane was shot down over Hamburg, Germany. Hadjes landed safely and the crew survived, but he was taken prisoner. Gen. George Patton liberated him in 1945. (Courtesy of Diane Vroulis.)

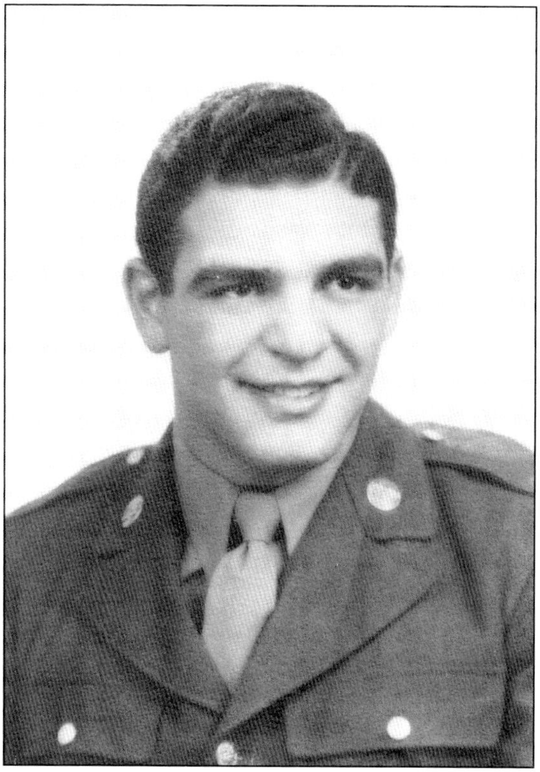

Thomas J. Lykos enlisted in the US Army and served in the 356th Medical Detachment in Candu, India, treating ill soldiers from 1943 to 1946. He graduated from the University of Texas with a law degree and settled in Houston. Tom served as president of the parish council for a total of five nonconsecutive terms (1954–1980). In 1954, the parish raised $18,000 for its annual mortgage payment under his leadership. (Courtesy of Irene and Thomas J. Lykos.)

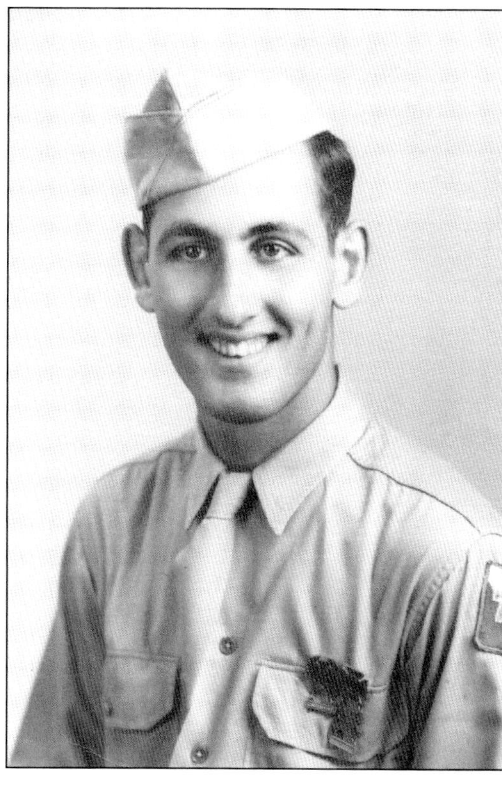

Jack Lymberry served in the US Army, 75th Infantry Division, from January 1944 to October 1945. Wounded twice, he received the Bronze Star and two Purple Hearts. While serving in Germany, he became a prisoner of war for two and a half months. In Houston, Jack served on the parish council (1977–1978). (Courtesy of Jack Lymberry and his daughter Christina Lymberry McIntyre.)

Serving from 1943, Michael P. Cokinos fought at the Battle of the Bulge and in the Ardennes, Rhineland, as well as in Central Europe. He supervised 100,000 displaced persons in the Cumberland Area of Austria. He retired as a brigadier general of the Army Reserve Command in 1980, with the Silver Star, Purple Heart, Legion of Merit, World War II European theater with three Battle Stars, Occupational Medal (Germany), and the American Defense. (Courtesy of Katherine Cokinos.)

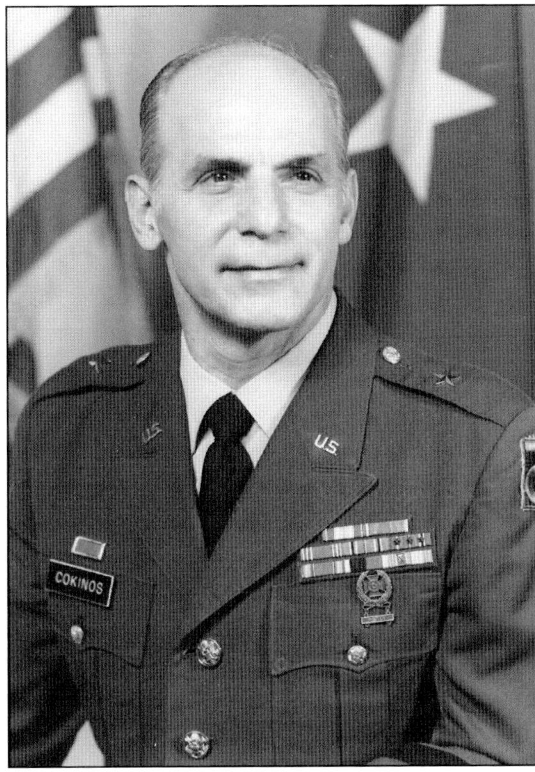

On January 26, 1945, 2nd Lt. Michael P. Cokinos received the Silver Star for gallantry in action while serving in Germany. As forward observer, Cokinos directed artillery for over 50 hours and organized medical evacuations. When his commander was wounded, Cokinos administered first aid, covered the officer with his body, and protected the commander's face with his helmet until the mortar barrage slackened. (Courtesy of Cokinos children.)

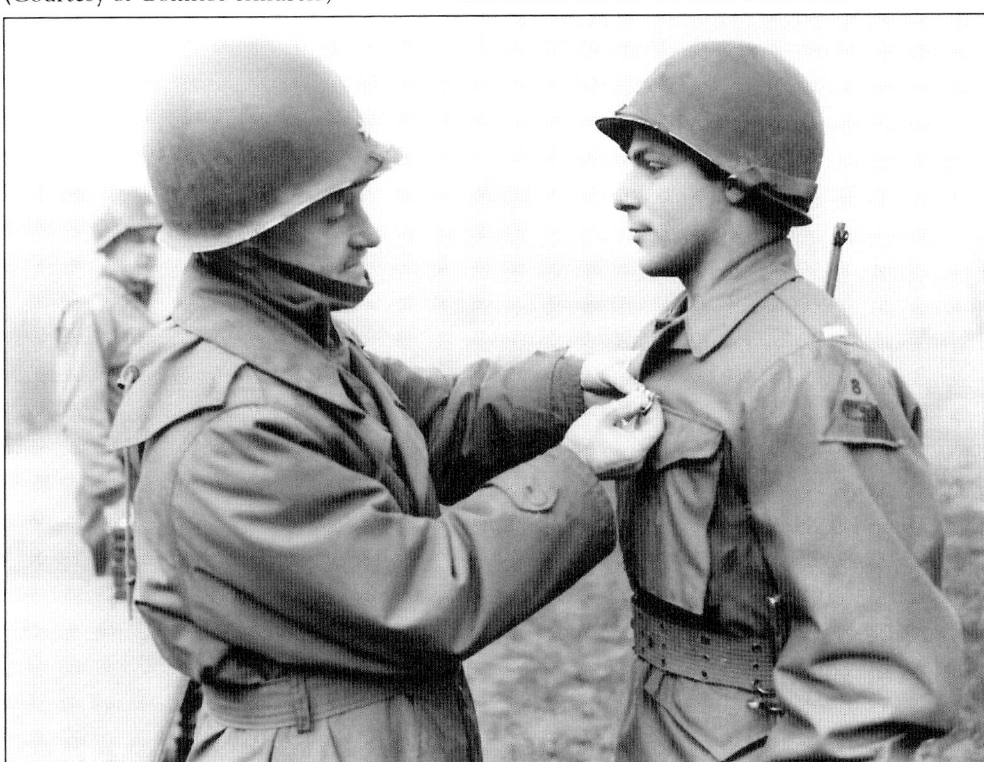

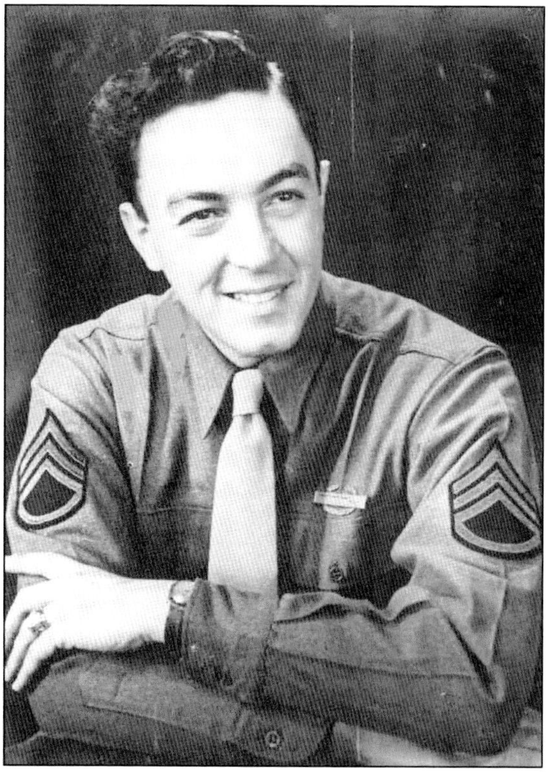

Houstonian Leonidas (Louis) Brailas graduated from Texas A&M University and served in the US Army in World War II as a private in the Infantry Artillery Unit. While serving in Ardennes, Rhineland, he and his half-brother Capt. Constantinos (Gus) Standish fought one mile apart from one another in the Battle of the Bulge but did not know it. Louis was wounded and received the Purple Heart. (Courtesy of Anastasia Poulos.)

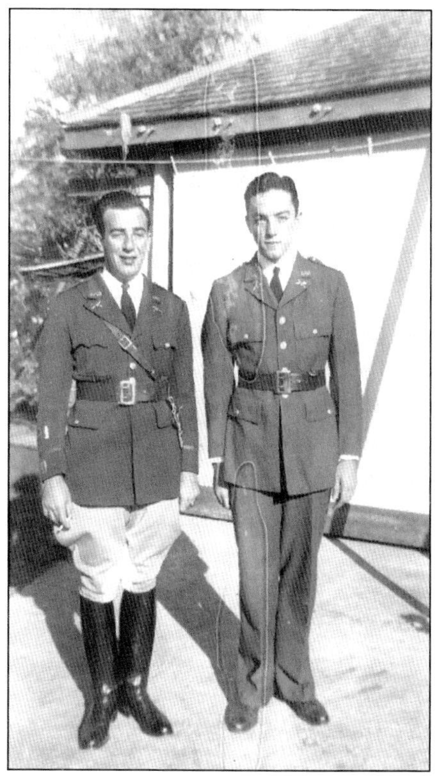

Pictured are Constantinos (Gus) Standish (left) and Leonidas (Louis) Brailas. Brailas was called upon again during the Korean Conflict, where he obtained the rank of lieutenant and was awarded the Bronze Star for acts of heroism. (Courtesy of Anastasia Poulos.)

Gus Kanakis joined the US Navy at the age of 17. He served as a petty officer in the South Pacific from 1944 to 1946. His unit was attached to the Antiaircraft Training Center for naval personnel. He was the cook for a unit of 250 men. After the war, Gus returned to Houston. An active member of the Annunciation community, he served on the parish council (1968–1970). (Courtesy of Gus Kanakis.)

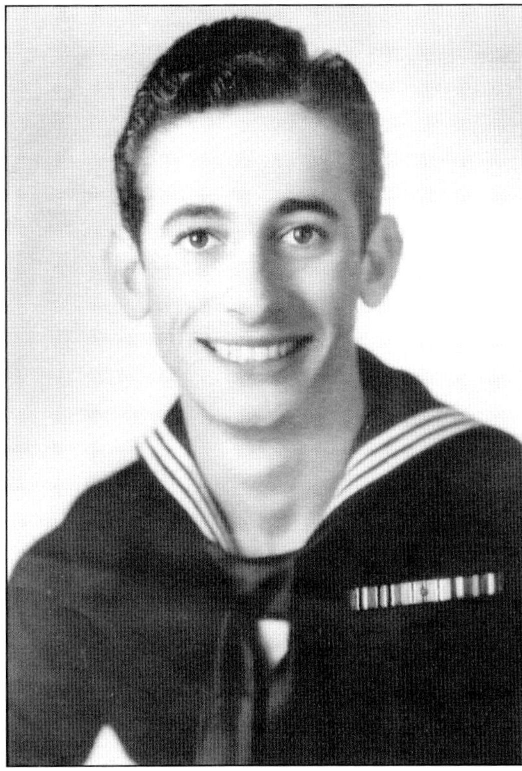

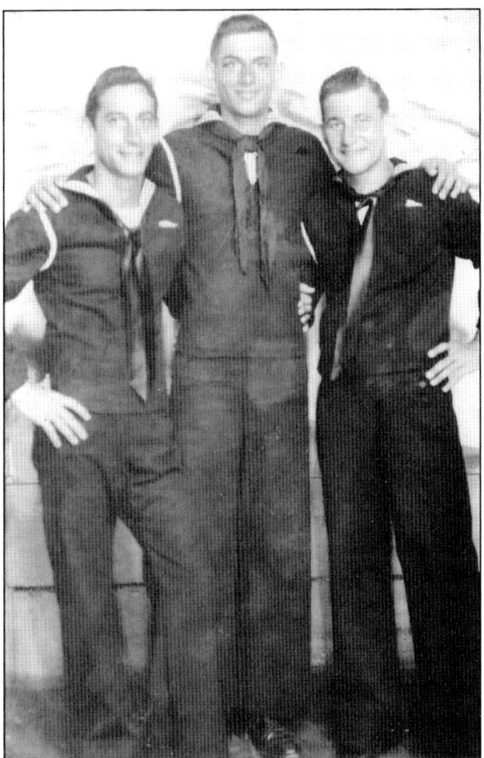

From left to right, Gus A. Kanakis, Peter Hademenos, and Spero Kefalas were three friends from Houston who joined the US Navy in 1944 and served in the South Pacific. On furlough, they accidently ran into each other on the street in San Diego. (Courtesy of Gus Kanakis.)

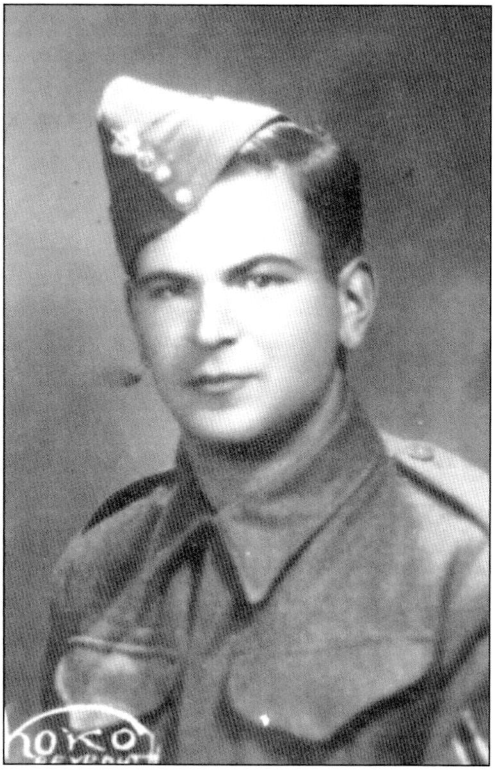

Kostas Ioannidis, from Samos, Greece, fought with the Allies in North Africa during World War II. He came to Houston in the late 1940s and attended the University of Houston. Kostas was active in the Annunciation community and served on the parish council (1974–1976). Kostas Ioannidis died in 1989. (Courtesy of the AGOC archives.)

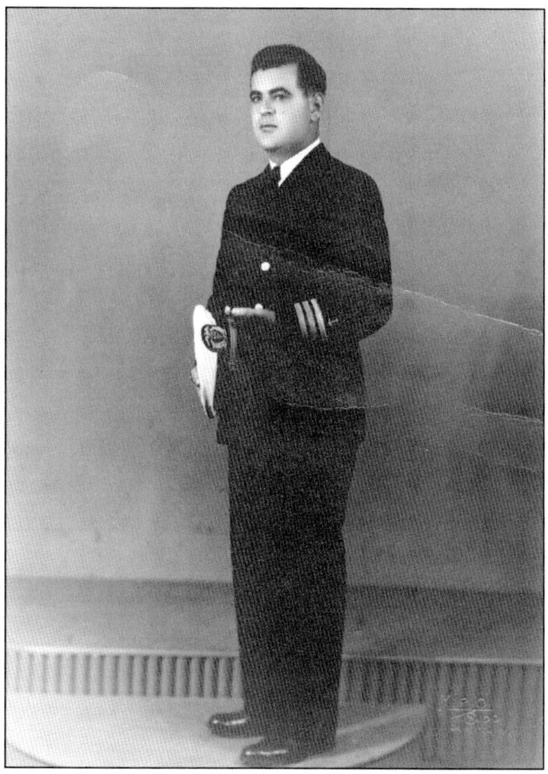

Adamantios (Diamanti) Georgandis was a captain in the US Navy during World War II. In 1947, he married Mary Damiris in the Hellenic Orthodox Church, which was later named the Annunciation Greek Orthodox Church, in Houston. His brother-in-law Peter Damiris served in World War I and was injured in France. (Courtesy of Argo Georgandis.)

George J. Pappas served in the US Army Air Force from 1942 to 1944. On August 7, 1944, the *Houston Press* reported that Lt. George J. Pappas, a copilot on his 17th mission, had been shot down in his B-17 and was reported missing in action. He had only been married for 14 months. George survived and was taken as a prisoner of war in Germany. (Courtesy of Dean and Kathy Pappas.)

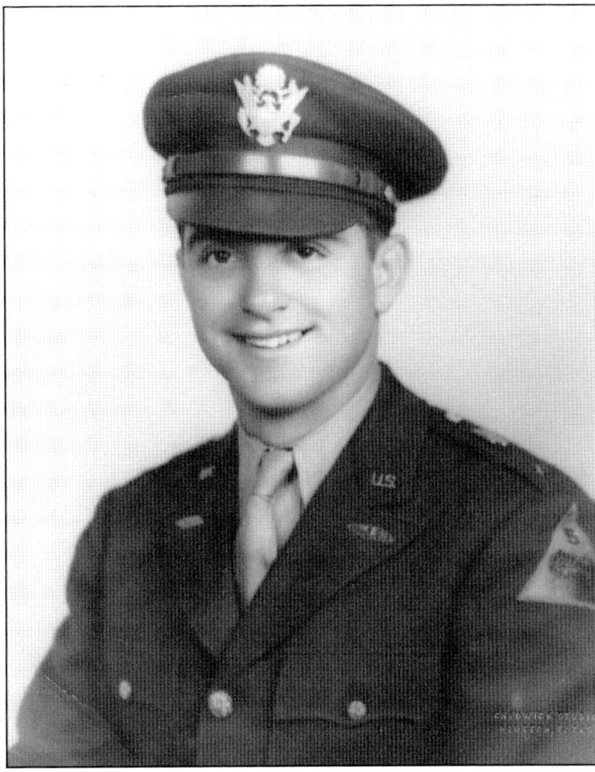

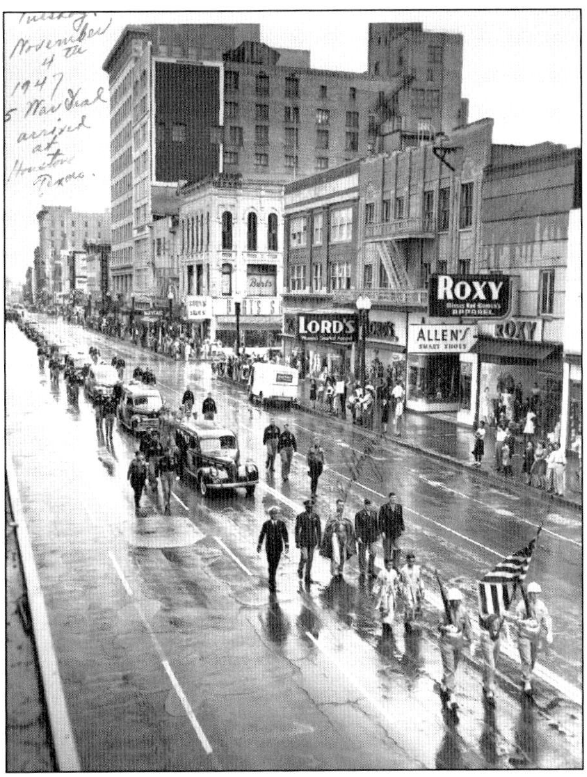

Greek Americans who were killed during World War II were received home on Tuesday, November 4, 1947, a somber, rainy day in Houston. The parade was led by a color guard, followed by two altar boys. Fr. Seraphim Haginas, flanked by members of the four branches of the military, led the procession. A military honor guard accompanied each of the five hearses; family members followed in a long line of limousines stretching down Main Street. (Courtesy of HMRC.)

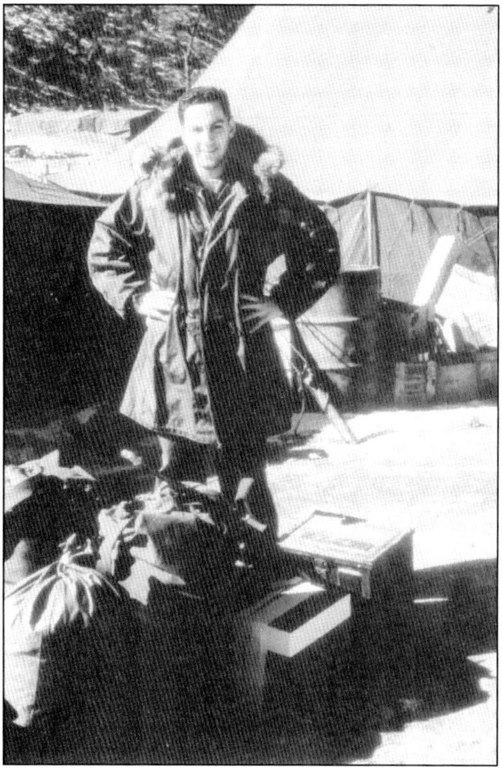

James (Jim) Bellos served in the US Army as a sergeant with the 40th Infantry Division as combat medic in the 115th Medical Battalion during the Korean War. Wounded in Inje, North Korea, on November 11, 1952, he was discharged from a MASH hospital on November 23 and received the Purple Heart. (Courtesy of James Bellos.)

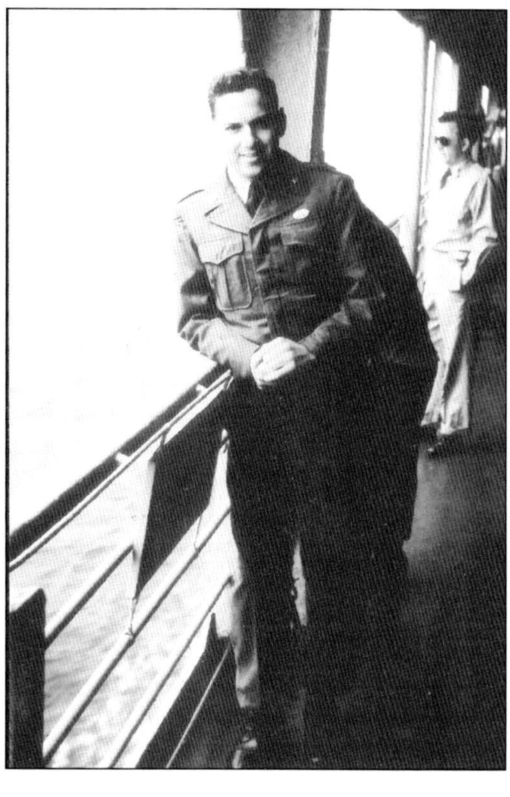

Jim Bellos graduated from the University of Texas at Austin (1946–1950) with a degree in pharmacy. He received the Commendation Ribbon with Medal Pendant and Combat Medic Badge for organizing the pharmacy section in his unit to treat the sick and wounded during the Korean War. He returned home on April 24, 1952. He married Mary Dabanlis, who served as director of the Sunday school at Annunciation Greek Orthodox Cathedral from 1972 to 1987. (Courtesy of James Bellos.)

Drafted at the age of 21, Emmanuel (Mike) Pantazis served as a corporal in the US Army during the Korean War. He was wounded and taken prisoner from May 18, 1951, to August 14, 1953. His parents, Nicholas and Cleopatra Pantazis, received a missing-in-action letter but did not know he was a prisoner of war until the Chinese government released the names at Christmas 1951. (Courtesy of Emmanuel Pantazis.)

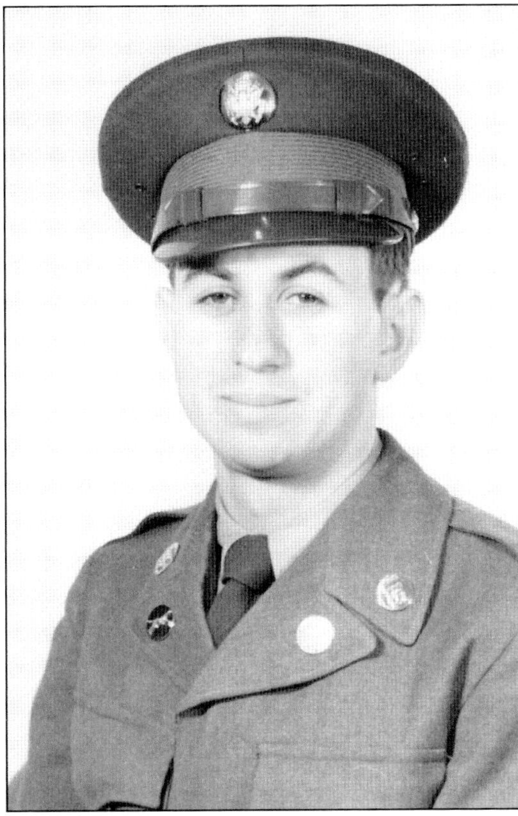

In 1953, Emmanuel (Mike) Pantazis sent his family a telegram telling them he was coming home. When he arrived at LaGuardia Airport, about 100 friends and relatives were waiting for him. His parents had arranged a welcome home party at St. Spyridon Church. Mike returned to Polytech Institute of Brooklyn and earned a degree in electrical engineering. In 1965, he came to Houston and began working for the National Aeronautics Space Administration (NASA). (Courtesy of Emmanuel Pantazis.)

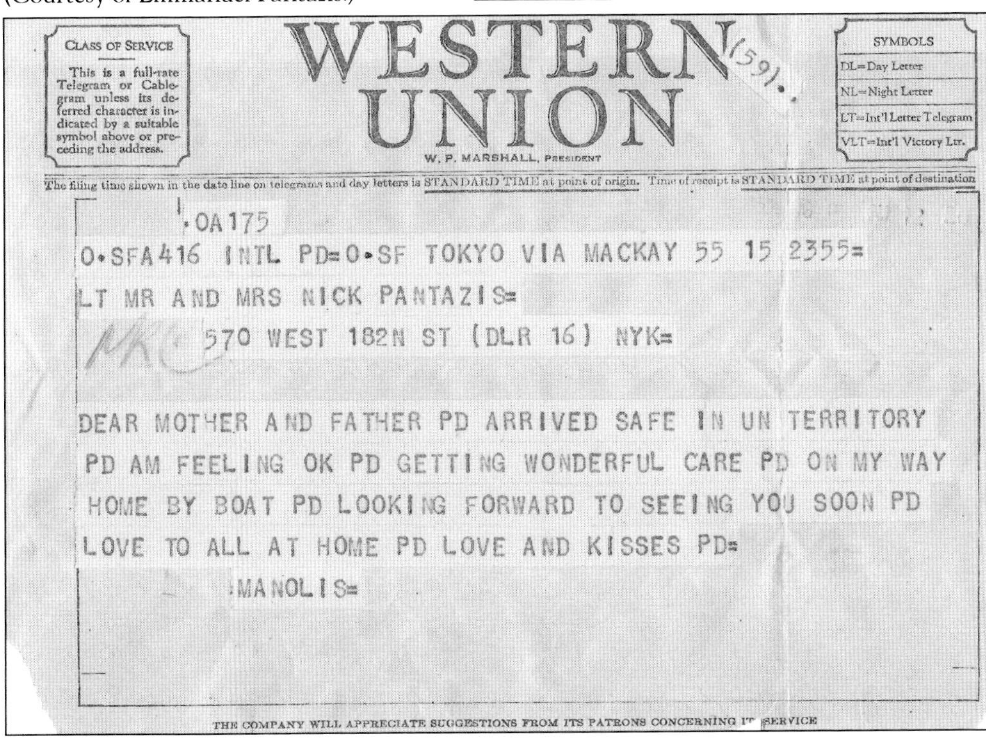

CLASS OF SERVICE

This is a full-rate Telegram or Cablegram unless its deferred character is indicated by a suitable symbol above or preceding the address.

WESTERN UNION (59)

W. P. MARSHALL, PRESIDENT

SYMBOLS

DL=Day Letter

NL=Night Letter

LT=Int'l Letter Telegram

VLT=Int'l Victory Ltr.

The filing time shown in the date line on telegrams and day letters is STANDARD TIME at point of origin. Time of receipt is STANDARD TIME at point of destination

.OA175

O.SFA416 INTL PD=O.SF TOKYO VIA MACKAY 55 15 2355=

LT MR AND MRS NICK PANTAZIS=

570 WEST 182N ST (DLR 16) NYK=

DEAR MOTHER AND FATHER PD ARRIVED SAFE IN UN TERRITORY PD AM FEELING OK PD GETTING WONDERFUL CARE PD ON MY WAY HOME BY BOAT PD LOOKING FORWARD TO SEEING YOU SOON PD LOVE TO ALL AT HOME PD LOVE AND KISSES PD=

MANOLIS=

THE COMPANY WILL APPRECIATE SUGGESTIONS FROM ITS PATRONS CONCERNING IT SERVICE

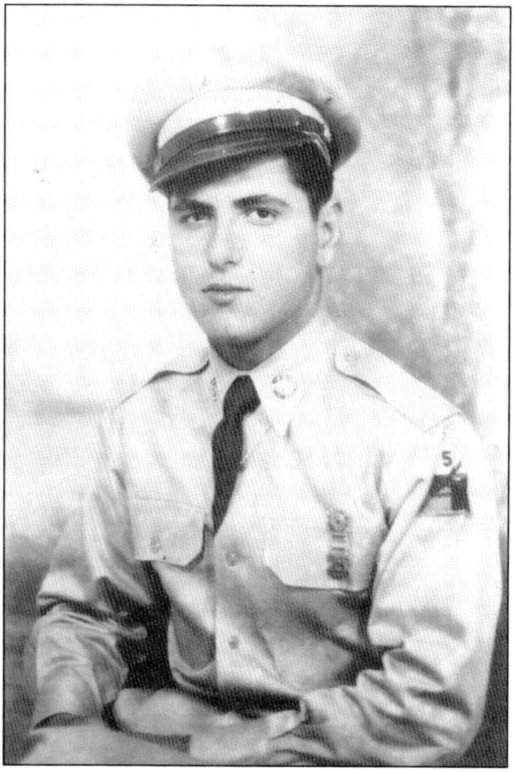

Harry Gazelas served in the US Army from 1950 to 1953 during the Korean War. He was wounded three times and received the Purple Heart each time. He was also a prisoner of war in Korea but managed to escape despite being wounded. (Courtesy of Toula Kaldanis.)

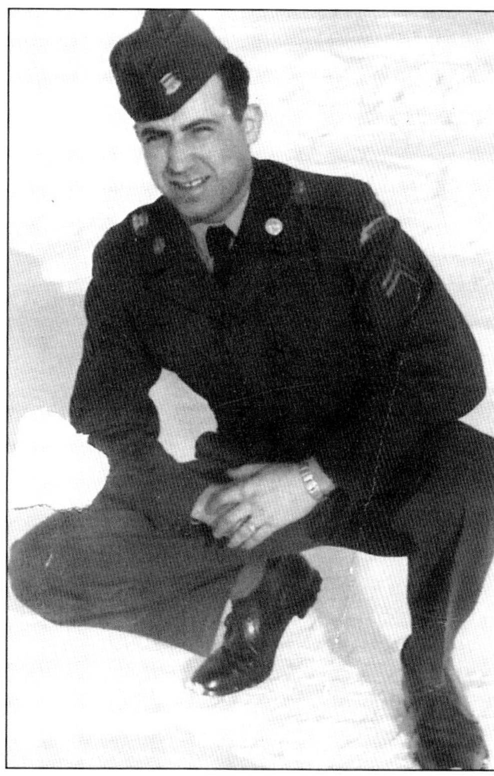

Stylianos (Steve) Liollio was drafted into the US Army and promoted to corporal during his service from 1950 to 1953. Stationed in Germany, Steve was trained as a machine gunner to identify enemy planes. Serving as best man for his friend Steve Kaldanis in Houston, he met and married Titika, the bride's sister. Because his future father-in-law stipulated that they could not marry unless they remained here, they settled in Houston. (Courtesy of Titika Liollio.)

Steve Kaldanis was born in Charleston, South Carolina. When he was a child, his parents returned to Epiros, Greece, but in 1950, Steve returned to Charleston where his sister resided. He was drafted into the US Army during the Korean War and served as a private who repaired generators from 1950 to 1953. He met and married Toula Gazelas in 1954 and moved to Houston. (Courtesy of Toula Kaldanis.)

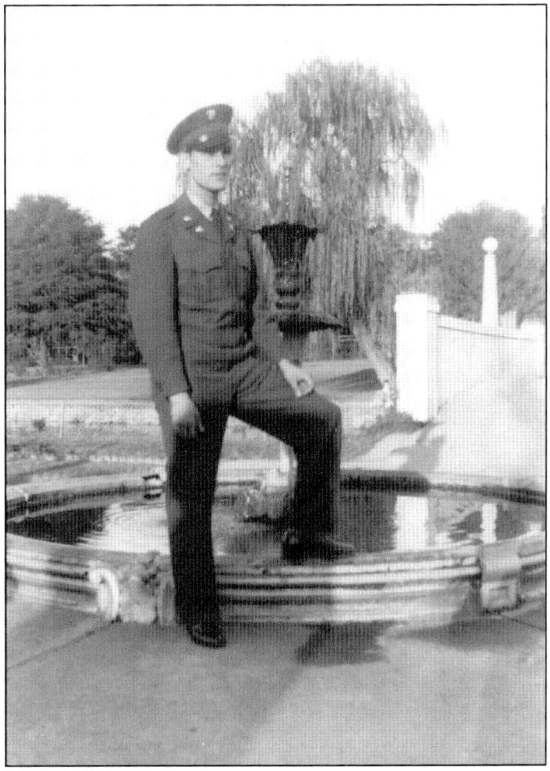

Diamantis John Cassis served in the US Army, first training recruits at Fort Knox, Kentucky, in 1959–1960, and then in the active Army Reserves from 1960 to 1987. He began his service in the Army as a second lieutenant. While in the reserves, he attended officer training schools and conducted training programs for armored units in the active Army. He retired with the rank of lieutenant colonel. (Courtesy of Irene Cassis.)

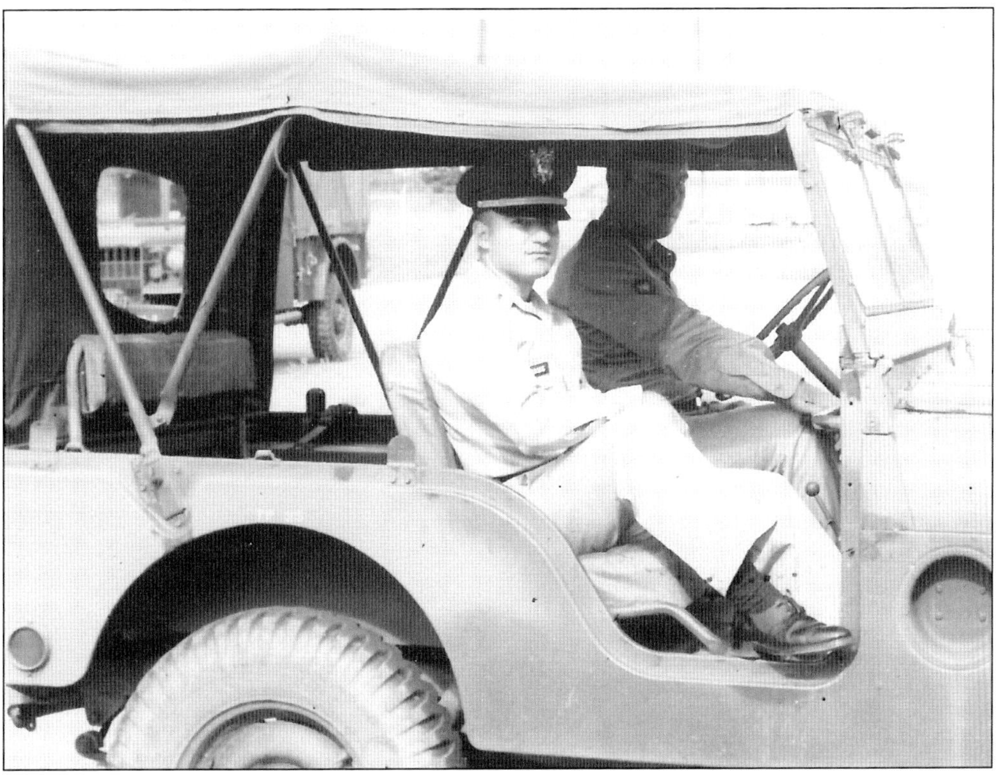

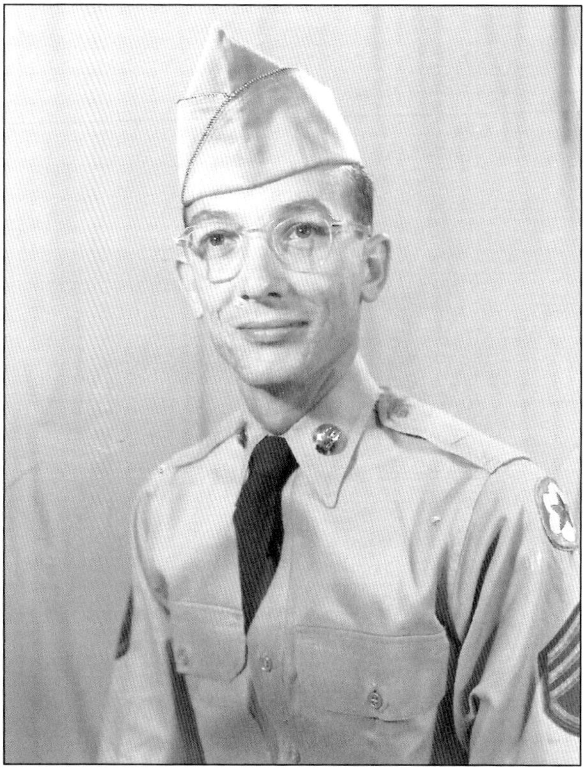

Alexander A. Jelson served in the US Army as a staff sergeant during the Korean War and served in Special Services doing laboratory work at William Beaumont Hospital in El Paso, Texas, from 1953 to 1955. Alex's father, Athanasios, was president of the parish council (1920). His brothers served in the Army during World War II: George was in the CIA, Angelo's ship was torpedoed going to India, and Johnny was injured in Europe. (Courtesy of Alexander A. Jelson.)

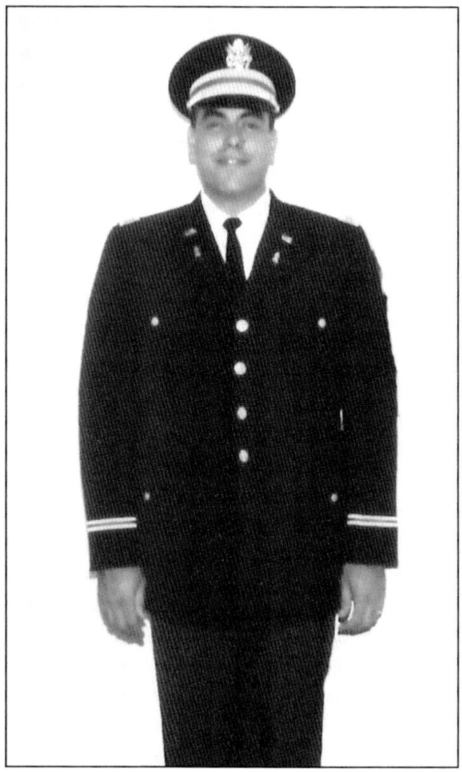

George Stefanidakis served in the US Army with the rank of captain from 1968 to 1974. Under the Ordinance Corps, he did research on chemical weapons in Edgewood, Maryland. At Annunciation, he was on the parish council and was the first activities chairman of the Greek Orthodox Community Center, organizing outdoor family activities in the early 1970s. He sings in the choir and also serves as a chanter. (Courtesy of Dr. George Stefanidakis.)

Six

Greek American Identity

The American Hellenic Educational Progressive Association (AHEPA) was formed on July 26, 1922, and believed that through education, Greeks could peacefully combat the prejudice perpetuated by the Ku Klux Klan. On December 17, 1923, the Greek American Progressive Association (GAPA) was established. Whereas a prerequisite for membership in AHEPA was American citizenship and only English was spoken at their meetings, GAPA adhered to its goals of preserving the Greek language, traditions, and religion. Youth organizations sponsored by AHEPA included the Sons of Pericles, the Daughters of Penelope, and the Maids of Athena. The GAPA women's chapter was Androniki, the men's chapter was Marcos Botsaris, and the young women's organization was Gamma Sigma Alpha (GSA).

Greek Orthodox Youth of America (GOYA) was founded in 1951. Originally for young adults from 18 to 25, GOYA later evolved into a teenage youth group. The Young Adult League (YAL), which welcomed those between the ages of 18 and 35, was formed in the 1970s. Spurred into action by the Turkish invasion of Cyprus, the Hellenic Professional Society was formed in January 1975 and immediately hosted a fundraising piano recital by Deno Gianopoulos for the refugees. Sponsoring cultural and educational events, the organization serves as a bridge between immigrants and Greek Americans.

The Women's Church Society, forerunner of today's Philoptochos, was established to support the church in every endeavor. By 1944, the Philoptochos Society was formed. The Women' s Church Society later dissolved and turned over its treasury of $2,000 to the parish council. Its members combined with Philoptochos to concentrate the efforts of the women in the parish.

Other types of clubs that began during this period evolved from groups of people who hailed from various parts of Greece. For example, Patmians formed the Patmian Society of St. John the Divine. Those from Chios began the Chios Society. Along with their generosity to their compatriots in Greece, these clubs were active in supporting their local church by implementing programs and maintaining traditions. In addition, they stressed the importance of becoming good American citizens and working toward success in their new homeland.

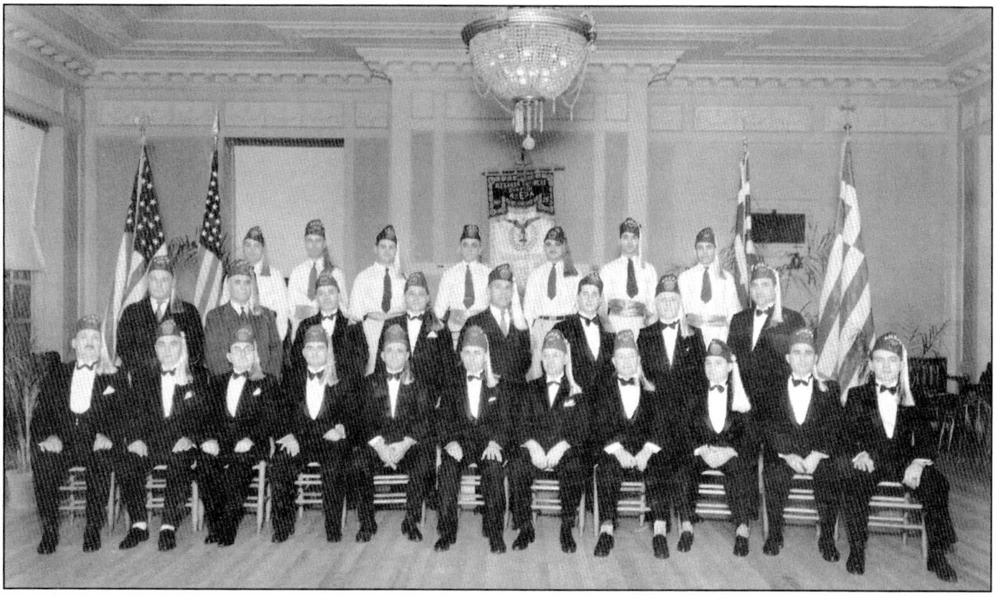

Newly elected officers and past officers of AHEPA Chapter No. 29, Alexander the Great, Houston, are pictured on February 4, 1934. AHEPA was organized in Houston in 1922. A newspaper article on AHEPA's purpose included participation in all worthwhile civic projects, promotion of the good of the city, and character building. Some of the early charter members were Jim Teflos, George Jelson (the second president), John Giannukos, Sam Giannukos, Jim Poulos, Angelo Jelson, Rudolph Harris, and Gus Malavansos. (Courtesy of HMRC.)

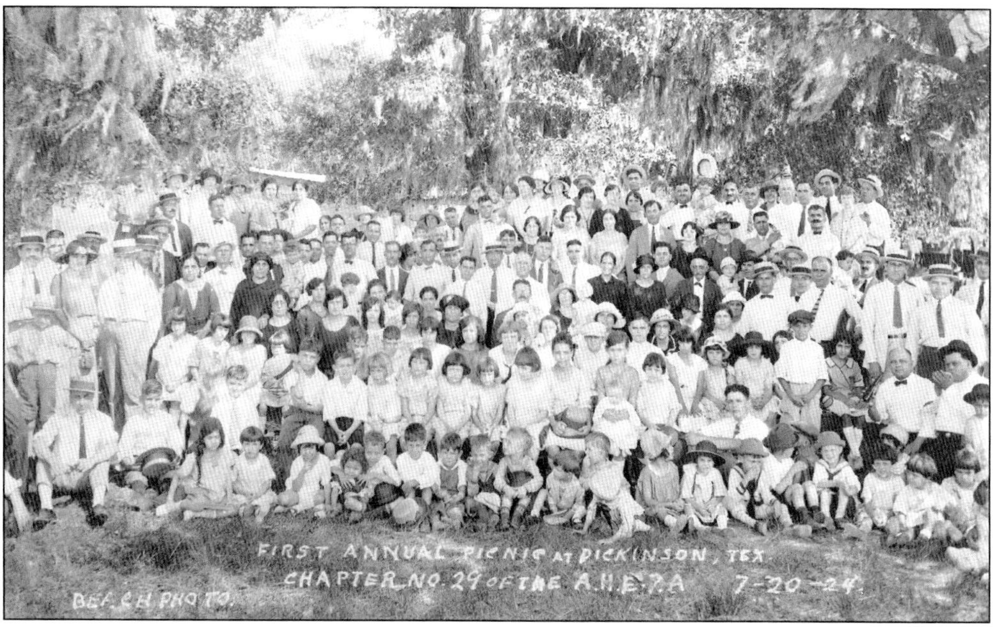

Here is the AHEPA first annual picnic in Dickinson, Texas, in 1924. Families from Houston and Galveston attended. Delicious food, prepared by the mothers and yiayias, was set under the pavilion and shared by everyone. Men played softball, and children competed in relay races. These picnics were mostly family affairs; many single men did not attend because they knew they would not find a *nymphe* (bride) there. (Courtesy of HMRC.)

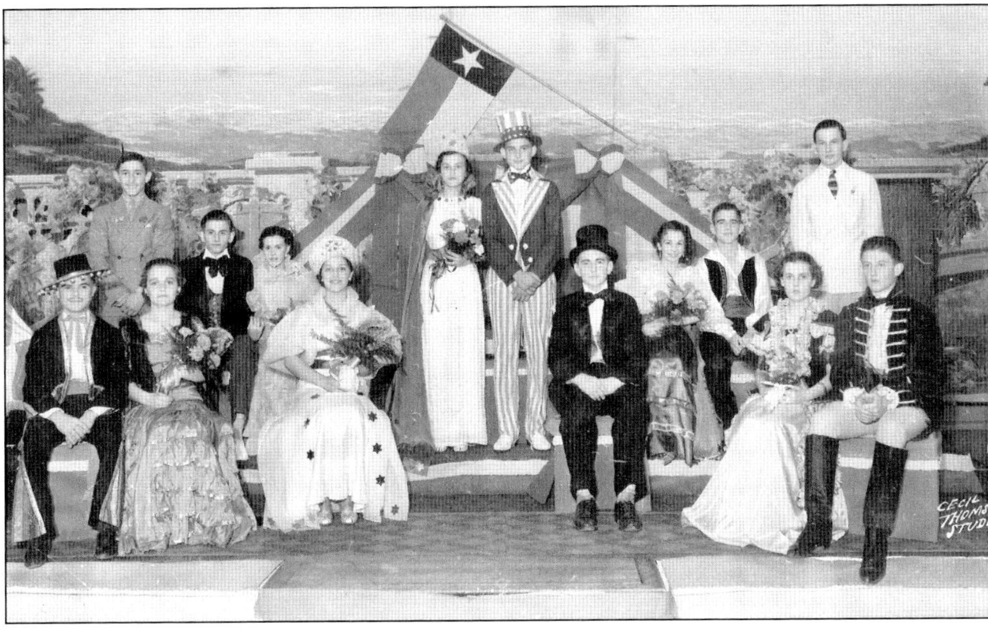

An important step toward securing future members of AHEPA was the creation of the Sons of Pericles in 1934. The American Hellenic Women's Society, which later became the Daughters of Penelope, and the young women's branch of AHEPA, the Maids of Athena, were also formed in the 1930s. King Angelo Verges and Queen Anastacia Catsinas are shown at the Sons of Pericles May Fete to commemorate the Texas centennial year in 1936. (Courtesy of HMRC.)

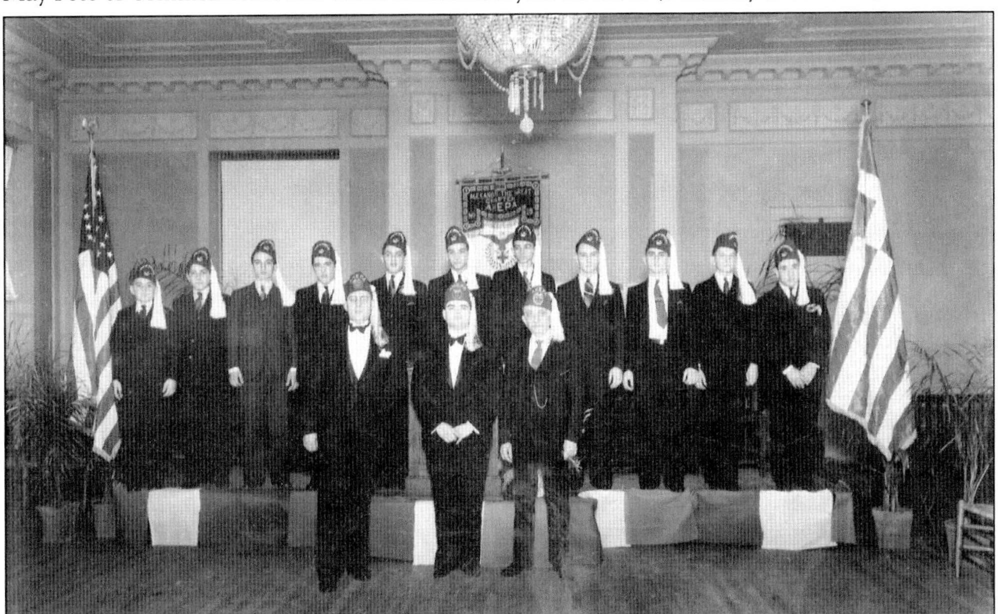

Here are members of the Sons of Pericles Junior Order of AHEPA Sam Houston Chapter No. 89, Houston, on February 4, 1934. Although AHEPA was organized in 1922, the Sons of Pericles did not organize until 1933–1934. Their purpose was to further the principles of the senior organization. An AHEPA committee appointed George Manthos as the first president of the Sons of Pericles. (Courtesy of HMRC.)

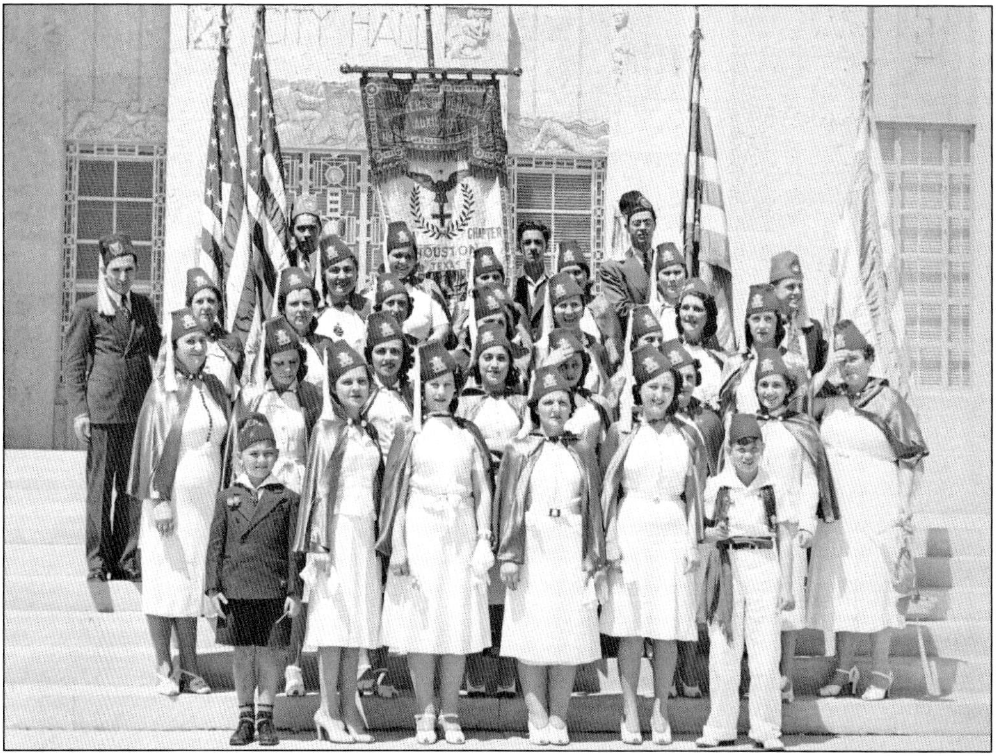

Daughters of Penelope, Houston Chapter, is seen in front of city hall in the 1940s. Mary M. Verges describes the Houston chapter as one of the largest and most fruitful in the domain. The Houston chapter has produced the greatest number of achievers on the national level of the Daughters of Penelope, with two international grand presidents, Becky Demeris and Mary M. Verges, and five National Penelopes of the Year, Sara Angelos, Thalia Vassiliades, Georgia Apostol, Sophie Papas, and Marie Harris. (Courtesy of Mary M. Verges.)

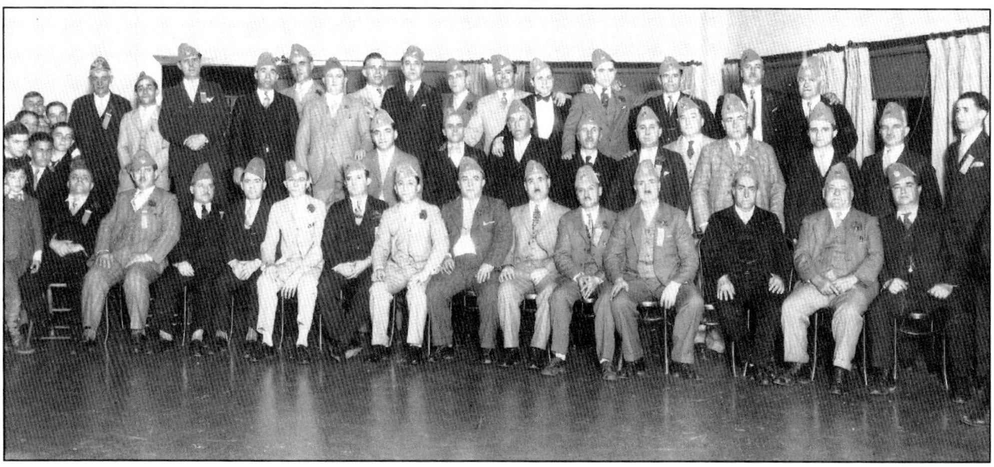

The Greek American Progressive Association (GAPA) was established on December 17, 1923. Its goals were the preservation of the Greek language and traditions and the Greek Orthodox Church. Many mistrusted and criticized the intentions of AHEPA, whose emphasis on good American citizenship as well as speaking English was thought to constitute an abandonment of all that was Greek. (Courtesy of the AGOC archives.)

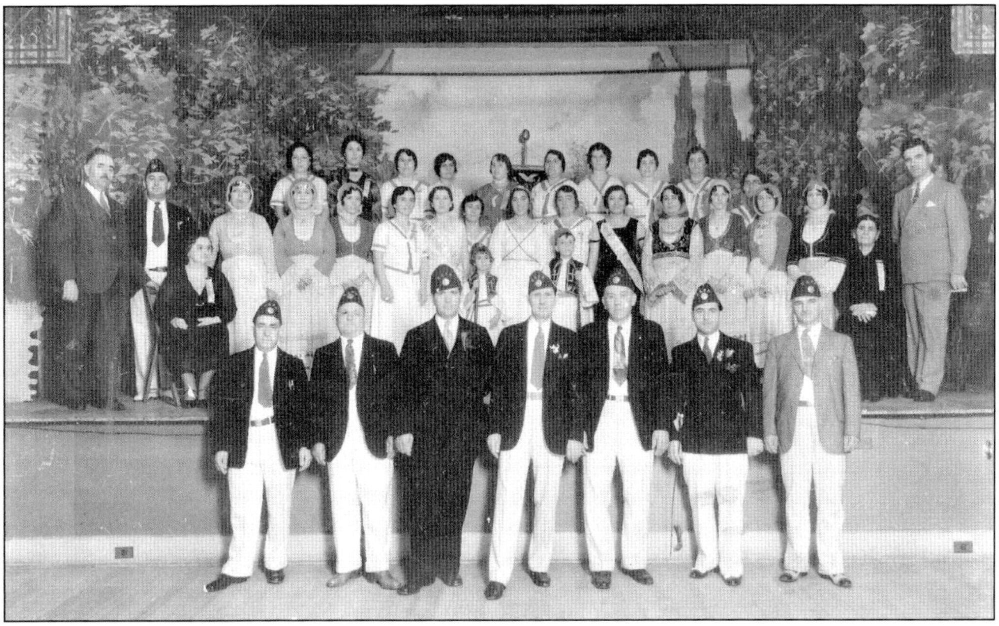

GAPA was never as successful as AHEPA, locally or nationally. One could not be a member of both clubs. Spats and rivalries between the two groups developed, but they were not intense in Houston. Often, the Greek community turned out for functions sponsored by one or the other organization. Pictured is the Andronica of GAPA, Houston, on October 30, 1932. In the first row at left is Basil Gazis; others are unidentified. (Courtesy of George Gazis.)

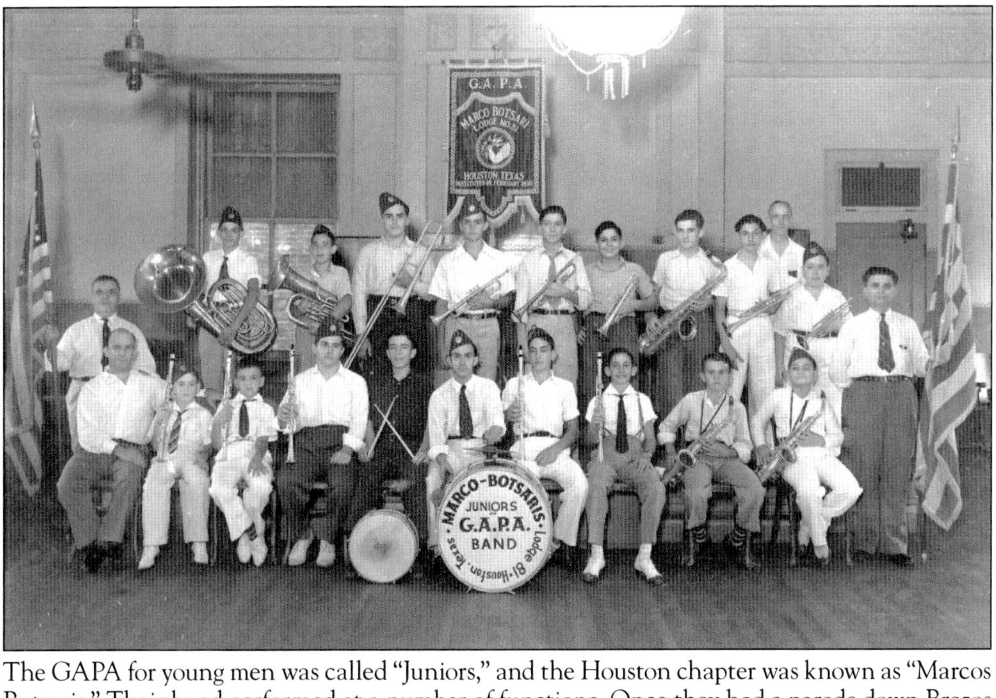

The GAPA for young men was called "Juniors," and the Houston chapter was known as "Marcos Botsaris." Their band performed at a number of functions. Once they had a parade down Brazos Street playing the Marine song. "It was so badly out of tune, but we thought they were great!" said Fofo DeClaris. (Courtesy of HMRC.)

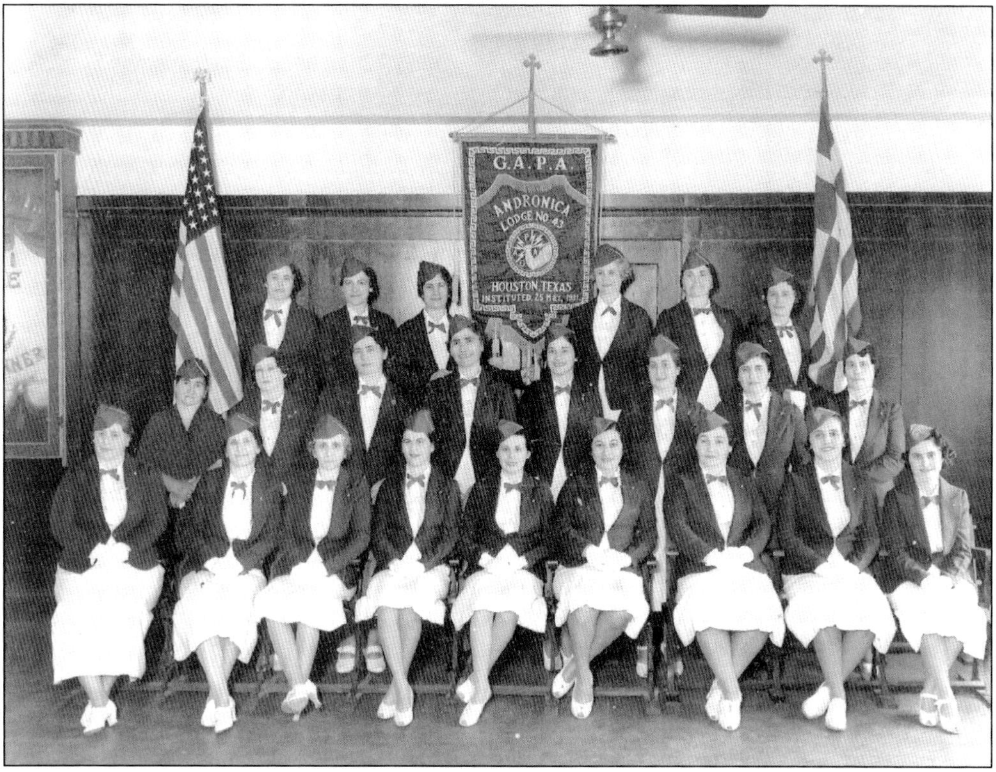

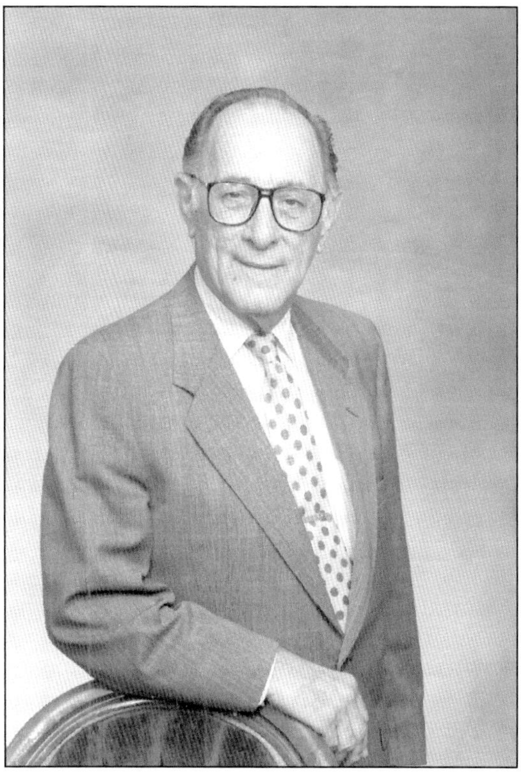

In the Houston parish, GAPA served its purpose for many immigrant Greek women. Alexandra Zografos recalls the following about GAPA: "Everyone was very warm, especially the old ladies. Mrs. Gazelas, Mrs. Panos, Mrs. Brailas, Mrs. Papajohn, Mrs. Poulos—I found here my second mothers. They took me into the GAPA. I really liked it because I could not speak English and they were speaking the Greek language." (Courtesy of George Gazis.)

James G. Petheriotes, a World War II veteran, graduate of the University of Houston, and co-owner of Petheriotes Brothers Coffee Company, was a member of Annunciation and president of the parish council (1986). Known as "Mr. AHEPA," James served on all levels and was elected supreme national treasurer. He is one of only four members of AHEPA to be awarded the Lifetime Achievement Award. In 1998, he was awarded the Ellis Island Medal of Honor. (Courtesy of Anthony Kouzounis.)

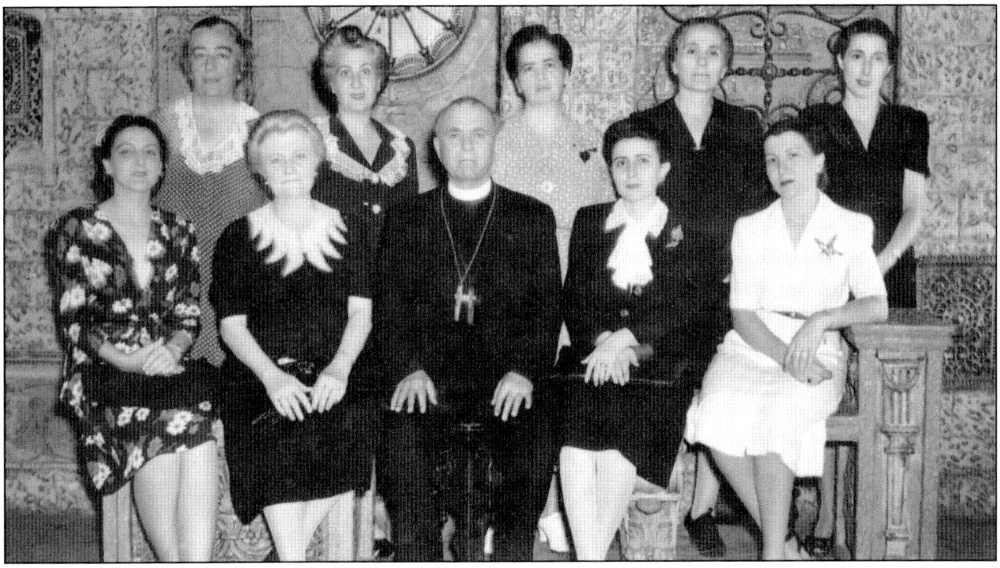

The Women's Church Society formed shortly after the church was built in 1917. Raising much needed money gave the members a greater role in the church. In November 1931, the late Ecumenical Patriarch Athenagoras I, who was serving as archbishop of North and South America, established the Ladies Philoptochos Society. Fr. Chris Nanopoulos founded Philoptochos at Annunciation in 1944. The Women's Church Society then joined the Philoptochos Society. (Courtesy of HMRC.)

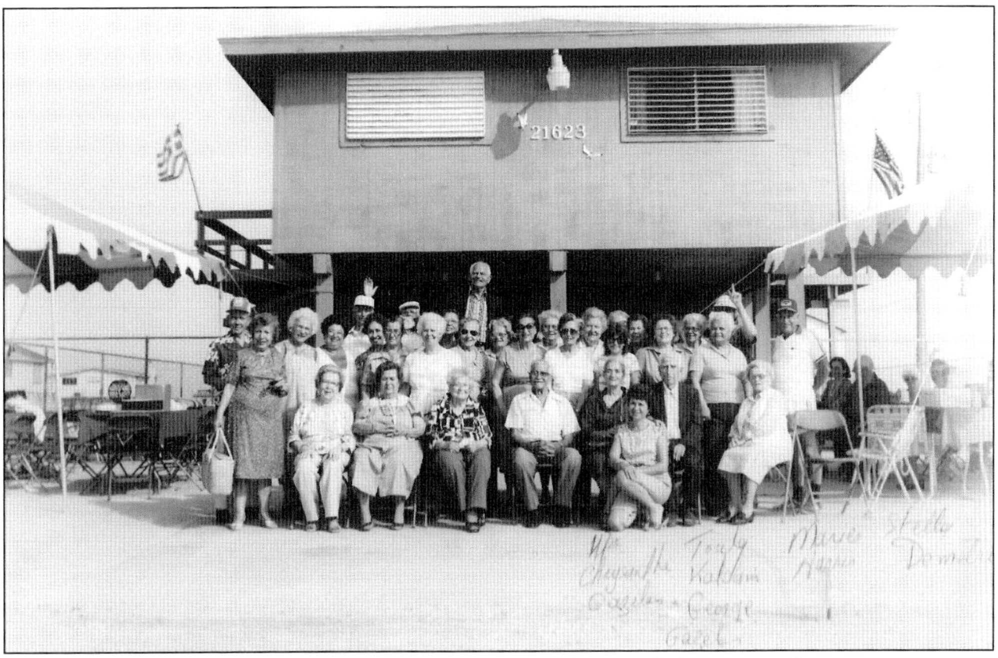

Fr. Nicholas C. Triantafilou approached Margaret Jelson with his vision for a senior citizens ministry in the 1970s. Beginning with only 12 members, today they number 150. They meet twice a month for fun and fellowship. They initially created crafts to sell at the Greek Festival to become financially independent. Eventually, the Philoptochos Society embraced the senior citizens as one of its ministries. (Courtesy of Margaret Jelson.)

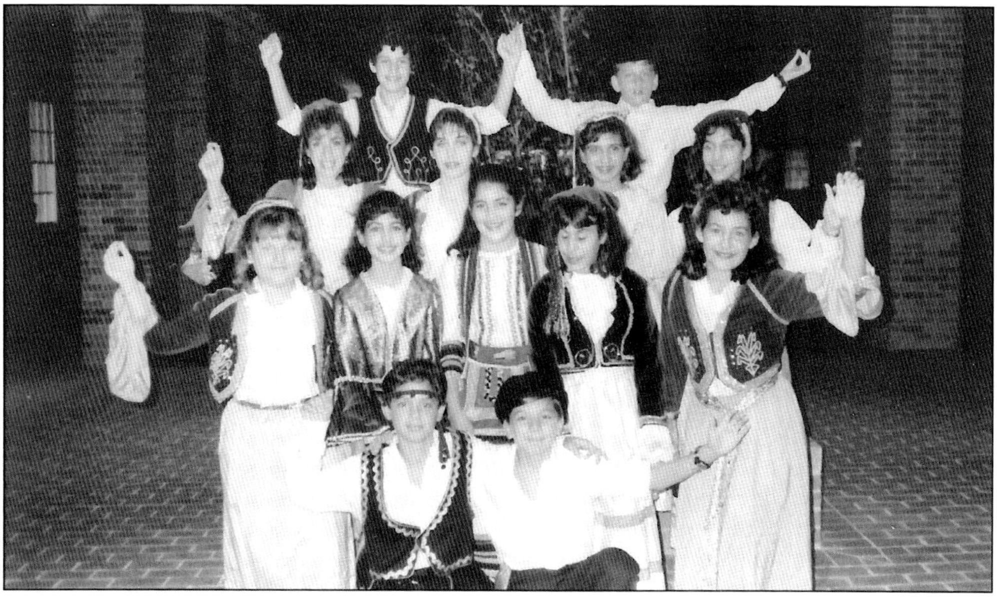

The Greek Orthodox Youth Association (GOYA) was founded during the 1950s. It was an Archdiocesan program started under the direction of Metropolitan Michael of Corinth, who succeeded Archbishop Athenagoras. The Houston chapter was founded in 1951 as an 18-to-25-year-old young adult group. Later, this group evolved into a teenage youth group. Children, teens, and young adults loved to dance in the Greek Festival. (Courtesy of the AGOC archives.)

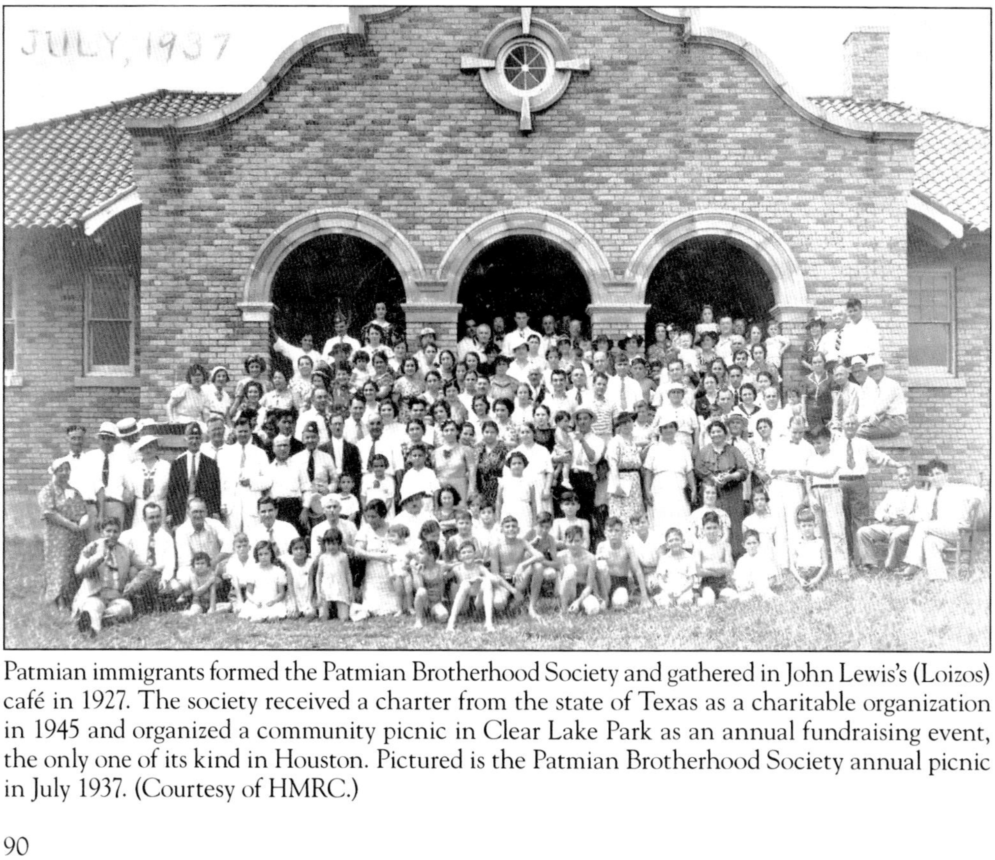

Patmian immigrants formed the Patmian Brotherhood Society and gathered in John Lewis's (Loizos) café in 1927. The society received a charter from the state of Texas as a charitable organization in 1945 and organized a community picnic in Clear Lake Park as an annual fundraising event, the only one of its kind in Houston. Pictured is the Patmian Brotherhood Society annual picnic in July 1937. (Courtesy of HMRC.)

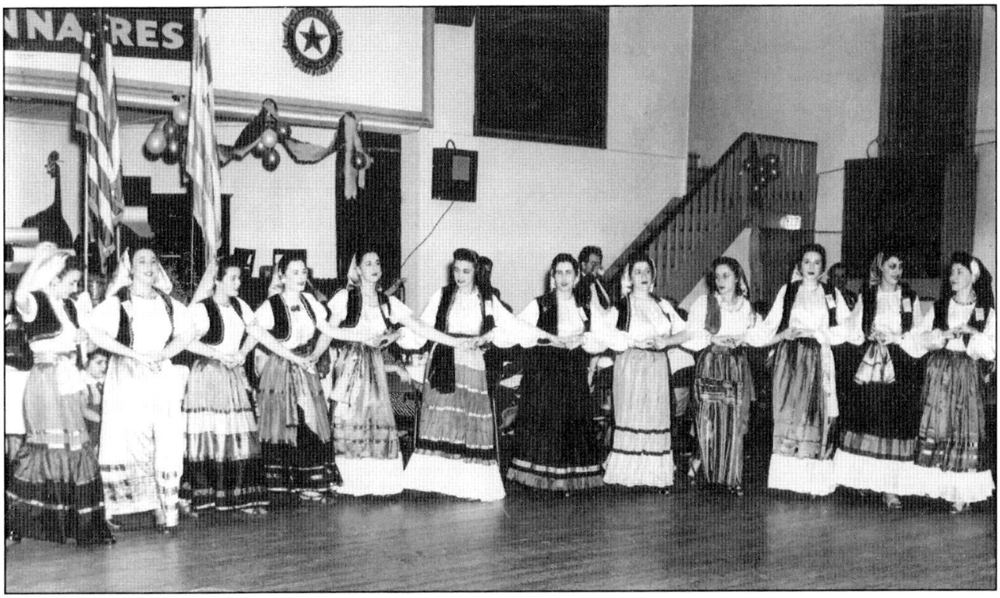

The Patmian Society of Houston Masquerade Ball is pictured in 1948. From left to right are Mary Gazis, Mary Kefalas, Dolly Manikas, Ann Manikas, Sophie Rose, two unidentified, Irene Fotinos, Mary Coronis, Stamatia Rose, Irene Margolis, and Stavroula Gouras. (Courtesy of the AGOC archives.)

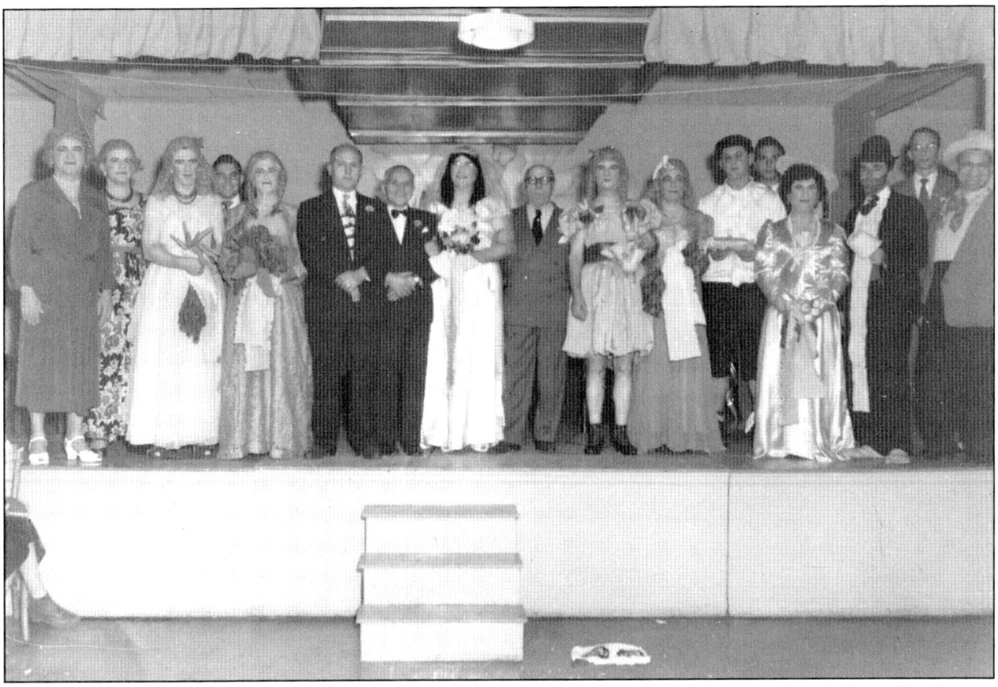

A hilarious mock wedding was presented by AHEPA. The skit was put on as a benefit dance, perhaps to raise money for one of its charities. From left to right are James Menutes, the manager of several downtown theaters; Nick Peet, organizer of this event; George Galanos and Willie Peet, "mothers" of the bride; groom Gus Angelos; bride Angelo Pontikes; best man John Grivas; and ring bearer Steve Demetre. (Courtesy of HMRC.)

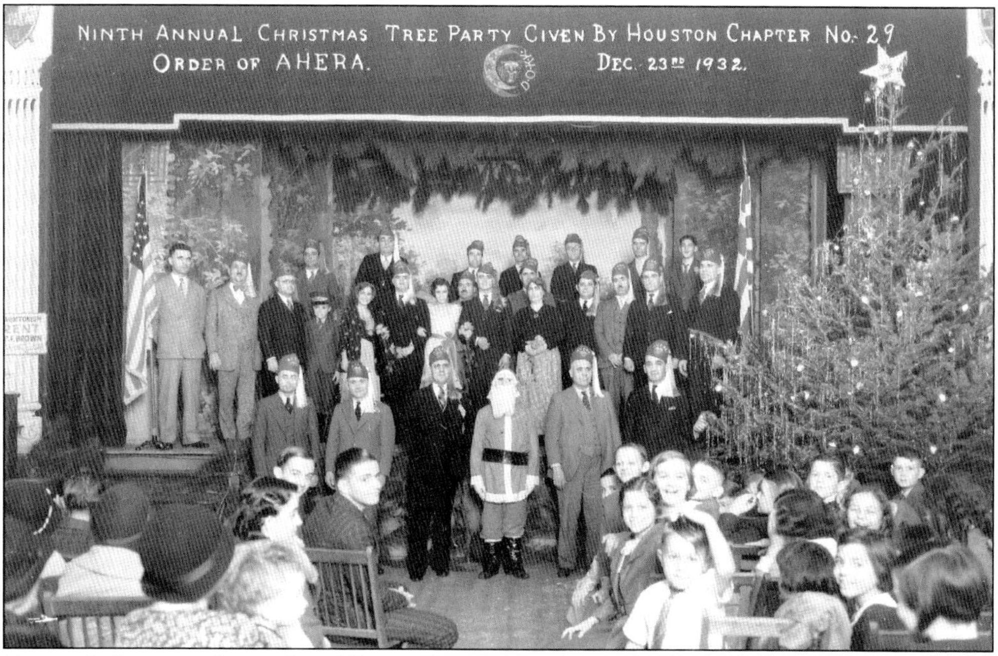

George Petheriotes always played Santa Claus for the parish children of all ages. He took his role very seriously and had his own Santa suit. He is pictured here in front of the stage at the ninth annual AHEPA Christmas Tree Party on December 23, 1932. George was president of the parish council from 1921 to 1922. (Courtesy of HMRC.)

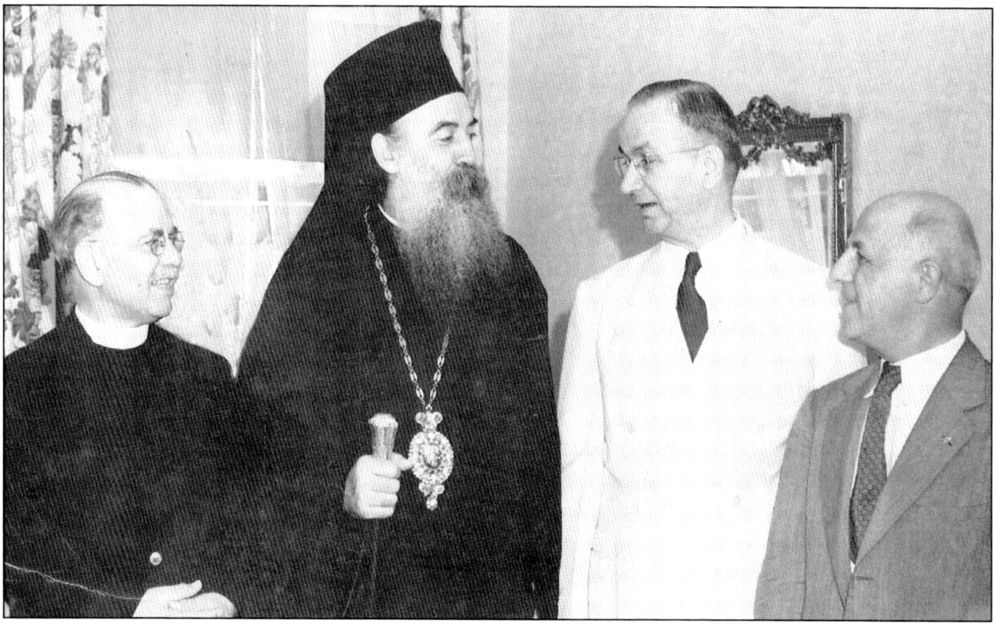

His Eminence Archbishop Athenagoras is posing with AHEPA delegates on June 26, 1941. From left to right are Fr. Chris Nanopoulos, priest of the Annunciation Greek Orthodox Church; the most Rev. Spyron Athenagoras, archbishop of the Greek Orthodox Church in North and South America; D.G. Harris, president of the parish council; and George Petheriotes, a trustee of the church. (Courtesy of the AGOC archives.)

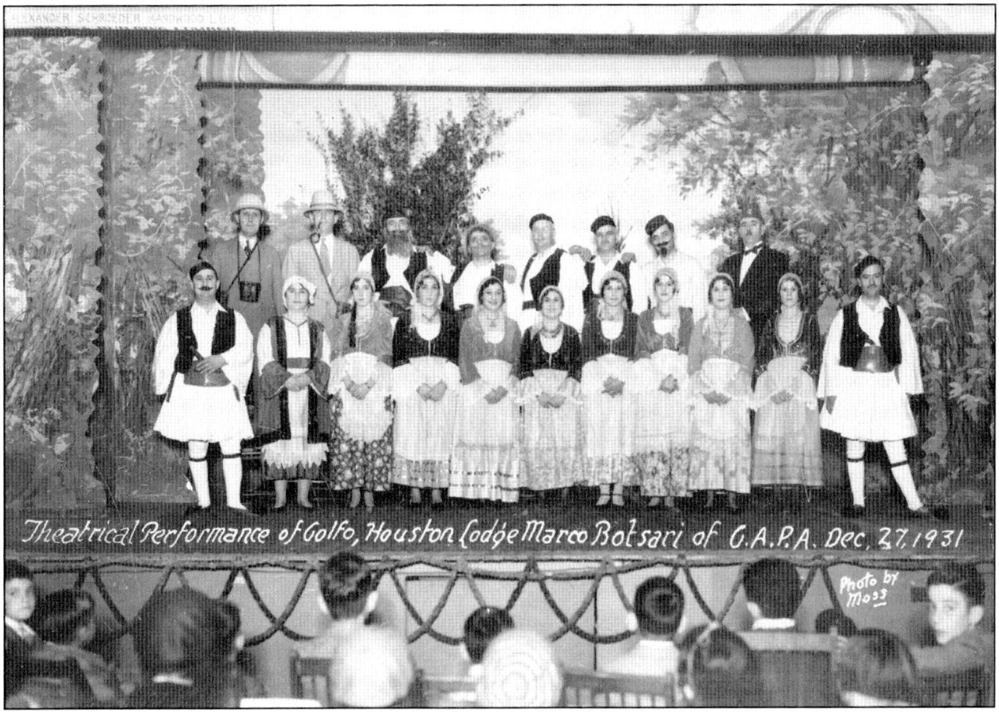

A theatrical performance of "Golfo" by the Greek American Progressive Association (GAPA) on December 27, 1931, is pictured. Plays were often given in the Greek community during this time of adjustment to their new country. Many members of the audience did not speak English and were anxious for entertainment in their own language. (Courtesy of HMRC.)

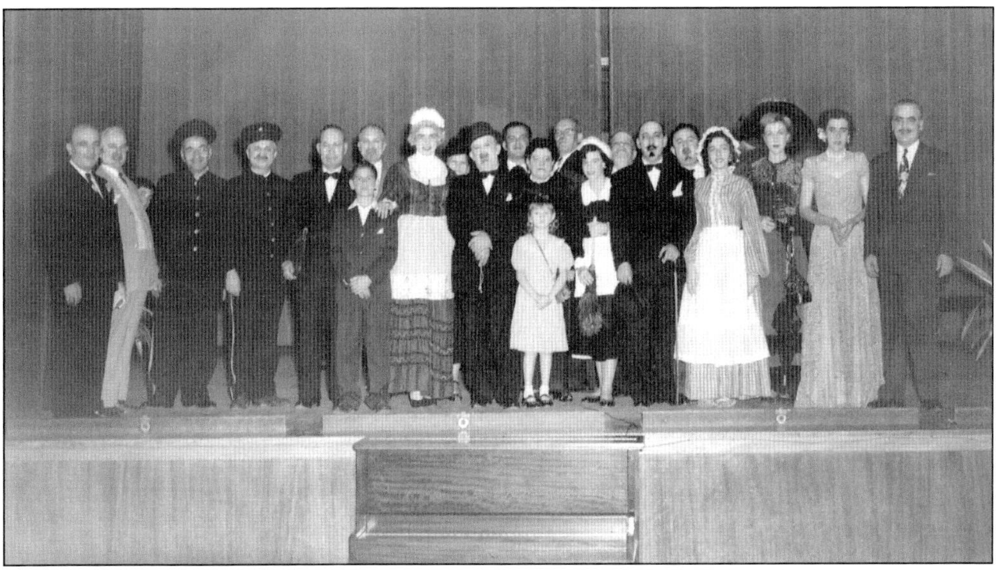

"Agnostos," a modern Greek drama, was presented under the auspices of the United Lodges of the Greek American Progressive Association of Houston at San Jacinto High School auditorium on April 15, 1951. This event benefitted the local GAPA chapters, Marcos Botsaris No. 81 and Androniki No. 43. Funds from this performance were also designated for the new Greek Orthodox church. (Courtesy of HMRC.)

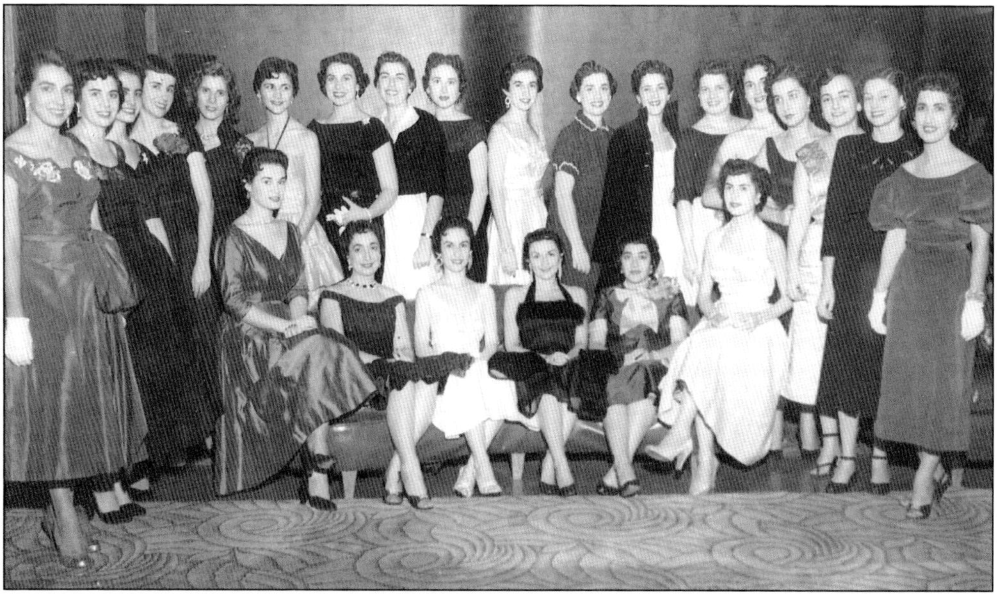

Gamma Sigma Alpha (GAPA girls) Shamrock Christmas Party is pictured in 1953. Shown are, from left to right, (first row) Dolly Manakis, Betty Pappas (Antonellos), Dorothy Panagos (Pappas), Tina Pappas, Dorothy Pratley (Brailas), and Toula Gazelas (Kaldanis); (second row) Helen Daskas (Standish), Mary Malavansos, Evelyn Theocharides (Boulafendis), Polly Callas, Betty Maduros Paul, Mary Ann Pavlides (Sterling), Evelyn Sinathis (Makris), Fofo Catsinas (Lewis), Stamatia Rose, Jeannie Panagos (Colias), Sophie Menutes Hadjes, Helen Beys (Catsinas), Marie Jacobs Harris, Sophie Rose (Stenis), Beulah Menutes, Becky Batmanis, Lea Peet (Kostas), and Matina Pappas (Peet). (Courtesy of the AGOC archives.)

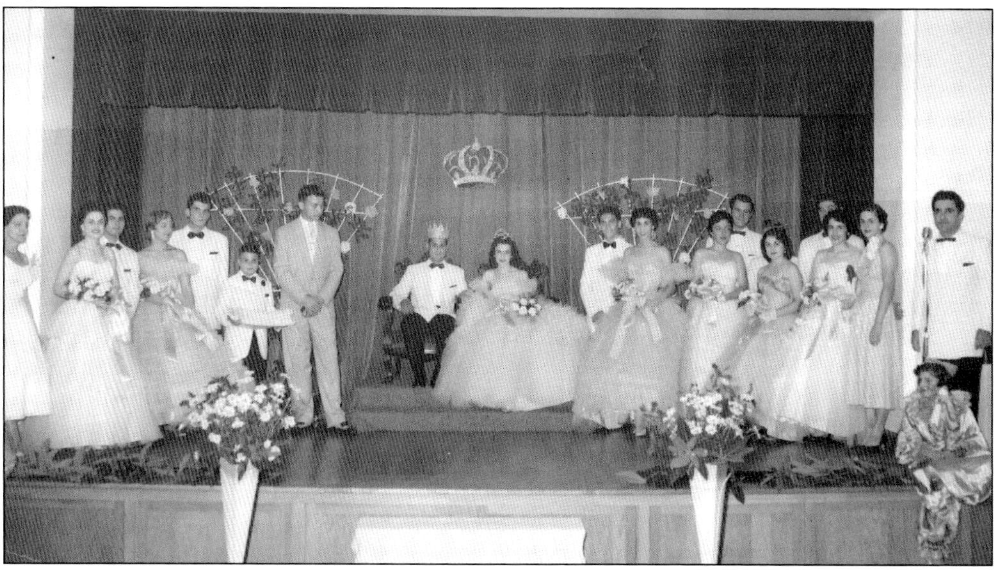

The Sons of Pericles 1954 May Fete was held at the S.P. Martel Auditorium. King Tony Pacheris and queen Elaine Butos (Stefanidis) were chosen by a panel of three celebrity judges from local radio and television stations. After the king and queen were crowned, a dance followed. The Sons and Maids sold tickets to this event, and the entire church community was invited. (Courtesy of Elaine Stefanidis.)

Seven

A Greek Presence in Houston

Philoxenia (lover of strangers) is the perfect word to describe the outreach Annunciation Cathedral extended to the greater Houston community. Fr. George Kalpaxis initiated the televising of Greek Orthodox services on special occasions. Homebound parishioners could participate in the liturgy, but all of Houston could witness the spiritual beauty of Orthodoxy as well. He also brought Annunciation parish into the Houston Council of Churches, which was dedicated to ecumenical dialogue among Christian denominations and advocacy for social issues.

The 1960s also marked the beginning of the Philocardiac Ministry to the heart patients of Houston's Medical Center. Women of Philoptochos visited patients and often served as interpreters between them and their physicians. The Greek Festival was inaugurated in 1968 and has grown into the largest ethnic festival in Texas and the Southwest. Over three days every October, the Greek community shared its culture and faith with all of Houston.

In the 1970s, Annunciation took an active interest in the affairs of the wider Houston community and began participating in the Houston Metropolitan Ministries programs. These included the Hunger Pantry, which distributed food to the needy, and Meals on Wheels program, which delivered hot meals to shut-ins. Beginning in 1973, Mary Bellos involved many volunteers from the Annunciation parish to institute the Children's Art Project (CAP) at M.D. Anderson Cancer Hospital. Pediatric patients in weekly art classes created Christmas cards using their original drawings; the CAP project has since grown to include all holiday greetings and general note cards. Political involvement helped pass Cooley's Anemia Act, an initiative that provided research and treatment protocols for this disease, also known as thalassemia, which primarily affected individuals of Greek-Mediterranean descent.

Fr. Nick Triantafilou worked in areas outside the immediate parish as well. He moderated the radio program "Religion on the Line," a significant opportunity to witness for the Greek Orthodox faith. He served on the National Presbyters Council from 1970 to 1976 and was president for two of those years. As chairman of the Archdiocesan Stewardship Task Force, Father Nick traveled around the country to promote the program. A member of the Texas Conference of Churches, he advocated for social justice for all. In these capacities and as vicar of the Southwest Conference of the Eighth Archdiocesan District, Father Nick made Orthodoxy a visible, living faith to the entire country.

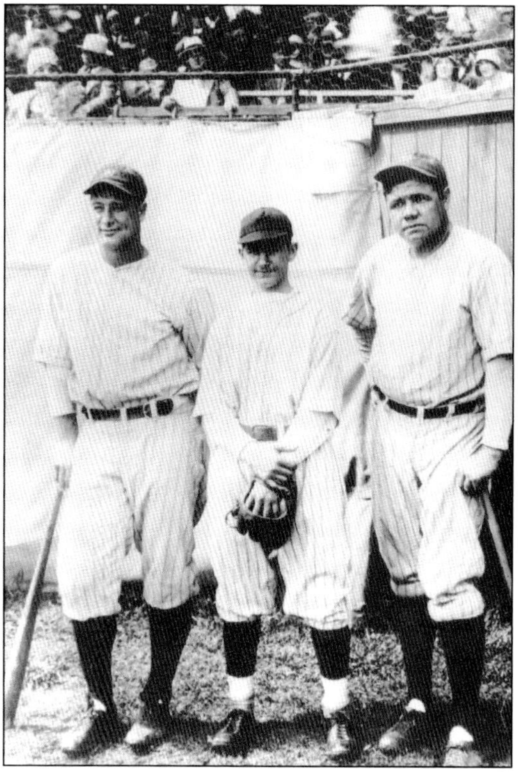

Louis P. Stathakis played for a minor league baseball team in 1927. He was an avid baseball player and earned the highest batting average. A picture event was arranged with Lou Gehrig and "Babe" Ruth. This picture is now in the National Baseball Hall of Fame. Louis P. Stathakis and his wife, Andromichae "Michae," both from Arkansas, made their home in Houston in 1964. (Courtesy of Andromichae Stathakis.)

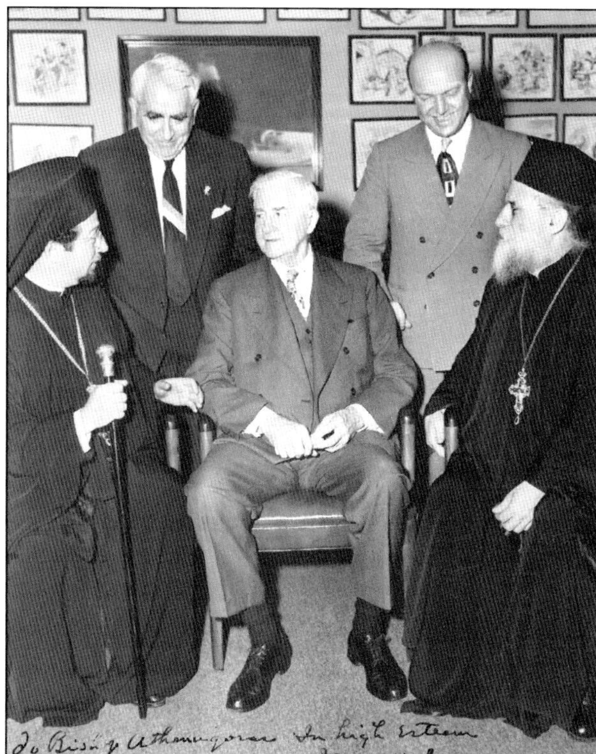

From left to right are an unidentified bishop; George P. Kelley, president of the parish council at Annunciation Church; Jesse Jones, philanthropist and secretary of commerce from 1940 to 1945; Chris Caridas; and His Grace Bishop Athenagoras. The photograph is signed, "To Bishop Athenagoras, In high esteem, Jesse Jones." (Courtesy of Evangeline Caridas.)

The *Houston Chronicle* reported that "Queen Frederika and King Paul of Greece came to Houston and paid a visit to the new $450,000 Annunciation Church on Yoakum Boulevard during their trip here." The cornerstone for the new church was a gift from the queen. Pictured on November 18, 1953, behind Queen Frederika is Mayor Roy Hofheinz. (Courtesy of Anthony Kouzounis.)

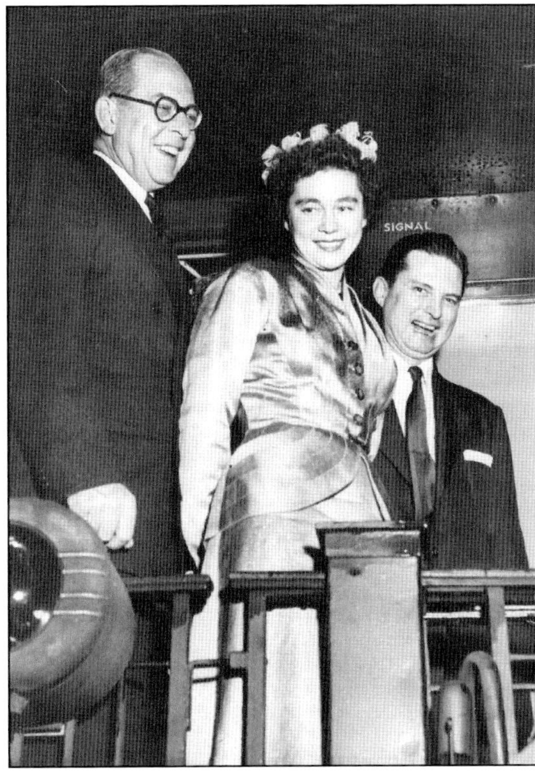

From left to right in the front row are King Paul, Queen Frederika, James Pappas, and his wife, Mary. When the royal couple visited the United States in 1953, the Annunciation Greek Orthodox parish provided them with cowboy outfits to wear to the rodeo; restaurateur Jim Pappas and his wife, Mary, accompanied the king and queen. (Courtesy of Chris Pappas.)

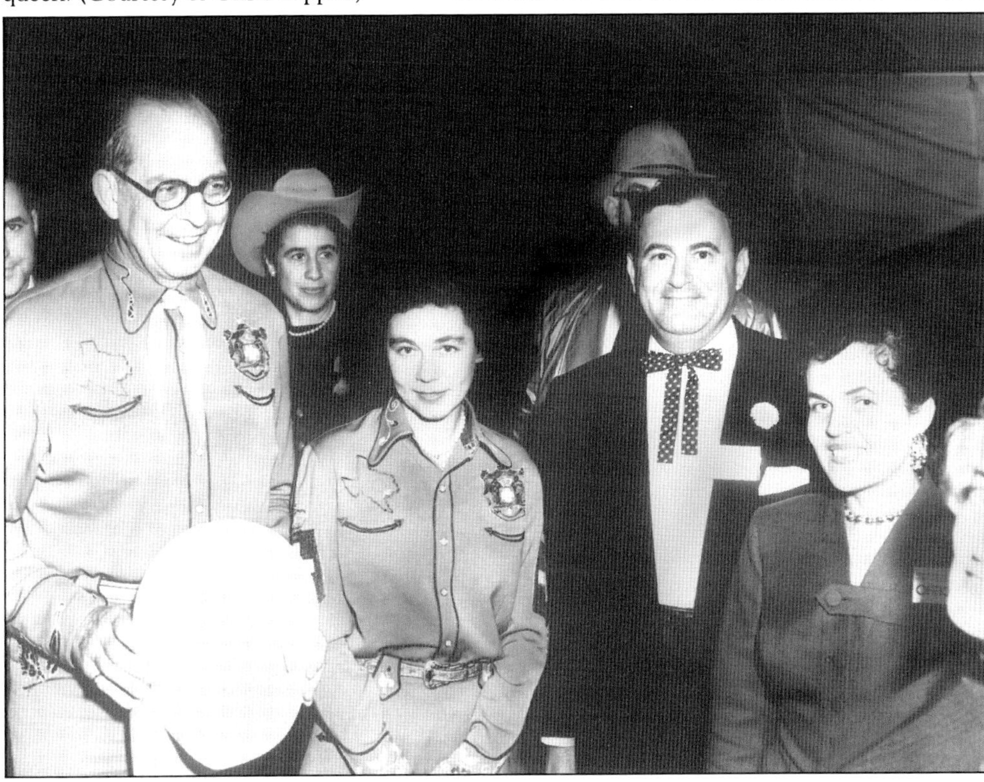

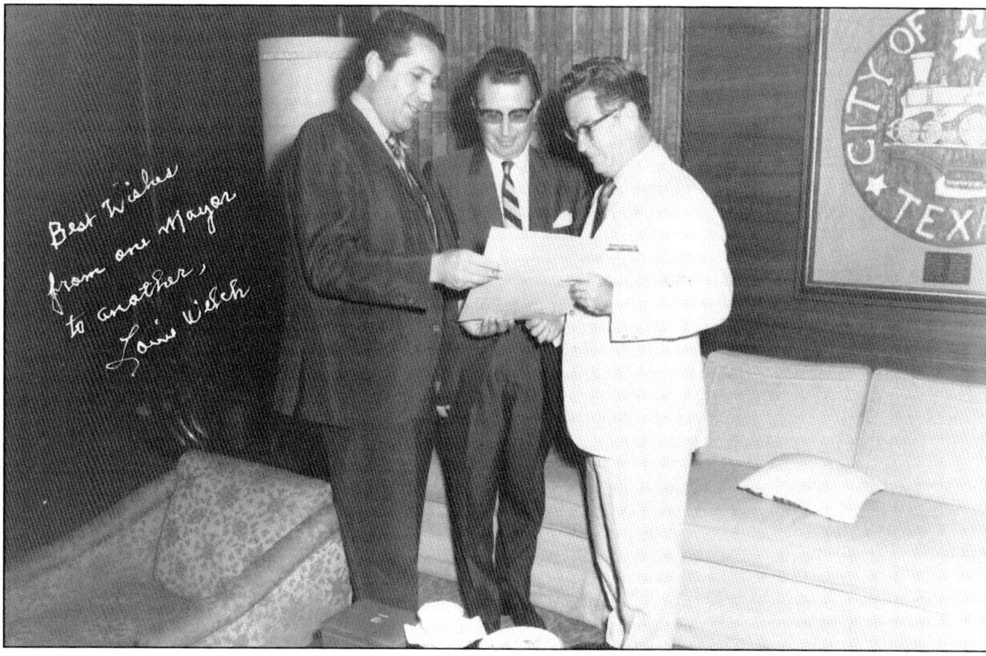

Leo Kalantzakis and Mayor Louie Welch were friends. When Leo's brother-in-law Nikos Kalogiannis, the mayor of Patmos, Greece, for 28 years, visited Houston in 1959, Mayor Louie Welch honored him by making Niko Kalogiannis an honorary citizen of the city of Houston. (Courtesy of Leo Kalantzakis.)

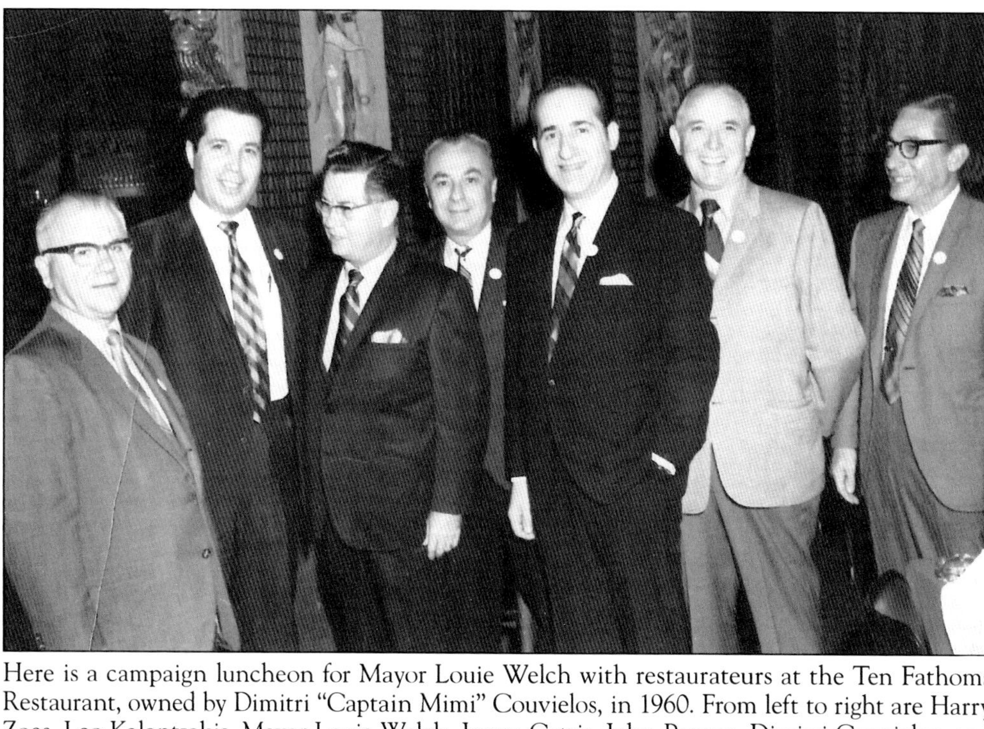

Here is a campaign luncheon for Mayor Louie Welch with restaurateurs at the Ten Fathoms Restaurant, owned by Dimitri "Captain Mimi" Couvielos, in 1960. From left to right are Harry Zoes, Leo Kalantzakis, Mayor Louie Welch, James Catsis, John Pappas, Dimitri Couvielos, and Gus Kanakis. (Courtesy of Leo Kalantzakis.)

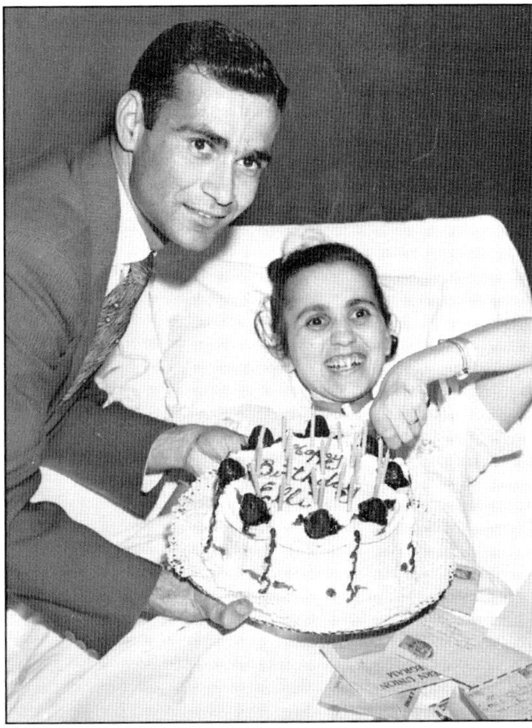

The Philoptochos Society took a special interest in Greek heart patients who came to Houston seeking help from Drs. Denton Cooley or Michael DeBakey. Elli Ioannou had lapsed into a coma, and Philoptochos wrote Pres. John F. Kennedy to expedite immigration procedures and allow Elli's brother to come from Cyprus to help her recovery. The president acted accordingly, and Elli Ioannou lived to celebrate her birthday in the early 1960s. (Courtesy of HMRC.)

The second annual Greek Festival took place in 1968 as a fundraiser to meet the increasing financial needs of the church. With Chris Nickolas as chairman and E.T. "Jelly" Nicolaou as cochairman (not pictured), many parishioners, including the youth, participated, and the festival was a tremendous success. From left to right are Thano Dameris, Chris Nickolas, Anthony Kouzounis, Charles Stamos, Gus Kanakis, and unidentified. (Courtesy of the AGOC archives.)

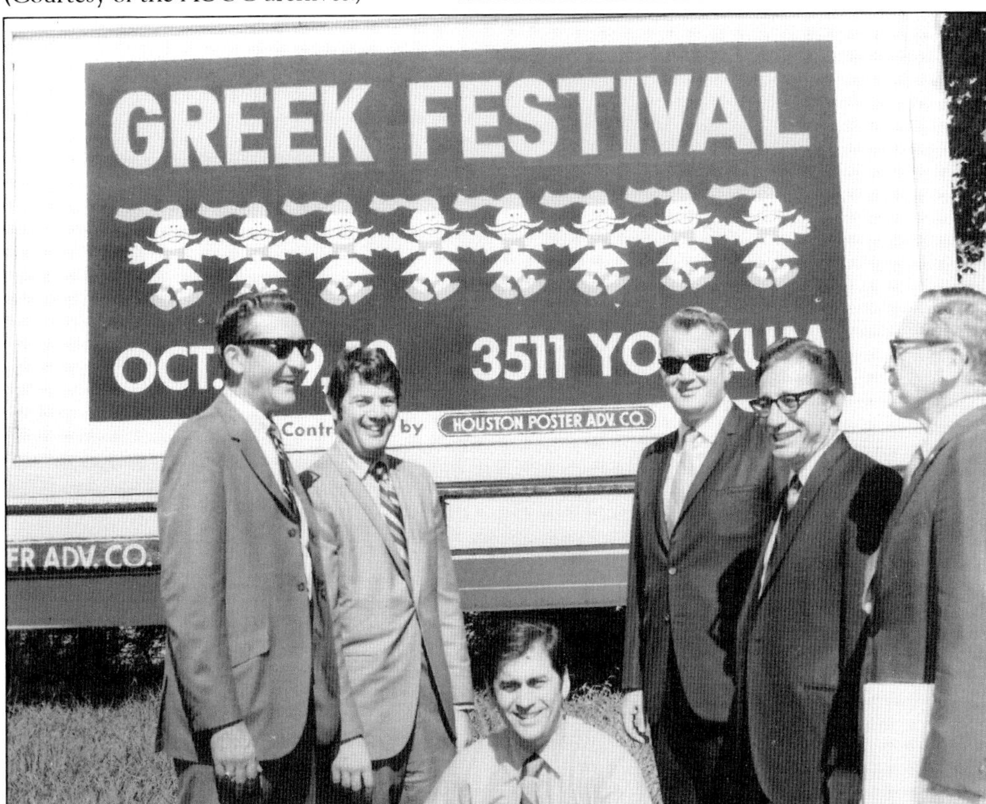

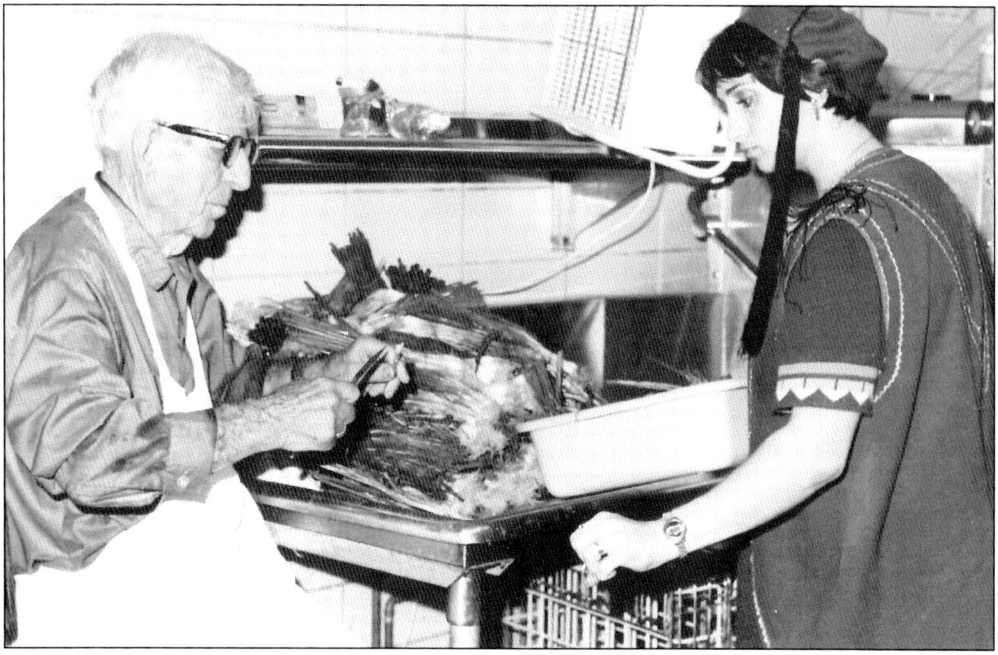

From the beginning of the Greek Festival up until his nineties, George Gazelas loved working with everyone to prepare for this event. His job was one that not too many volunteers wanted, cutting up countless fresh scallions by hand. After he died, the festival organizers purchased electric choppers. (Courtesy of the AGOC archives.)

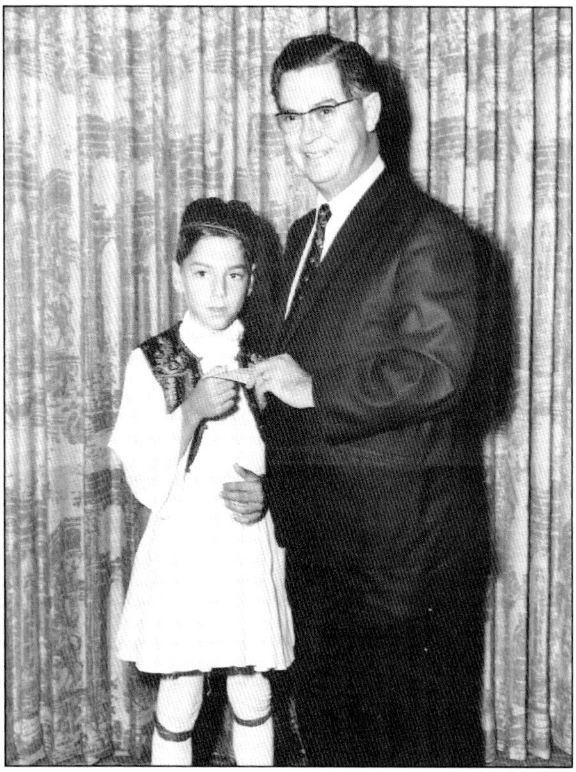

Many clever promotions were used to publicize the Greek Festival. Dignitaries and news media from the greater Houston community were invited for seated lunches the day before the festival began. Wearing an Evzone costume, the uniform of the Royal Palace Guards in Greece, Peter Bellos presents the first two tickets to the Greek Festival to Mayor Louis Welch. (Courtesy of the AGOC archives.)

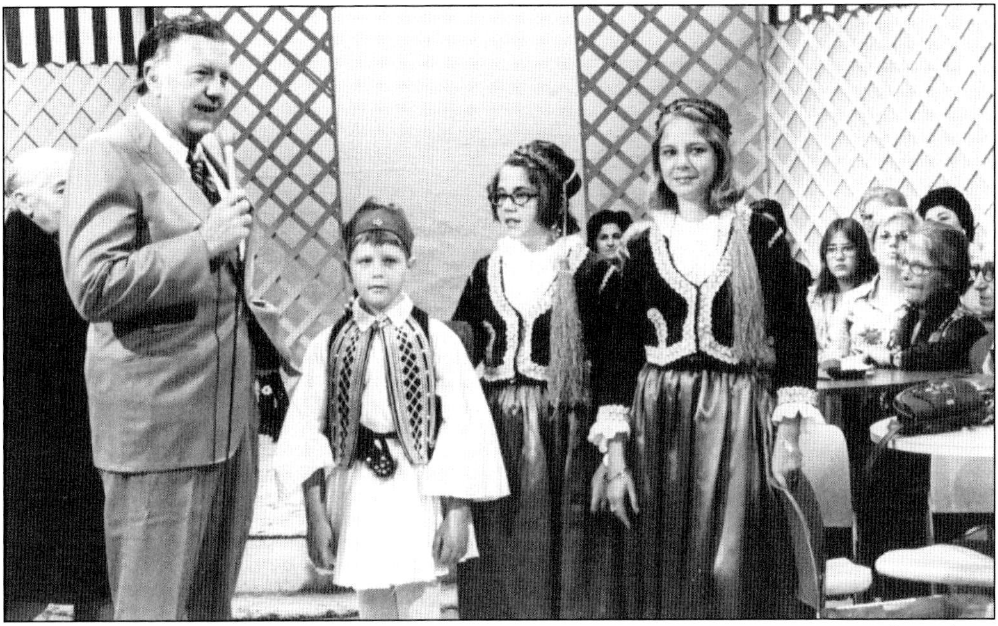

Don Mahoney and Jeana Clair's television show on channel 39 aired in 1970. Pictured are, from left to right, Don Mahoney, Chris Lum (age six), Maria Lum (age eight), and Helen Lum (age nine). Maria Lum Fink recalls, "This picture brought back so many good memories! Mama used to drag us to the TV tapings. We rehearsed once before the show aired. I also played the piano on the show." (Courtesy of the AGOC archives.)

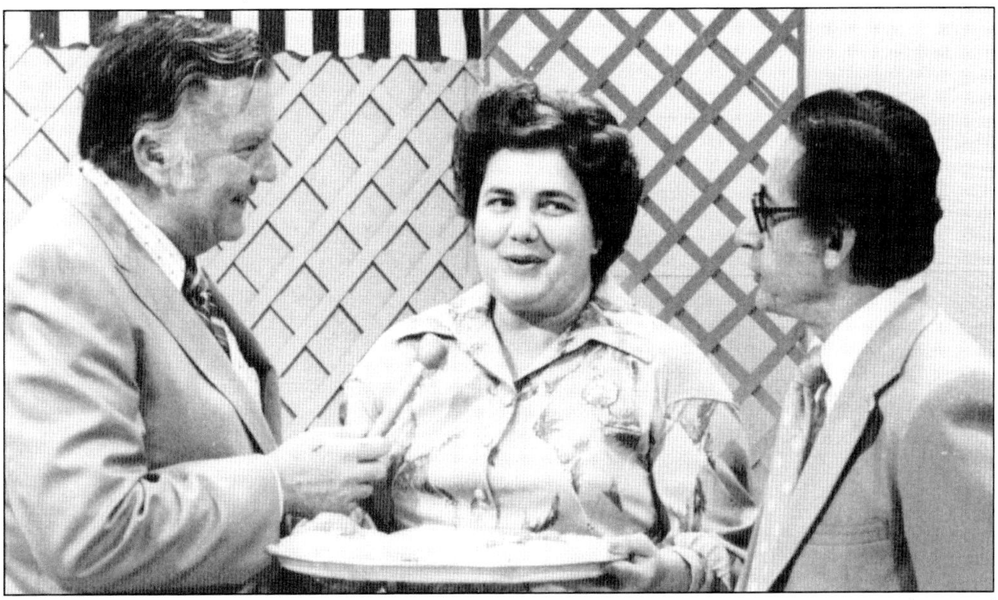

From left to right are Don Mahoney, Marie Harris, and Gus Kanakis. Marie was in charge of assessing and ordering the ingredients for food preparation for the Greek Festival. She was the parish Philoptochos president for several terms and the first Philoptochos president for the Diocese of Denver. She served on the Emergency Aid Coalition and SEARCH Homeless Services boards, which helped the destitute. Marie was awarded the Medal of St. Paul twice and the Philoptochos Agape Award in 2012 for her outstanding service. (Courtesy of the AGOC archives.)

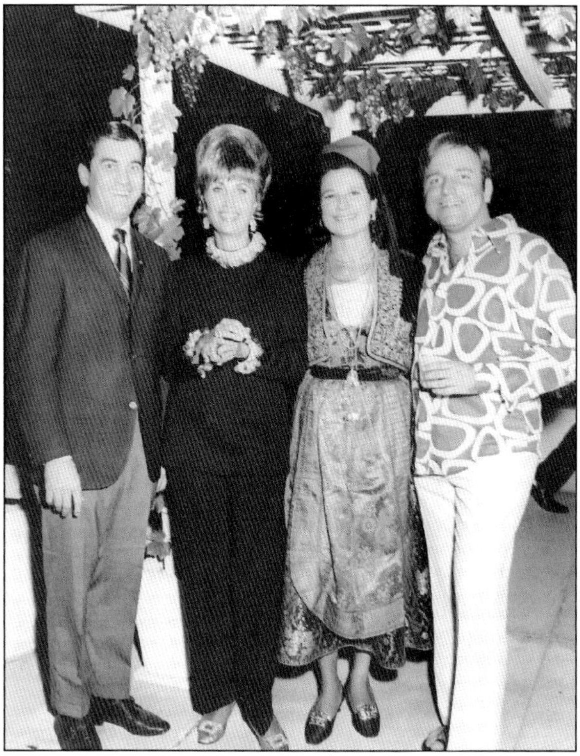

From left to right are Anthony Kouzounis, Evelyn Nickolas, Thomai Kandis, and Johnny Callas at the annual Season Kick-off at the Alley Theatre in September 1969. The Alley Theatre is one of the three oldest resident theaters in the United States. In 1996, the Alley won the Regional Theater Tony Award and is one of the most respected repertory companies in the country. (Courtesy of Anthony Kouzounis.)

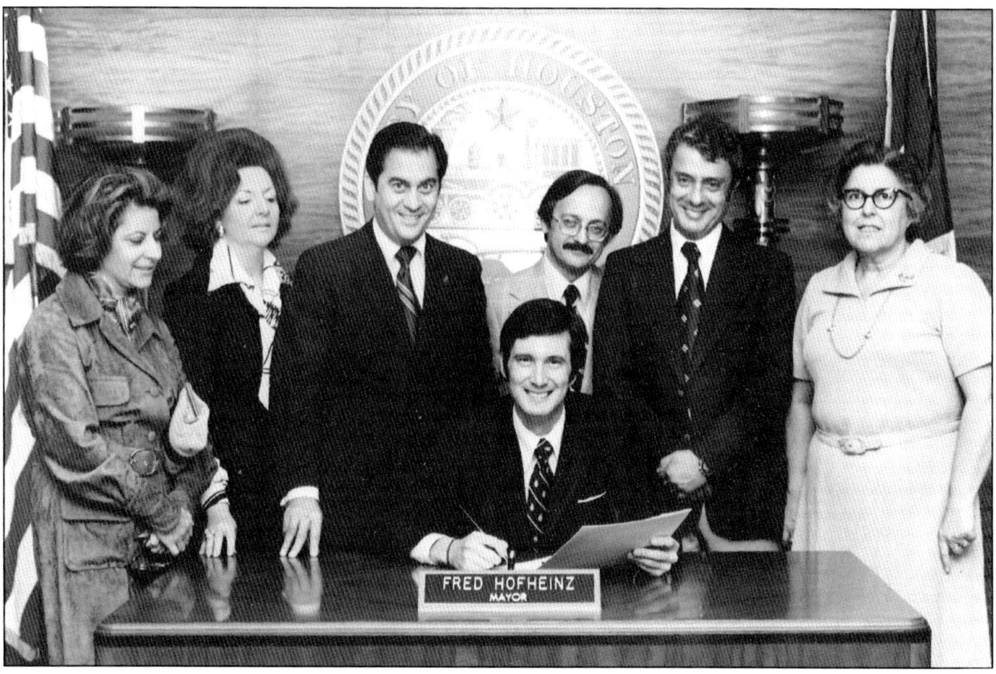

Mayor Fred Hofheinz is seated at this desk holding the Greek Independence Day Proclamation in the mid-1970s. Also pictured are, from left to right, Greek school director Nora Magazis, Becky Demeris, Anthony Kouzounis, George Blytas, George Magazis, and Thalia Vassiliadis. (Courtesy of Anthony Kouzounis.)

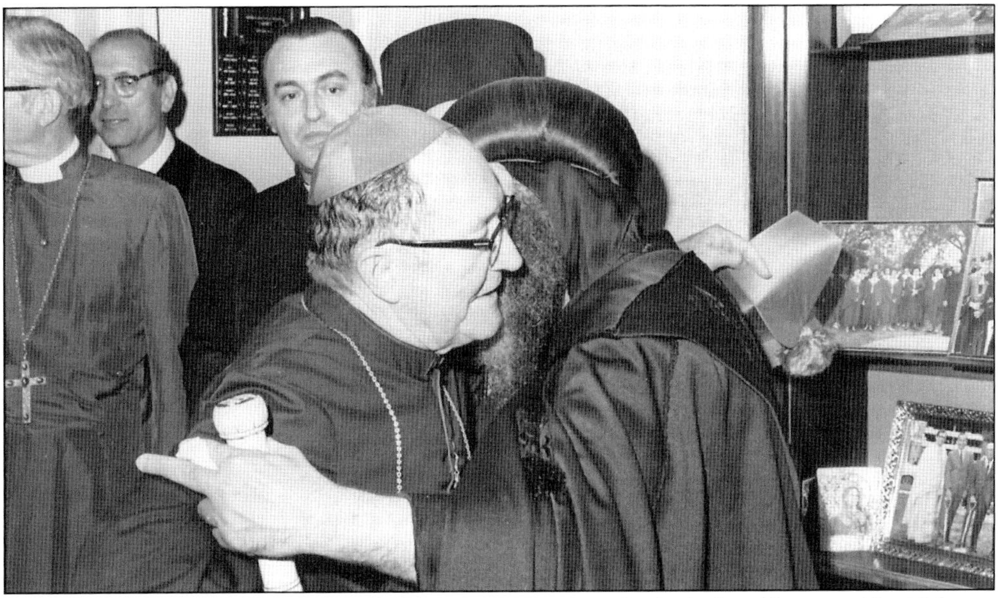

The 1973 ecumenical meeting was held at Annunciation Cathedral in Houston. His Holiness Pope Shenouda III (right) is embracing Bishop John L. Morkowski, apostolic administrator and coadjutor bishop of the Galveston-Houston diocese of the Catholic Church. Other clergy pictured are Fr. Demetrios Lokis (behind Bishop Morkowski), assistant priest at Annunciation from 1975 to 1980, and unidentified Protestant pastors. Meeting attendees included His Grace Bishop John of Thermon and Coptic Orthodox clergy. (Courtesy of the AGOC archives.)

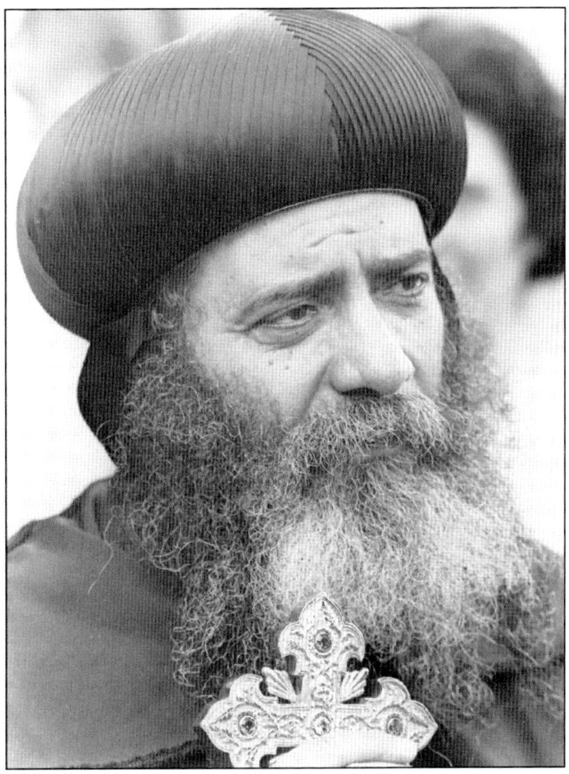

His Grace Bishop Shenouda was consecrated on November 14, 1971, as His Holiness Pope Shenouda III, the 117th pope of Alexandria and patriarch of the See of St. Mark. He is known for his commitment to Christian unity. Pope Shenouda asked Fr. Nicholas C. Triantafilou to coordinate ecumenical meetings that took place on February 12, 1973, because he did not speak English. (Courtesy of the AGOC archives.)

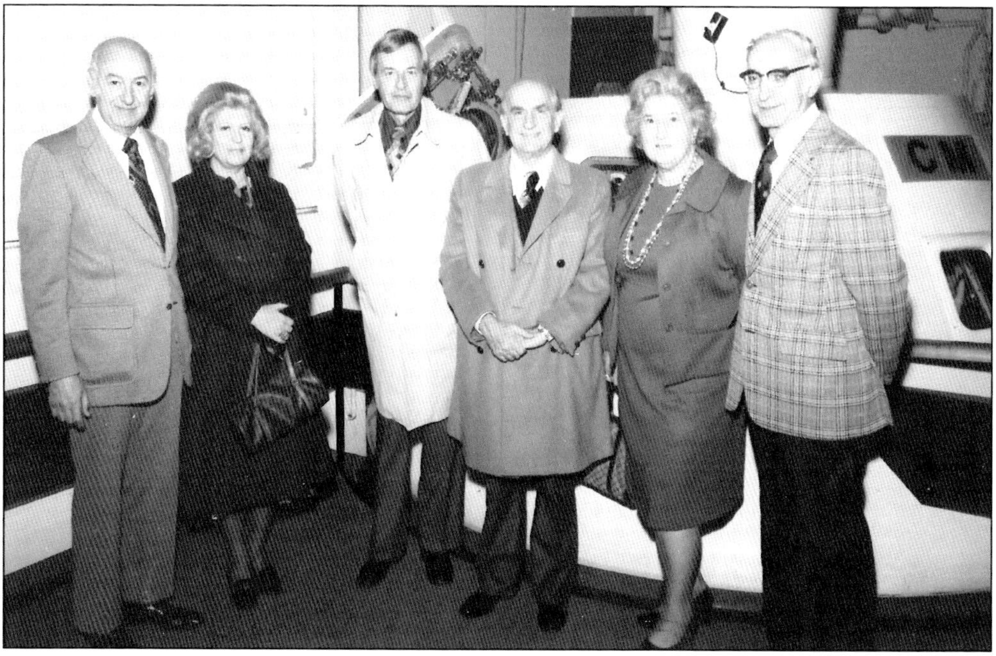

Ambassador Tosca of Greece visits the Johnson Space Center in January 1976. Pictured are Peter H. Pappas, Ambassador Tosca's wife, a space center technician, Ambassador Tosca, Virginia Nick of Dallas, and Aleck Bond, the assistant director for Program Support for the center. (Courtesy of the AGOC archives.)

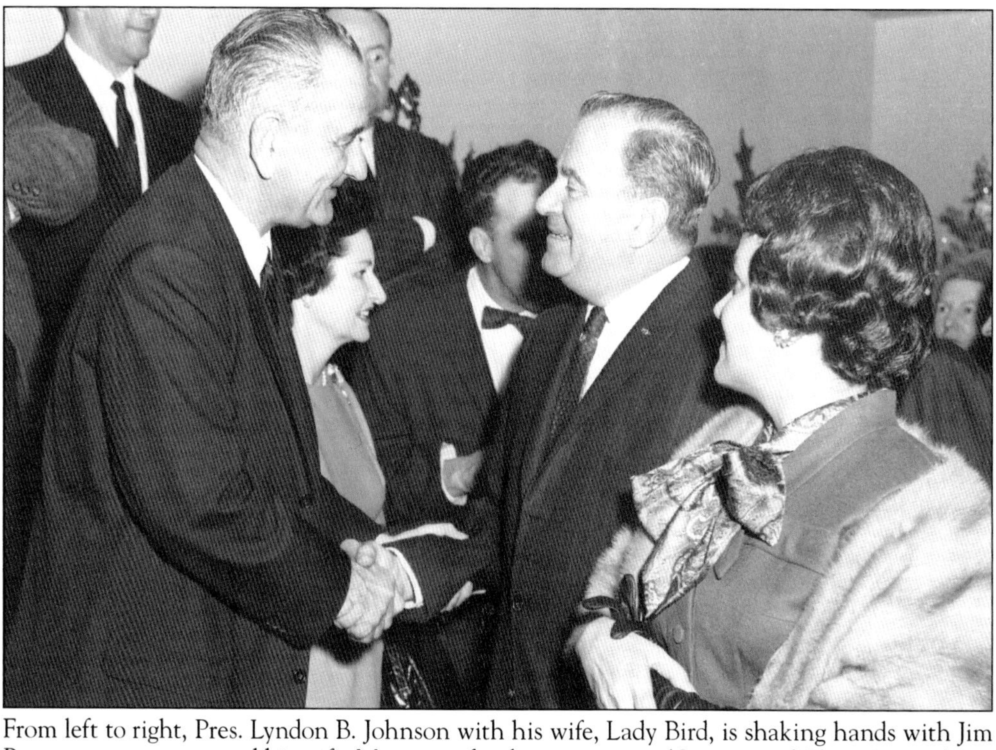

From left to right, Pres. Lyndon B. Johnson with his wife, Lady Bird, is shaking hands with Jim Pappas, restaurateur, and his wife, Mary, at a fundraising event. (Courtesy of Chris Pappas.)

The April 15, 1966, edition of the *Houston Post* reported that Thano Dameris, a Houston lawyer, was named as assistant to William W. Sherill, director of the Federal Deposit Insurance Corporation (FDIC). President Johnson appointed Sherill to the three-man governing body of the FDIC. (Courtesy of Catherine Dameris.)

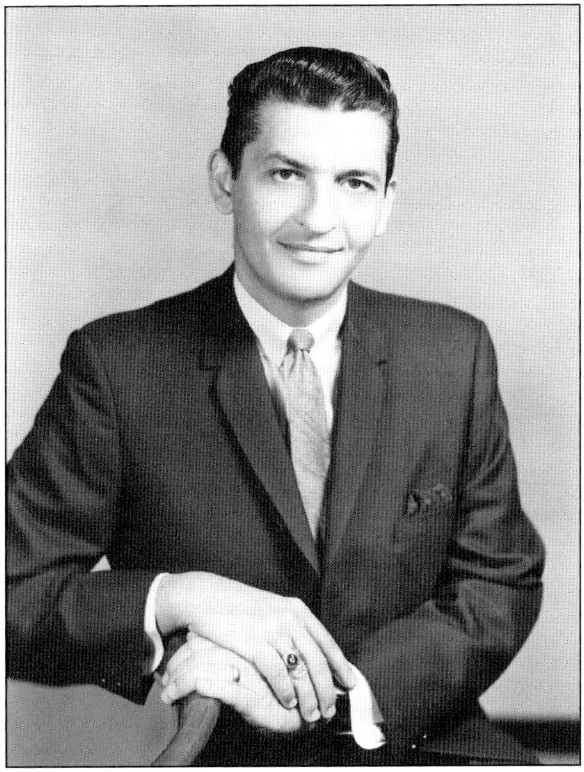

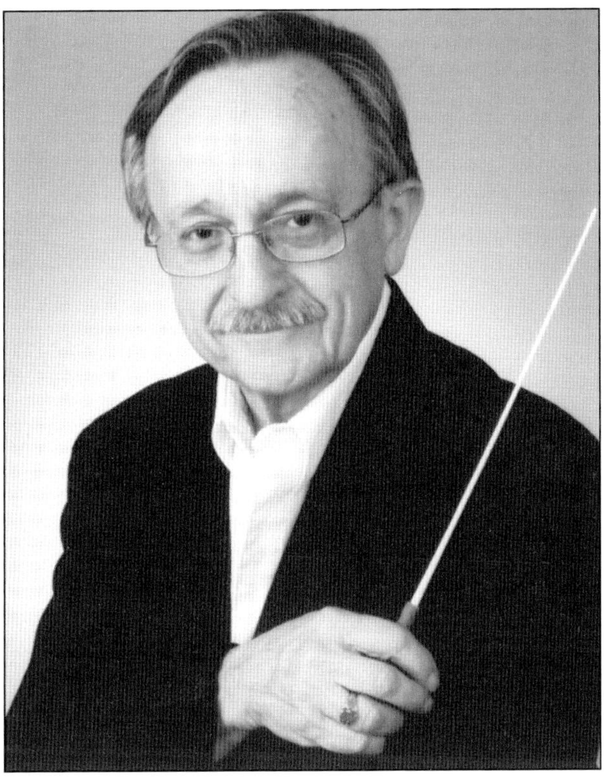

George Blytas, born in Cairo, Egypt, first pursued a career in music but ultimately earned a doctorate in physical chemistry and chemical engineering instead. In 1973, he formed a chamber group of amateur musicians, the Houston Sinfonietta, which, by 1979, evolved into an orchestra. Proud of his heritage and active in Annunciation Cathedral, Dr. Blytas founded the Hellenic Professional Society of Texas and was elected its first president in 1975. (Courtesy of the AGOC archives.)

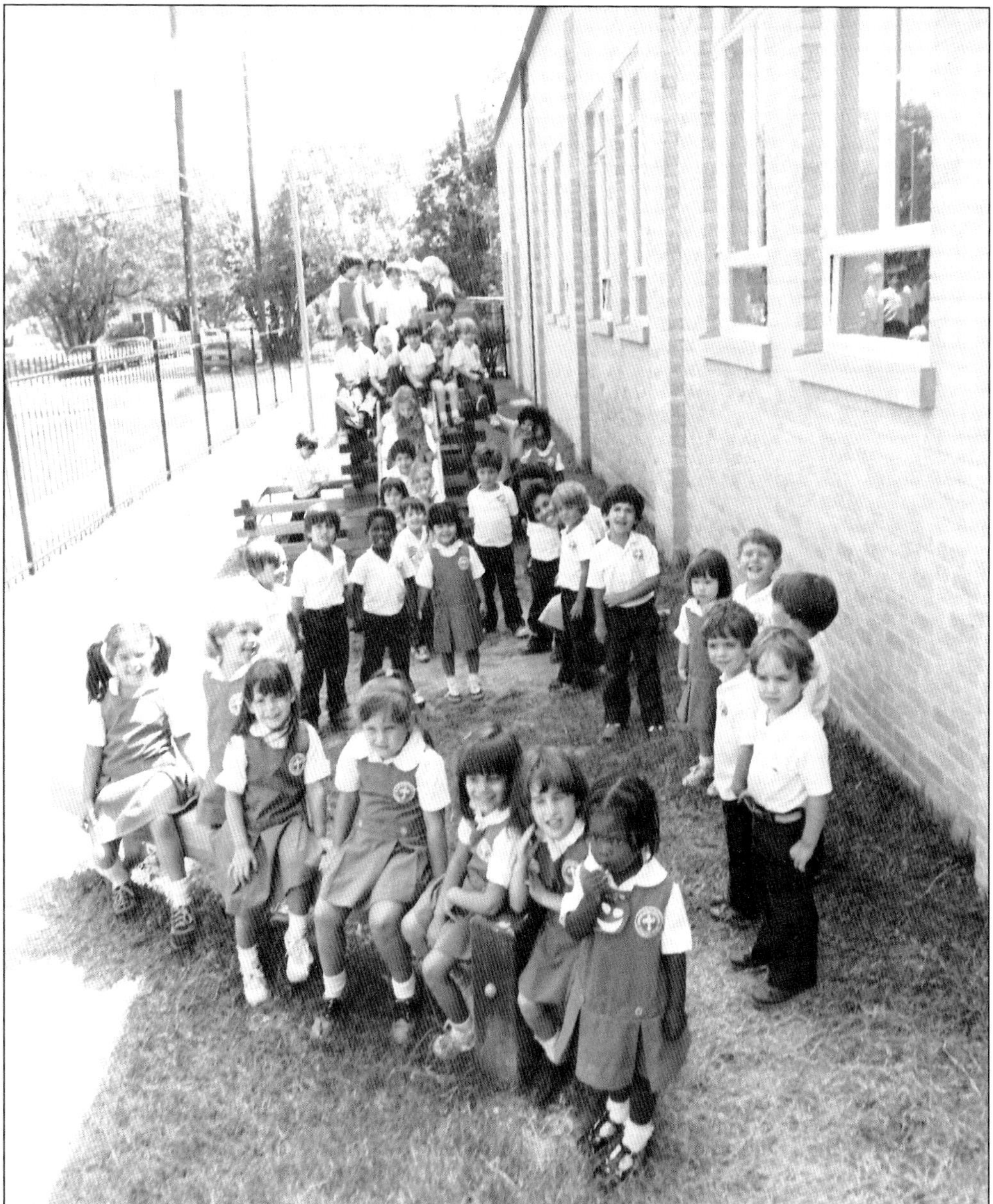

Fr. Nicholas C. Triantafilou and Presbytera Diane founded Annunciation Orthodox School (AOS), a private school for the children of the parish and the Houston greater community in 1970. Presbytera Diane, a certified teacher, donated her services the first year. The school opened its doors to 10 preschool children and was located in the Annunciation Greek Orthodox Cathedral's Polemanakos Educational Building. Gradually, AOS grew to include the eighth grade. To accommodate its growing student body, the school added the Jesse H. and Mary Gibbs Jones Early Childhood Development Center and the Katherine E. Veletsos Lower School building. In honor of her husband, Georgia Caloudas donated the funds for the Steve G. Caloudas Activity Center. With its outstanding curricula, AOS was accepted, by acclamation, into the prestigious Independent Schools Association of the Southwest and is accredited with commendations in 21 areas. (Courtesy of the AGOC archives.)

Eight

The Church Flourishes

The dream for a bigger church with educational and fellowship facilities began to crystallize in the minds and hearts of the community. The people united to gather the finances and talents to make their dream a reality. With this Byzantine church, the Greeks would make a statement to the city of their faith and heritage as well as build for their own posterity.

On March 1, 1946, the *Houston Chronicle* reported that, after years of meetings and discussions, the community purchased half a block of land on Yoakum Boulevard for $20,000 from the Wilkin-Parker Lumber Company. Under the leadership of Fr. Seraphim Haginas, he and the parish council, the building fund, and the finance committee worked closely with the parish to bring about the dream. Though the methods used to raise the necessary funds were essentially the same, a new strategy was implemented when the fundraisers went out to organizations, such as United Way and various churches and synagogues, to get ideas. Monies were raised from within the community as well as through loans and outside contributions and donations from the various fraternal clubs and organizations. Built with the youth in mind, the Yoakum Boulevard church facilities were planned to meet both their educational and recreational needs.

The people continued to worship in the Walker Street church until 1952, when the Yoakum Boulevard church was completed. The Walker Street church was purchased by the city of Houston for $50,000 in 1951 and is commemorated as the first Greek Orthodox church in Texas with a plaque in today's Tranquility Park, at the site of the old church.

On the morning of Great Friday, April 18, 1952, the church was officially opened for services. The parish celebrated the Resurrection in their new church. In 1955, the state of Texas declared the Greek Orthodox Church a major faith.

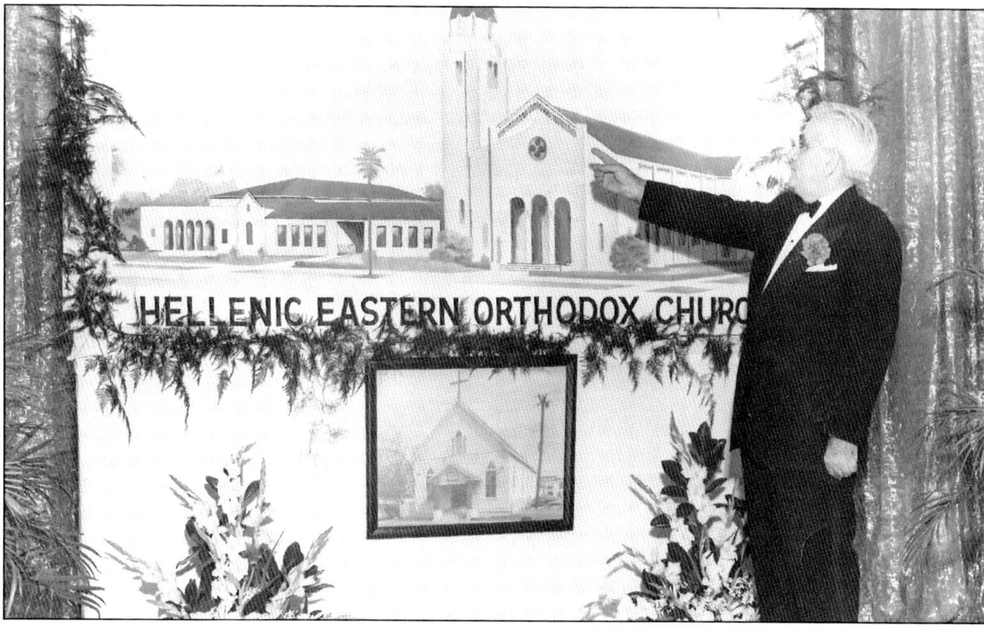

The need for a larger church building had been recognized shortly after the Walker Street church was built. The dream for a bigger church with educational and fellowship facilities crystallized in their minds and hearts, and the people once again took a leap of faith. Here, George P. Kelley, president of the parish council (1950–1952), shows the plans for the new church on Yoakum Boulevard. (Courtesy of the AGOC archives.)

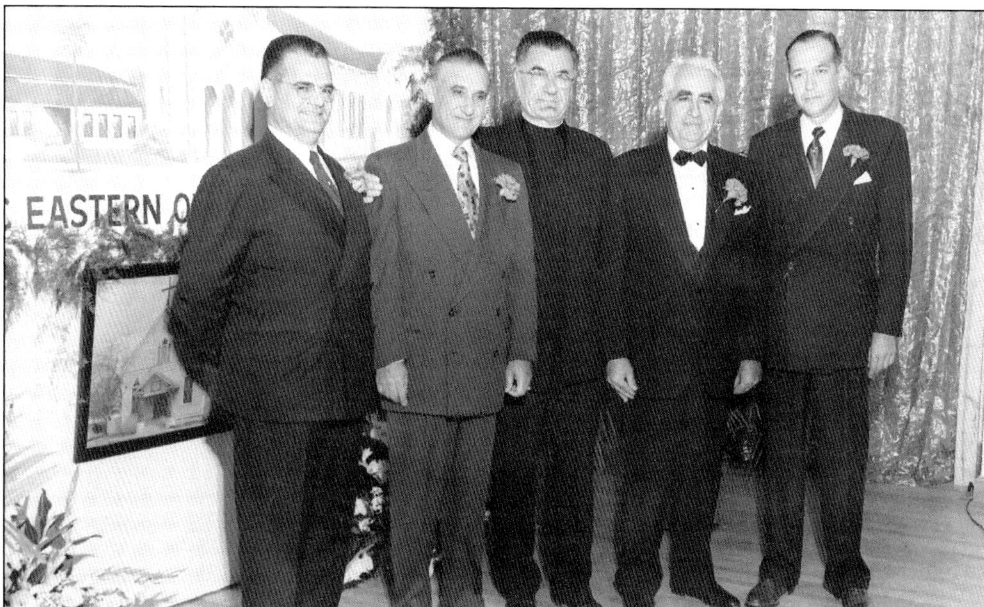

From left to right, Nick Peet, Spero P. Martel (after whom the church auditorium is named), Fr. Seraphim Haginas (who served Annunciation Church from 1946 to 1954), parish council president George P. Kelley, and Angelo Jelson are seen at a fundraising event held in the late 1940s to the early 1950s, prior to the ground breaking of the new church sanctuary on Yoakum Boulevard. (Courtesy of HMRC.)

Fr. Seraphim Haginas served Annunciation Church from 1946 to 1954. Aggressive, vibrant, and a hard worker, he wanted a new church with education buildings. He was the first priest to establish a class for adult Christian education. Father Haginas was also one of the first priests to have his own car to make home and hospital visitations. Most of his predecessors rode buses. (Courtesy of Elaine Stefanidis.)

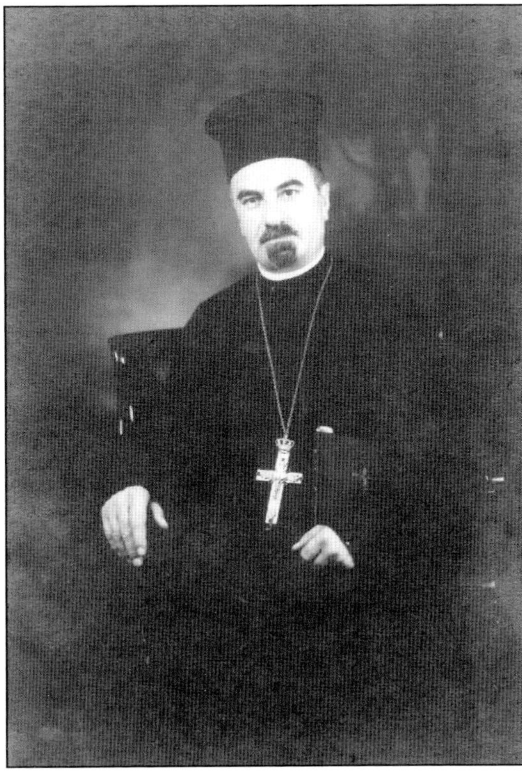

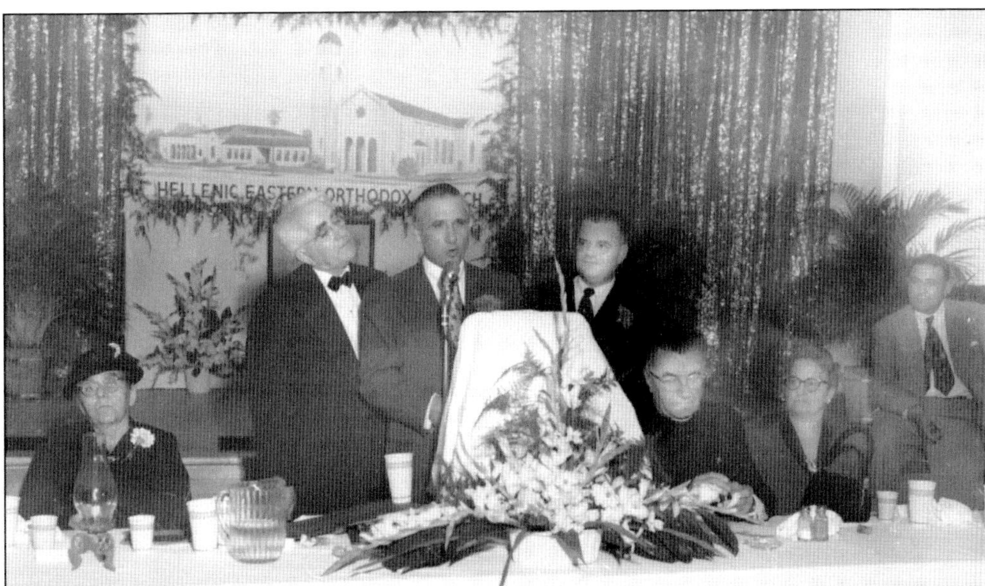

Here is the dedication of the S.P. Martel Auditorium, at which the attendees were shown a projection of what the church would look like. Until the new sanctuary was completed, services were held in the S.P. Martel Auditorium. On the morning of Great Friday, April 18, 1952, the church was officially opened. From left to right are Constantina Peet, George P. Kelley, Spero Martel, Nick Peet, Fr. Seraphim Haginas, Presbytera Elizabeth (Sigalas) Haginas, and Gus Fress. (Courtesy of HMRC.)

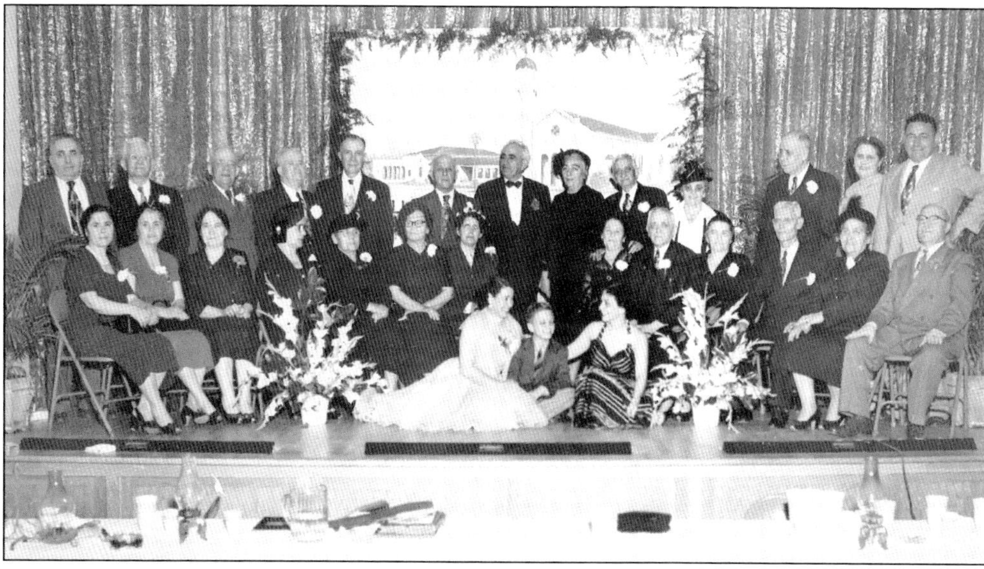

Here is the dedication of S.P. Martel Auditorium in 1952. Pictured are, from left to right, (first row) Bessie Spillios, Nick Giannukos, and Olga Manthos (Nash); (second row) Rallia Boozalis, Anna Picramenos, Nota Kousakis, Maria Menutes, Constantina Peet, Despina Malavansos, Sophia Petheriotes, Demetra Jelson, James Angelos, Constantina and George Tsangalakis, Mary Fress, and Bill Kousakis; (third row) Victor Boozalis, George Picramenos, Angelo Mytilen, John Papazoglakis, Nick Spillios, George Petheriotes, George P. Kelley, Glycaria Brailas, Athanasios Jelson, Anastasia Chickenis, Theo Peet, Anastasia Zgourides, and Gus Fress. (Courtesy of HMRC.)

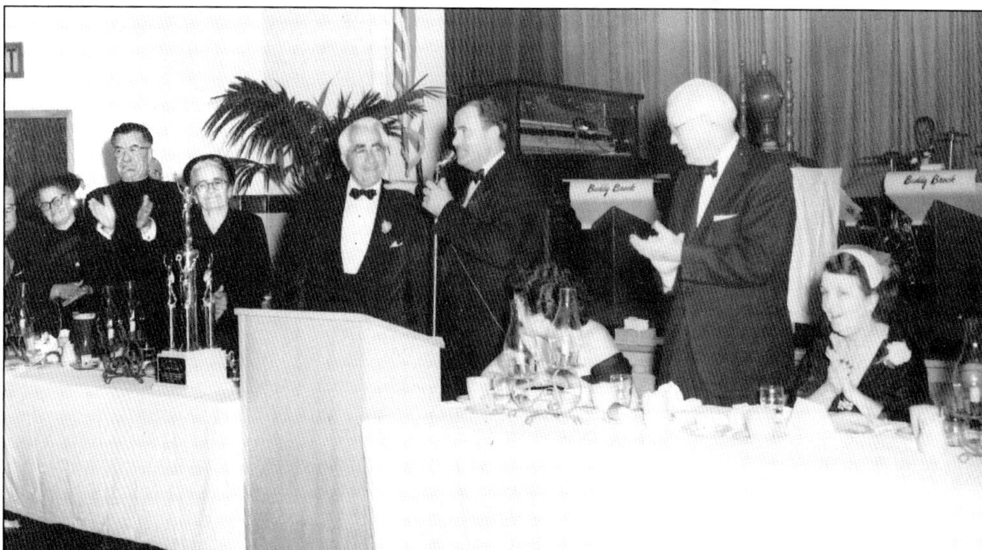

Here is the banquet celebrating the completion of the S.P. Martel Auditorium, named after Speros Martel in appreciation "for his generosity and tireless efforts in the completion of the Yoakum Church." Martel founded the Marian and Speros P. Martel Foundation in 1956, which donated to Annunciation Cathedral, Annunciation Orthodox School, and Rice University. From left to right are Presbytera Elizabeth (Sigalas) Haginas, Fr. Seraphim Haginas, unidentified, parish council president George P. Kelley, James Pappas at the podium, and three unidentified. (Courtesy of the AGOC archives.)

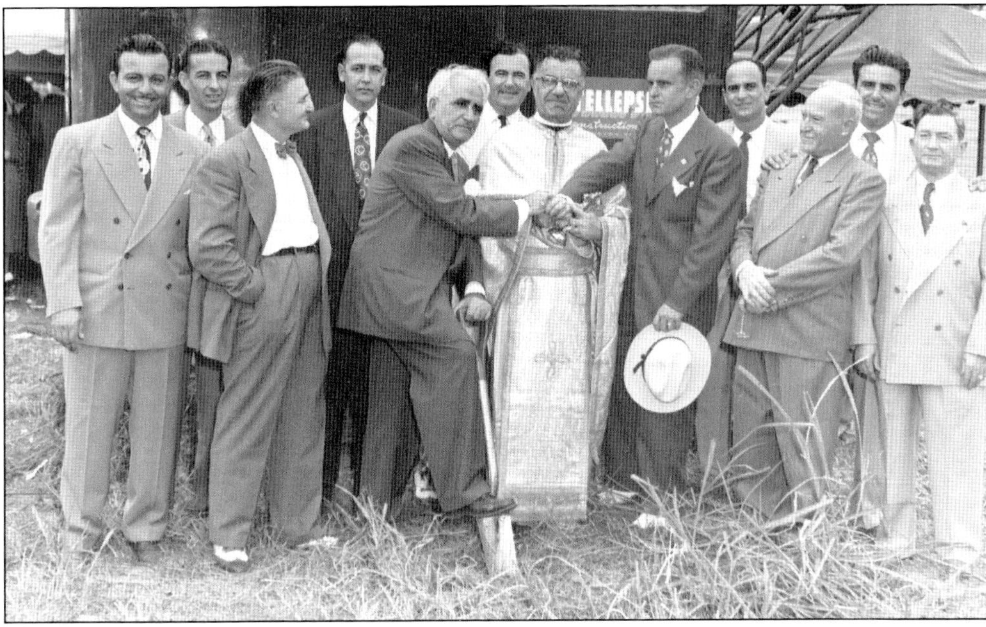

Ground breaking of the new location of the Annunciation Greek Orthodox Church at 3511 Yoakum Boulevard occurred in 1951. From left to right are Nick Pappas, Sam Kamas, James Prappas, Angelo Jelson, parish council president George P. Kelley, James Pappas, Fr. Seraphim Haginas, three unidentified, Victor Pappas, and Tom Arapolis. (Courtesy of HMRC.)

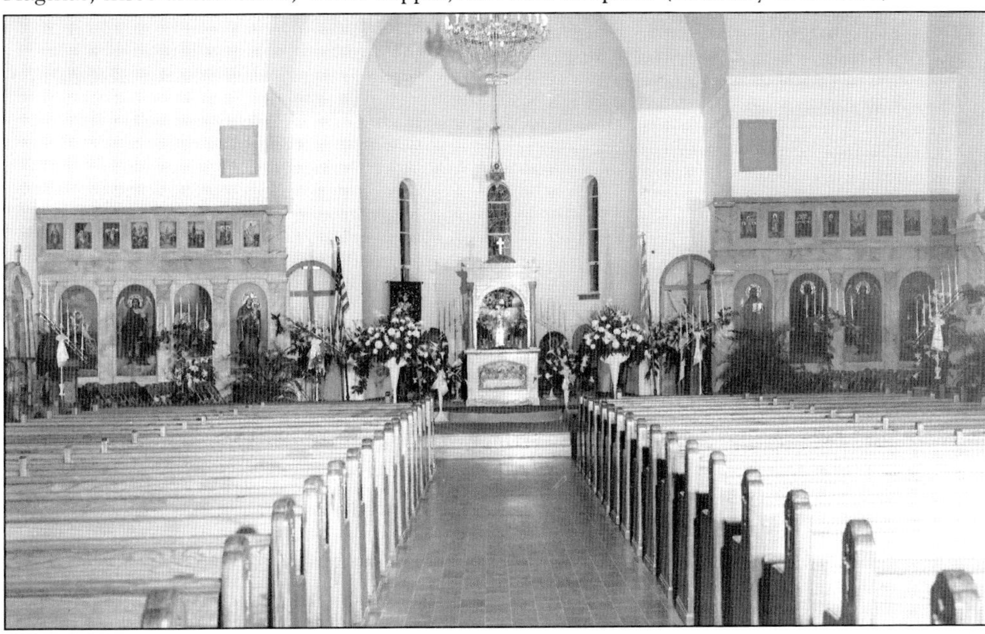

Here is the Annunciation Greek Orthodox Church on Yoakum Boulevard before iconography and royal doors were added in 1952. The icons and the chandeliers from the Walker Street church were retrieved just before the building was demolished. The icons were then installed in the iconostasion of the new church. New icons have been added in the sanctuary by iconographers such as Stelios Maris and Diamantis Cassis, but the icon screen remains the same. (Courtesy of the AGOC archives.)

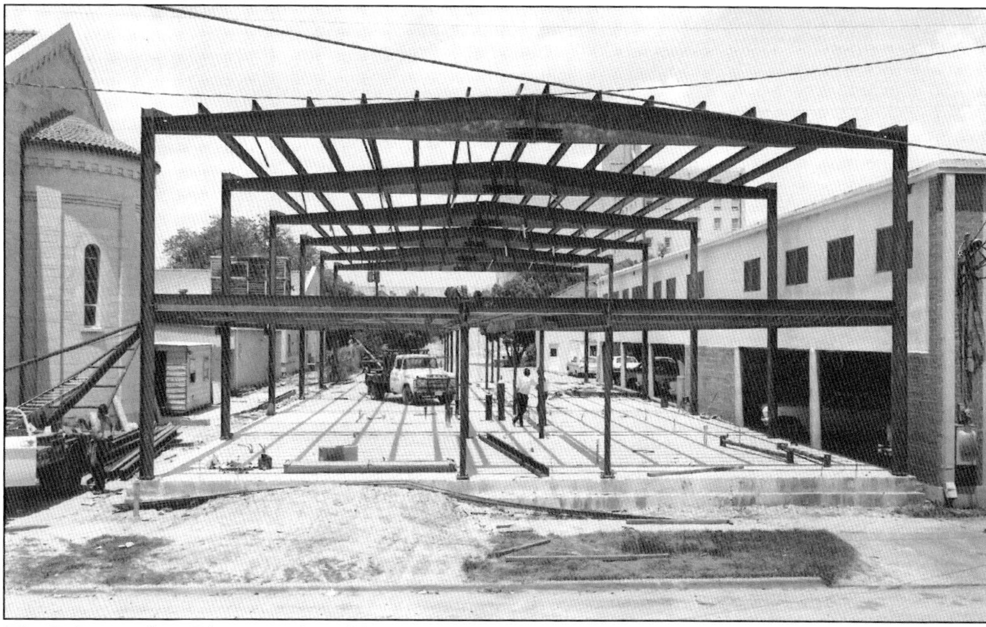

The Polemanakos Educational Building was under construction in 1968. When a larger church was built on Yoakum Boulevard, Theo and Nick Polemanakos, the remaining brothers, paid $107,000 of the $300,000 cost of the educational building. This facility was built with the youth in mind. It exceeded the current educational and recreational needs of the community in anticipation of its continued growth. (Courtesy of the AGOC archives.)

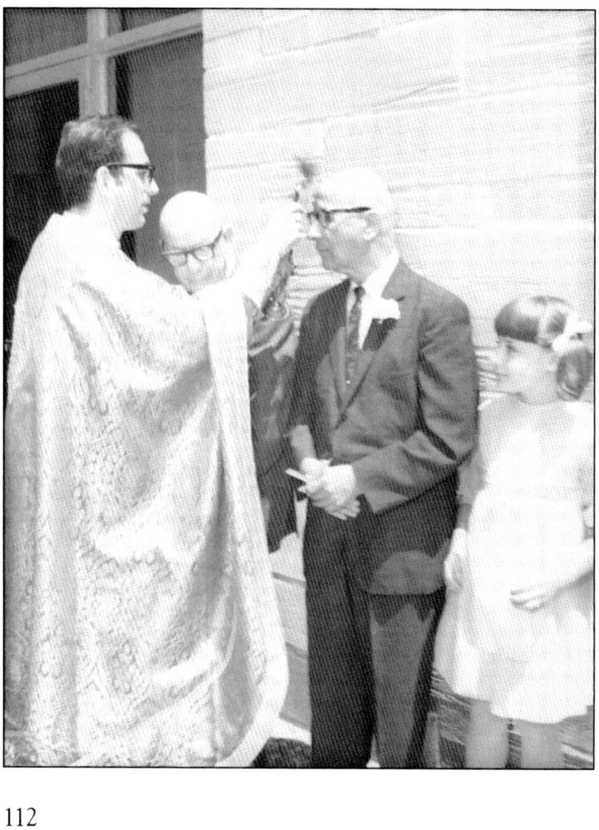

From left to right are Fr. Nicholas C. Triantafilou, Theo Polemanakos, Nick Polemanakos, and Wanita Hadjes. Father Nick blesses the Polemanakos brothers, benefactors of the church, attending the Polemanakos Educational Building ribbon-cutting event in 1968. In the 1970s, His Eminence Archbishop Iakovos honored Nick Polemanakos with the Medal of St. Paul, the highest honor the Greek Orthodox Archdiocese bestows on a layperson, in recognition of his Christian faith and love. (Courtesy of the AGOC archives.)

Nine

A Radical Decade

In the 1960s, the community grew in number and size and it became impossible for one priest to minister to the expanding population. In 1965, Fr. Nicholas C. Triantafilou was named assistant priest to Fr. George Kalpaxis. Two years later, Father Kalpaxis was reassigned and Father Nick was elevated to the rank of *proistamenos* (dean). That same year, Houston became the See of the Eighth Archdiocesan District when the headquarters were moved from New Orleans, and the Annunciation Church was elevated to the status of a cathedral in 1967.

Father Nick was an innovative leader. In a presentation to the board of trustees, he requested that an altar fund be established. Any gratuities given to priests for sacraments or visitations were to be deposited into this fund. The board approved this plan, and the altar fund became a source of aid to needy individuals and families. Father Nick continued to offer adult catechism and began neighborhood Bible studies. He and Presbytera Diane instituted Friday Lenten Suppers to encourage young people to participate in the five Salutation Services and teach them about Great Lent. Working hand in hand with Father Nick, the Ladies Philoptochos Society Philocardiac ministry visited Greek patients in the Texas Medical Center to assist them in any way possible.

The parish celebrated its 50th anniversary in 1967 with festivities that included a Greek Night, which was so successful that in 1968, the parish held its second annual Greek Festival. The four-day festival enables the Greek community to share its culture and religion and uses the profits to expand its charitable ministries.

Despite the financial success of the festival, the parish wanted to assume a more personal responsibility for the church. In 1969, the Fair Share Commitment program replaced annual dues. Now, parishioners made a more personal commitment of time, talent, and treasure to the church. Houston presented this program to the archdiocese, and Father Nick was asked to introduce this unique Biblical concept to all the churches in the Greek Orthodox Archdiocese. Father Nick spent the next two and a half years leading the Archdiocesan Stewardship Program.

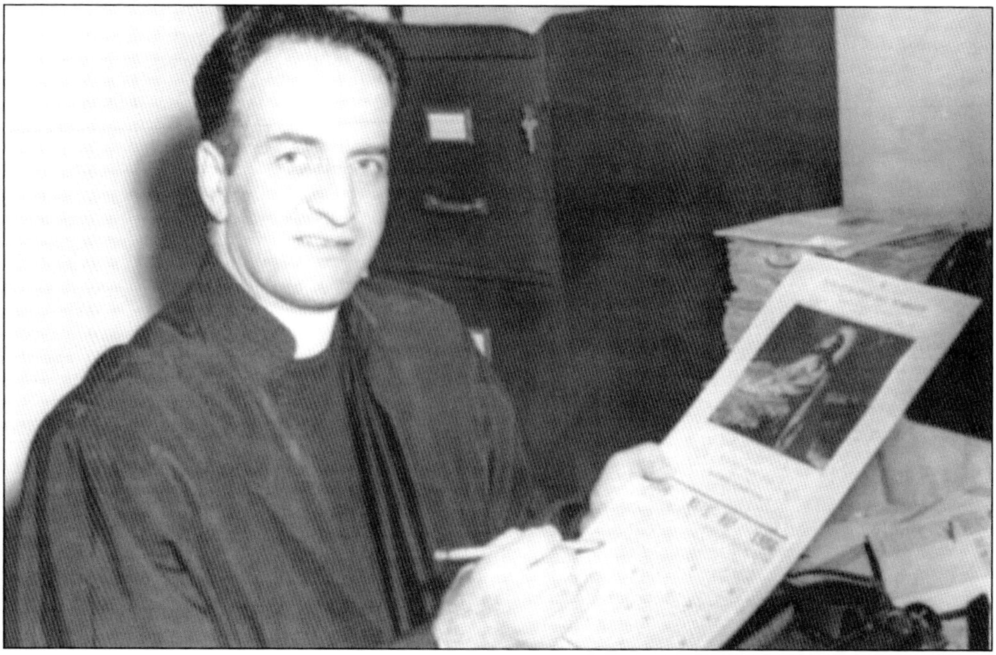

By 1960, given the unparalleled growth in the church and the vast distances Fr. George Kalpaxis (1954–1966, pictured) traveled to minister to parishioners, the need arose for a second priest to help serve the church community. The parish council requested an assistant priest from Archbishop Iakovos. His Eminence appointed Rev. Nicholas C. Triantafilou (1965–1987). (Courtesy of Anita Kalpaxis Jones.)

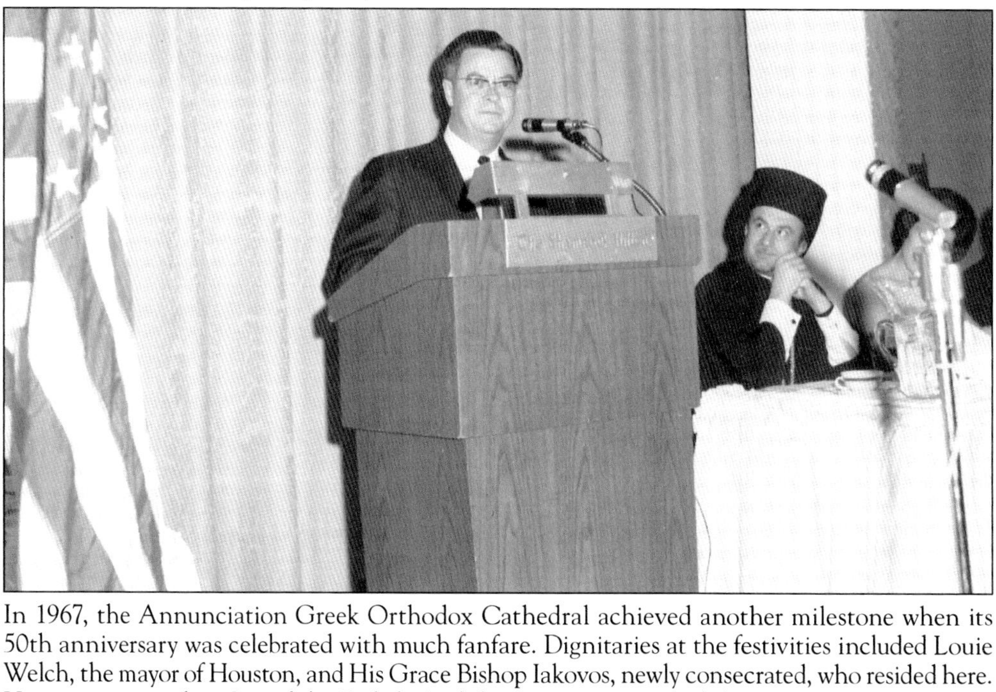

In 1967, the Annunciation Greek Orthodox Cathedral achieved another milestone when its 50th anniversary was celebrated with much fanfare. Dignitaries at the festivities included Louie Welch, the mayor of Houston, and His Grace Bishop Iakovos, newly consecrated, who resided here. Houston was made a See of the Eighth Archdiocesan District, and the Annunciation Church was elevated to the status of cathedral. (Courtesy of the AGOC archives.)

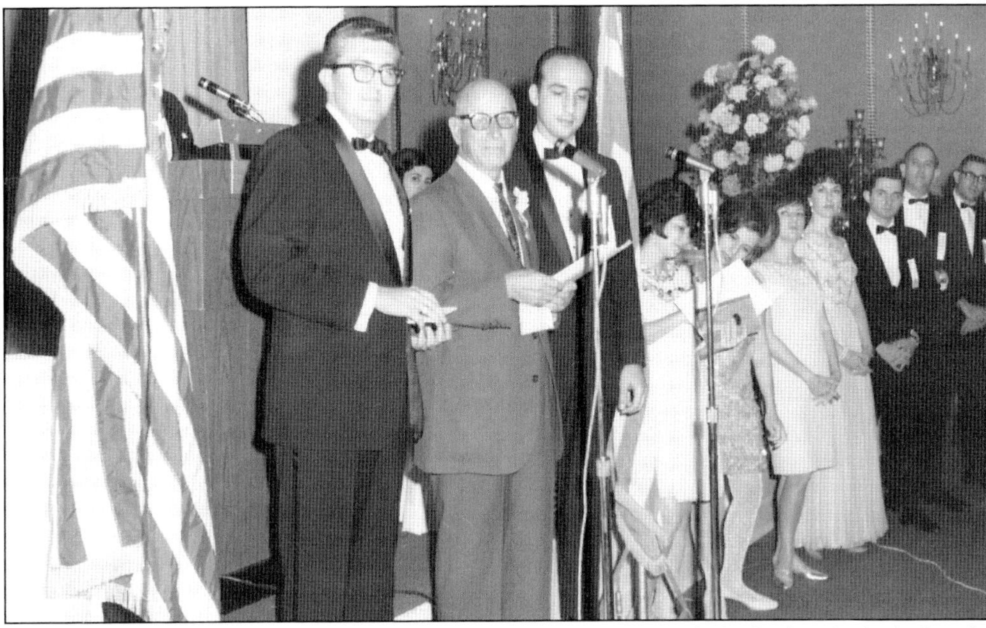

The parish celebrated the 50th anniversary of Annunciation Greek Orthodox Cathedral at the Shamrock Hilton Hotel. At left is Nick T. Dameris, cochair of the 50th anniversary along with Greg Catsinas (not shown). Others pictured are, from left to right, Nick Polemanakos, Paul Voinis, Mary Bellos, Kallie Nicolaou, Stella Harrison, Mary Poulos, James Papadakis, Jerry Kaler, and Art Makris. (Courtesy of the AGOC archives.)

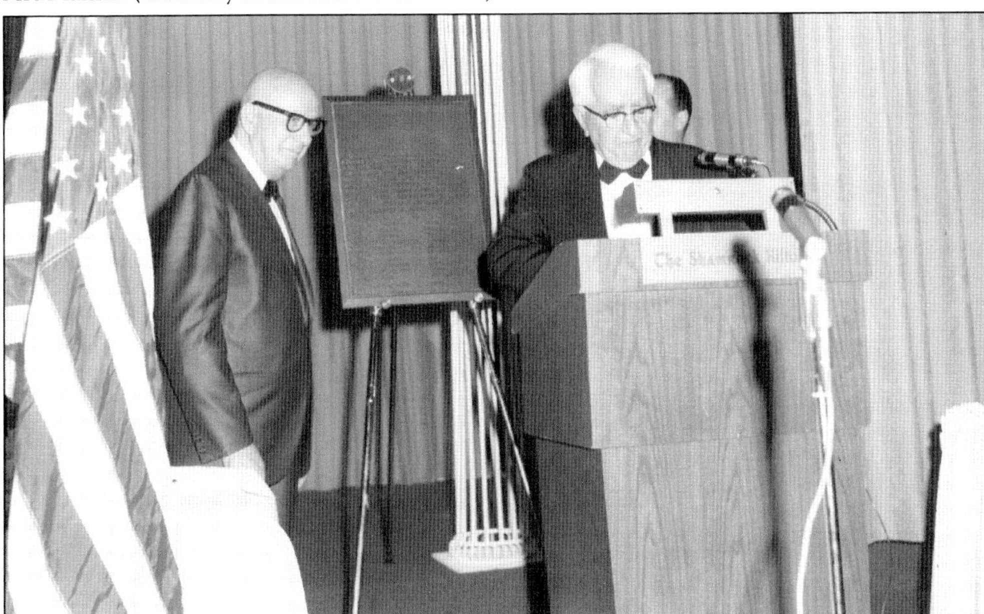

Annunciation Greek Orthodox Cathedral celebrated its 50th anniversary at the Shamrock Hilton Hotel in 1967. Theo Polemanakos, on the left, was recognized for his generosity to the church. George P. Kelley, a prominent member of the church and one of the presidents of the community, is standing at the podium. The master of ceremonies, behind Kelley, was Fred Nahas. (Courtesy of the AGOC archives.)

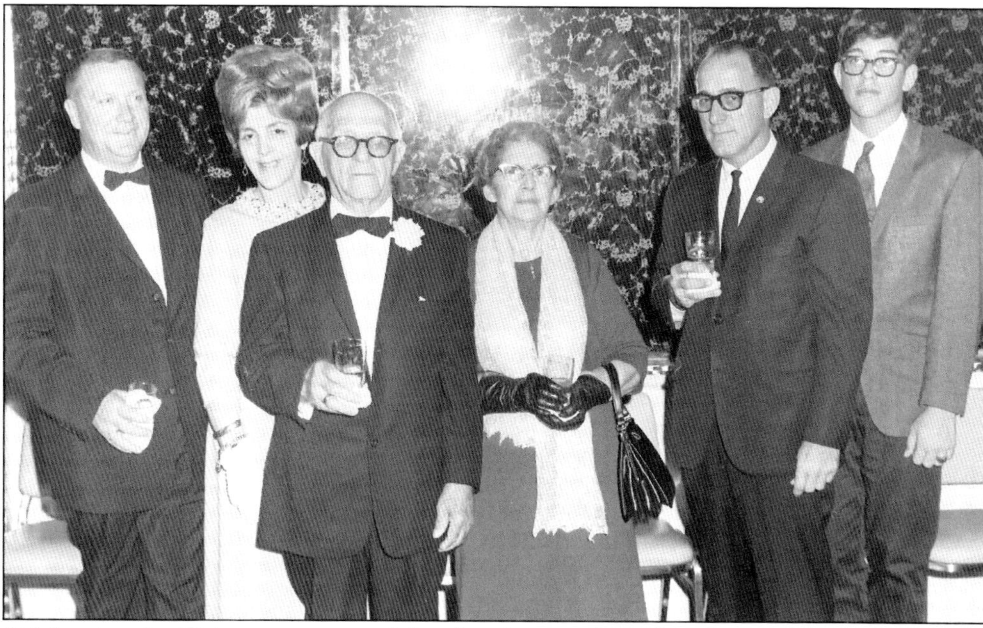

Celebrating the 50th anniversary of the church in 1967 at the Shamrock Hilton Hotel are unidentified, Katherine Matandos, George and Sophia Petheriotes, their son James Petheriotes, and Michael Matandos. George Petheriotes was president of the parish council in 1921–1922. (Courtesy of the AGOC archives.)

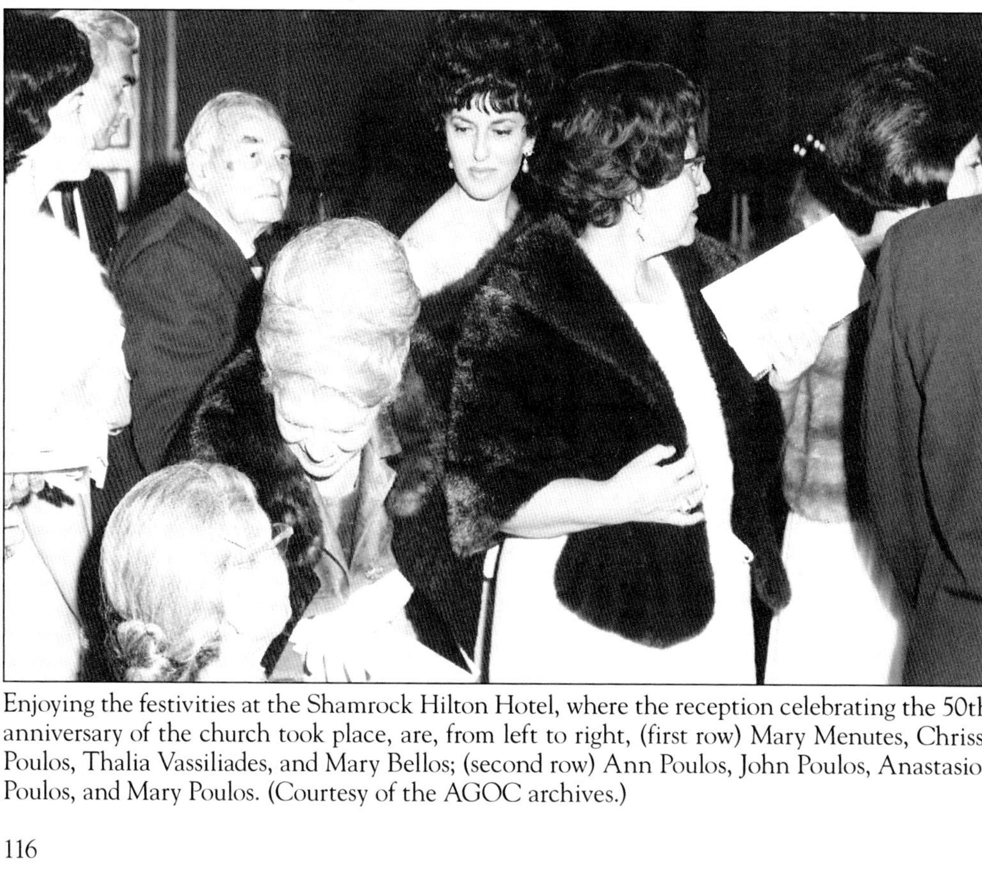

Enjoying the festivities at the Shamrock Hilton Hotel, where the reception celebrating the 50th anniversary of the church took place, are, from left to right, (first row) Mary Menutes, Chrissi Poulos, Thalia Vassiliades, and Mary Bellos; (second row) Ann Poulos, John Poulos, Anastasios Poulos, and Mary Poulos. (Courtesy of the AGOC archives.)

Houston became the home of His Grace Bishop Iacovos of Catania, the first bishop of the Greek Orthodox Diocese of Houston (1967–1969). He was appointed bishop when the diocese was relocated to Houston from New Orleans, effective December 1, 1967. Temporary headquarters for the Houston Diocese was Annunciation Greek Orthodox Cathedral at 3511 Yoakum Boulevard. The bishop arrived in Houston in time to participate in the 50th anniversary festivities for Annunciation. (Courtesy of the AGOC archives.)

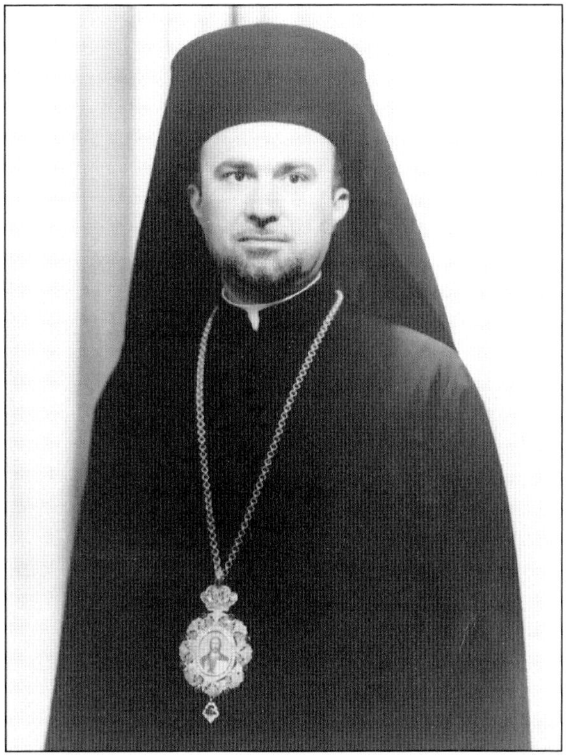

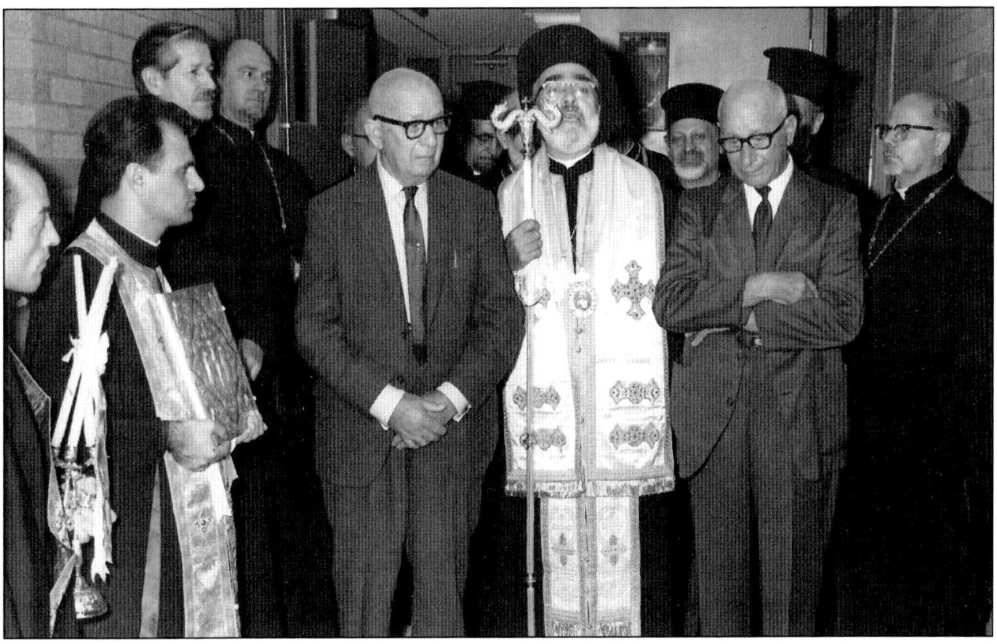

Pictured are ceremonies in Brookline, Massachusetts, for the newly built Polemanakos Educational Building at Hellenic College Holy Cross in 1968. His Eminence Archbishop Iakovos is shown with Theo and Nick Polemanakos, Fr. Leonidas Contos, and many others. As generous benefactors of their faith, the Polemanakos brothers supported their church in Houston as well as the seminary by building new dormitories for the student body. (Courtesy of the AGOC archives.)

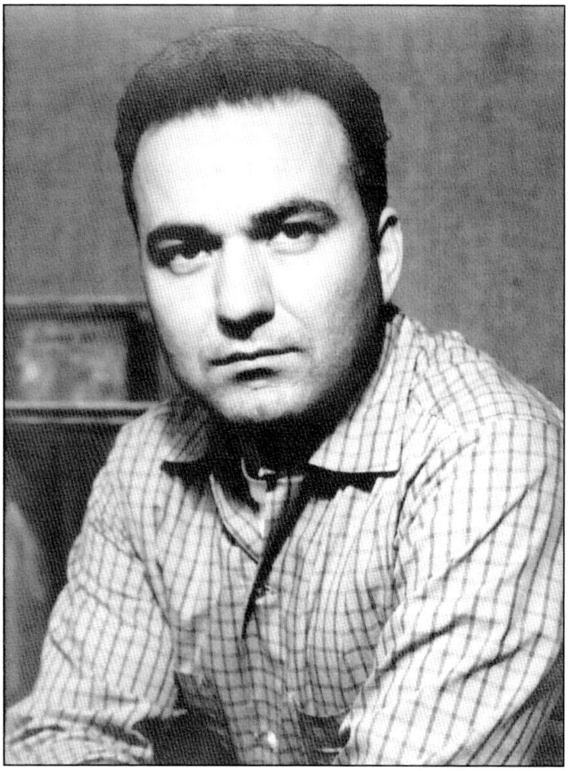

Diamantis (Dan) Cassis and his mother immigrated from Galaxidi, Greece, to Shreveport, Louisiana, to join his father in 1946. The art teacher and artist discovered Byzantine iconography in the early 1960s and chose to specialize in this unique form of Orthodox religious art. In 1961, he married Irene Gazelas and moved to Houston, where she resided. Dan produces icons for churches and homes throughout the United States. (Courtesy of Irene Cassis.)

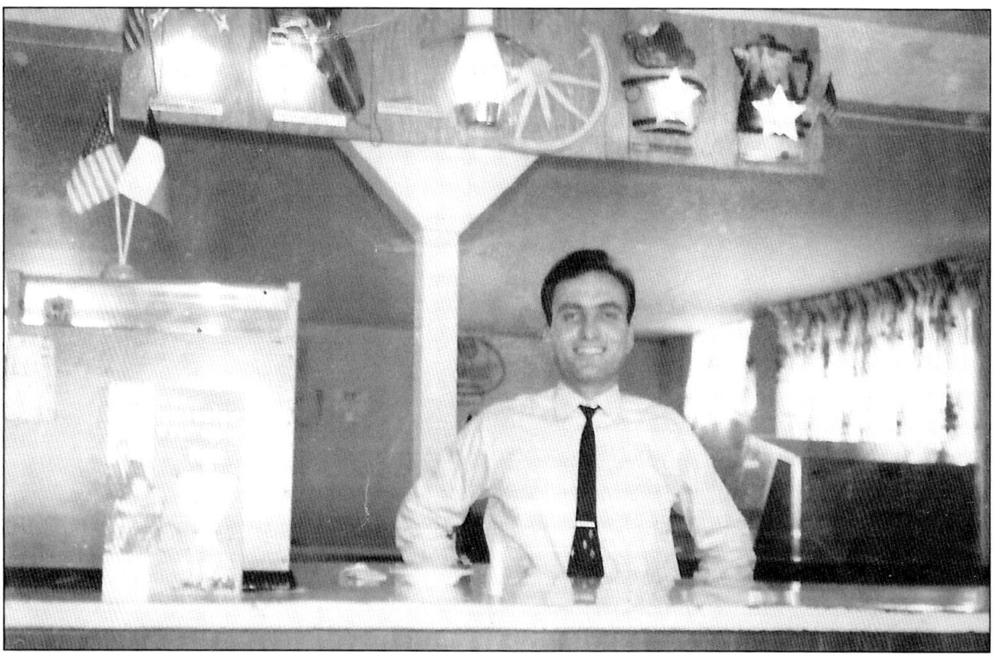

Sotirios (Steve) Vionis came from Naoussa, Macedonia, Greece. He worked on cargo freighters before coming to the United States. In 1961, he bought the Athens Bar & Grill, a tiny bar in the port of Houston, and expanded it. It quickly became a successful Greek restaurant with live entertainment that was popular with Greeks, sailors, and Americans. (Courtesy of Nikolaos Vionis.)

Here is the opening of the Chart Room at the Watergate Yachting Center in Kemah, Texas, in 1967. From left to right are Jim Pappas, owner of Pappas Refrigeration Company, who later became a restaurateur; Leo Kalantzakis, owner of the Chart Room; and Vicki Pappas (Giannukos). Leo bought restaurant equipment and furniture for his restaurants from Jim Pappas. (Courtesy of Leo Kalantzakis.)

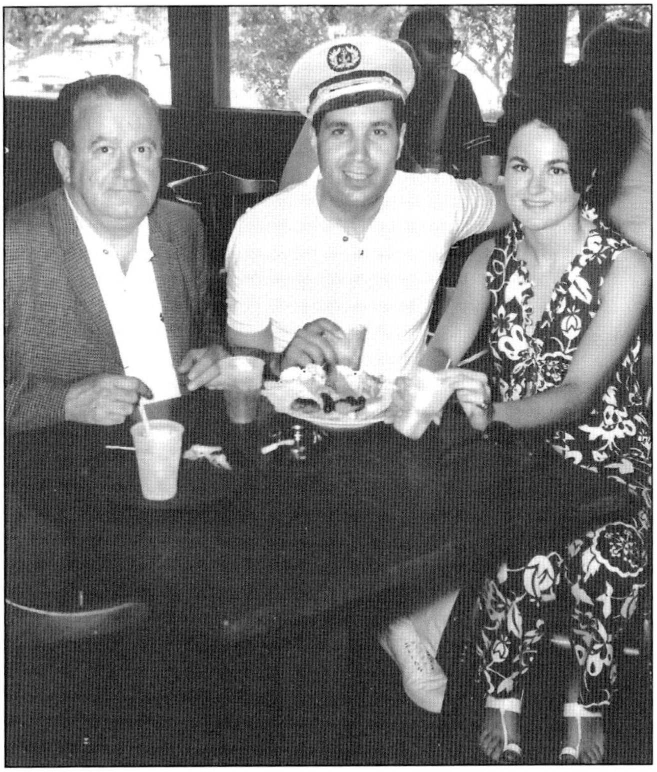

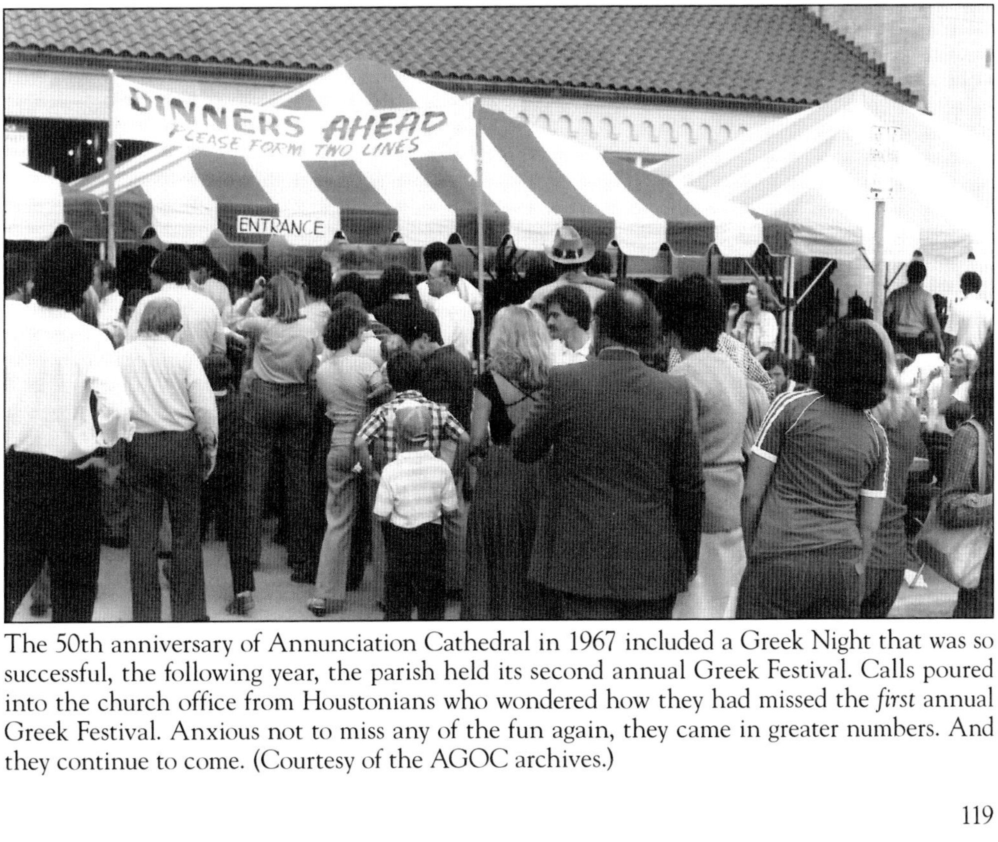

The 50th anniversary of Annunciation Cathedral in 1967 included a Greek Night that was so successful, the following year, the parish held its second annual Greek Festival. Calls poured into the church office from Houstonians who wondered how they had missed the *first* annual Greek Festival. Anxious not to miss any of the fun again, they came in greater numbers. And they continue to come. (Courtesy of the AGOC archives.)

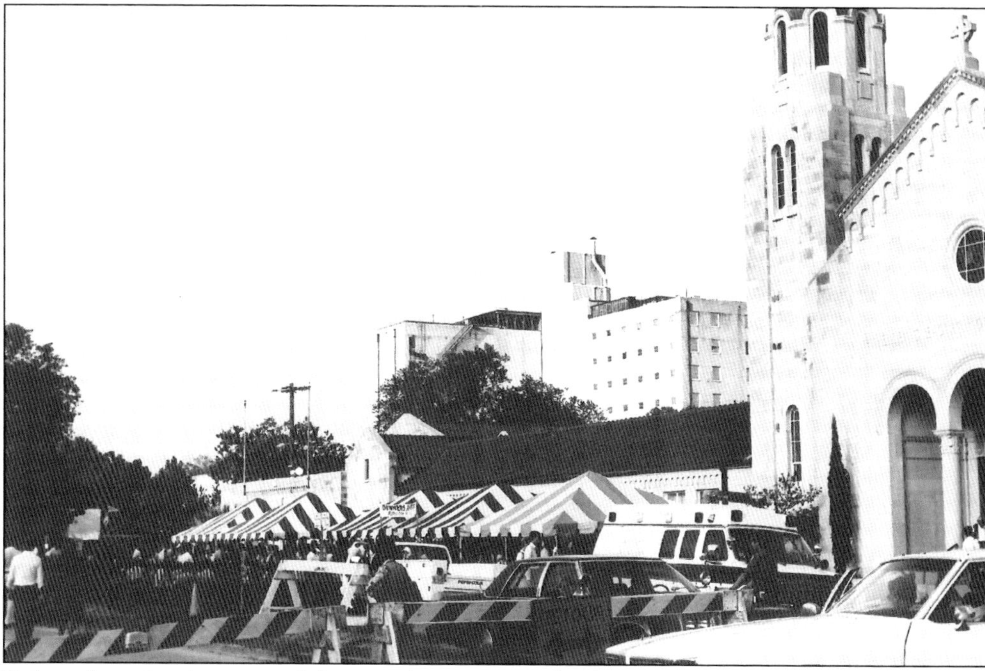

Before the redevelopment of the complex in 2000, the festival was confined to the courtyard connecting the cathedral to the Martel Auditorium. The city of Houston closed streets, and tables were set up in front of the cathedral so visitors could enjoy their meals. In 1987, a fourth day was added to the festival to accommodate the 50,000 guests. (Courtesy of the AGOC archives.)

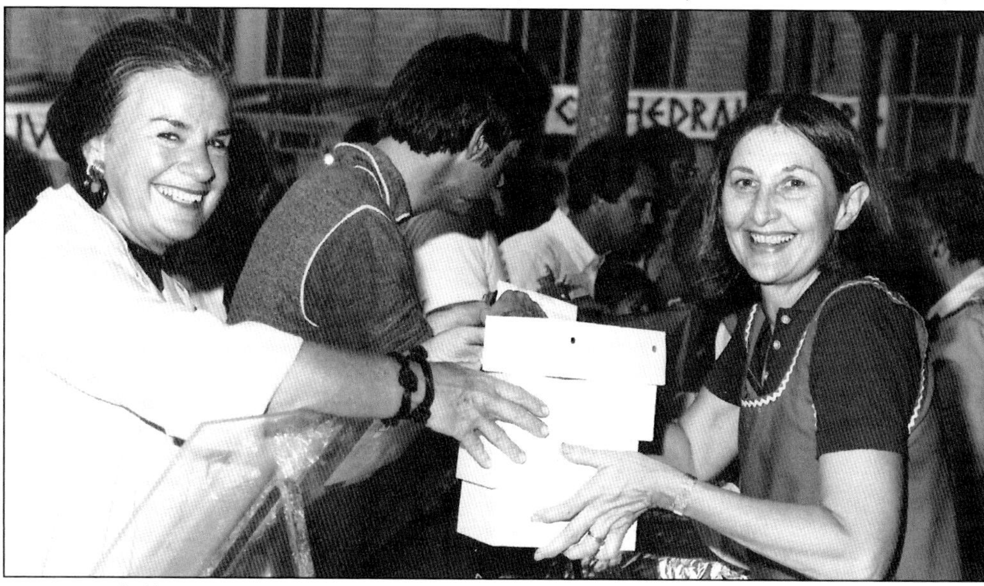

Maria Mitchell Ballantyne (left) is picking up boxes of sweets from Mary Prappas at the annual Greek Festival. In preparation for the festival, 18,000 *koulourakia*, 17,000 *kourambiethes*, 16,000 *finikia*, and 22,000 pieces of baklava, a total of 73,000 sweets, are baked and sold. Eventually, the festival added *loukoumathes* (honey balls), *rizogalo* (rice pudding), and *tsourekia* (sweet Easter bread) to the dessert menu. Close to 6,000 orders of *loukoumathes* and *rizogalo* are sold, and festival workers bake 820 loaves of bread. (Courtesy of Paul Voinis.)

Ten

THE JOURNEY CONTINUES

The 1970s saw a succession of young assistant priests serve as youth ministers. But older, more experienced priests also served the growing community in this capacity. Fr. Costas J. Kouklis worked tirelessly at the Seamen's Center, and Fr. Demetrios Lokis helped new immigrants with translations of documents they needed for employment and citizenship applications. Dedicated parishioners who built upon a tradition of lay involvement in all aspects of the church's mission supported the efforts of the assistant priests. The leadership and participation of the laity has become one of the most progressive characteristics of the Houston church.

In 1970, Annunciation Orthodox School was conceived as a preschool by Father Nick and Presbytera Diane. Their goal was to create a spiritual environment for the children. The school opened with 10 students, and Presbytera Diane, a certified teacher, donated her services the first year. With the enthusiastic support of the parish, the school was expanded from preschool through the eighth grade. As a complement to the school, an extended day care center was created for working mothers, which enabled them to place their children in the Annunciation School.

At this time, the Polemanakos brothers offered the community eight acres of land in southwest Houston with the stipulation that parishioners raise $364,000 to construct recreational facilities. Through a successful land acquisition drive, the Greek Orthodox Community Center (GOCC) became a reality. The GOCC provided a swimming pool, picnic pavilion, tennis courts, sports facilities, and playgrounds. Now, the youth of the parish had their own athletic and recreational facility. Vacation Bible school was held at the center, providing the children with opportunities to view God's glory in their immediate surroundings. Special services were celebrated, including an Epiphany Cross Toss into the pool. Most important was the fellowship that flourished among families who played, swam, and ate together at the GOCC.

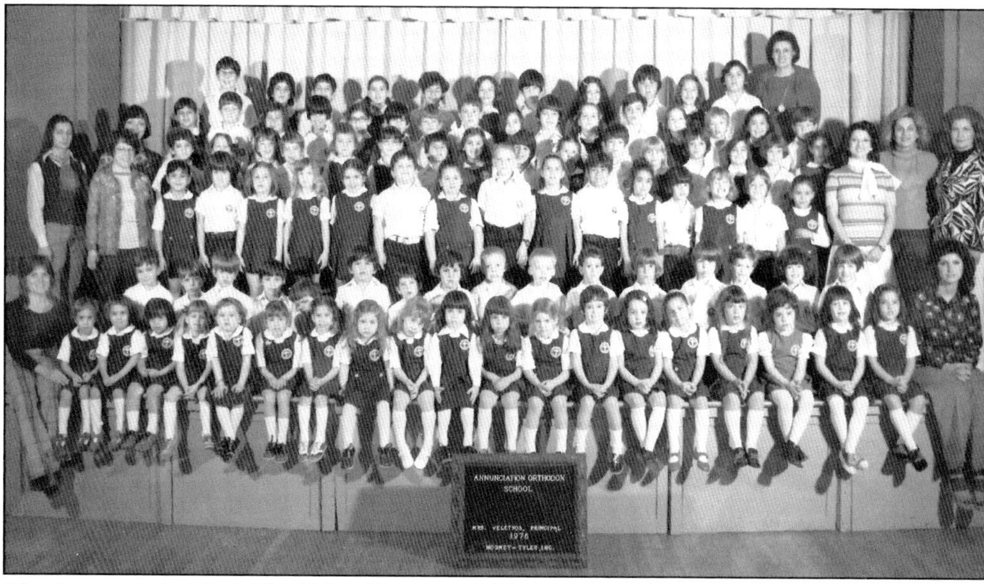

The Annunciation Orthodox School began in 1970 as a ministry of Annunciation Greek Orthodox Cathedral. Barbara Coyner was its first principal (1970), followed by Katherine Veletsos (1975). An extended day care was added, and as enrollment grew, the school added a grade level each year from preschool through the sixth grade. For the next 25 years, Veletsos worked tirelessly to achieve academic excellence while maintaining a nurturing and spiritual environment. Veletsos is pictured at the top right, along with the enrollment of the entire school and its faculty, in 1976. (Courtesy of the AGOC archives.)

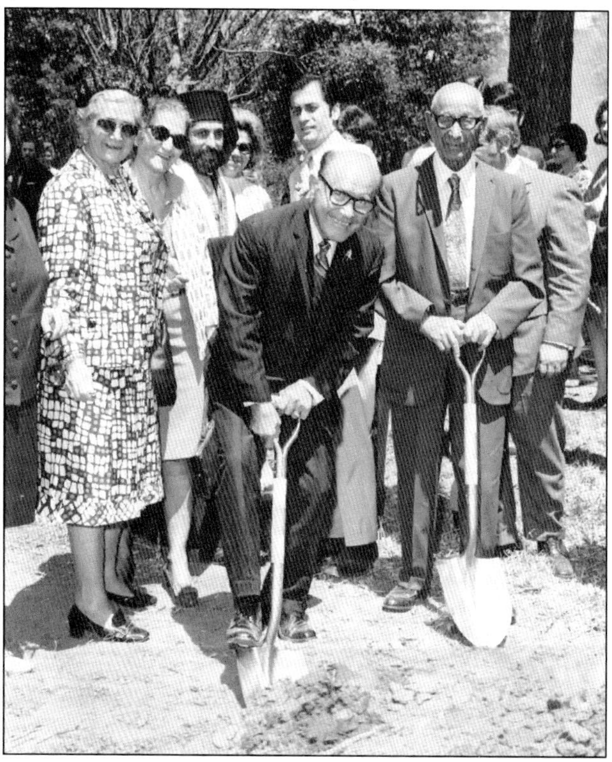

Ground breaking and blessing of the Greek Orthodox Community Center occurred in 1972. Pictured holding the shovels are Stavros (Steve) Panos and Nick Polemanakos. From left to right are Mercena Panos, Chrysanthe Gazelas, His Eminence Bishop John of Thermon, and Anthony Kouzounis, president of the parish council from 1972 to 1976. Fr. Nicholas C. Triantafilou (not pictured) and His Eminence Bishop John of Thermon offered prayers after the ground breaking. (Courtesy of the AGOC archives.)

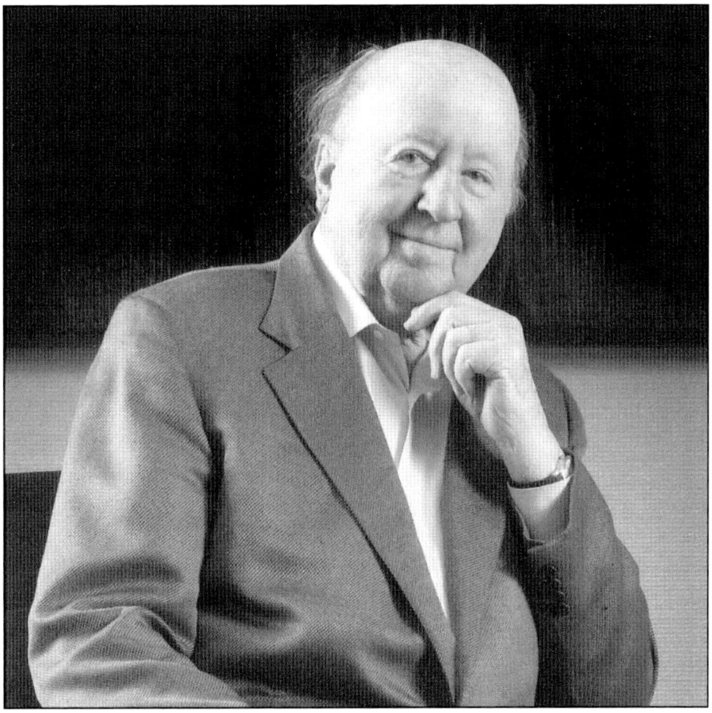

George Phydias Mitchell was born in Galveston to Greek immigrant parents. With a degree in petroleum engineering, he started Mitchell Energy & Development Corporation, an independent oil and gas company that grew into a Fortune 500 company. In 1974, Mitchell developed the Woodlands, a 25,000-acre planned community 27 miles north of downtown Houston. He and his wife, Cynthia, have played a major role in the revitalization of Galveston. (Courtesy of the AGOC archives.)

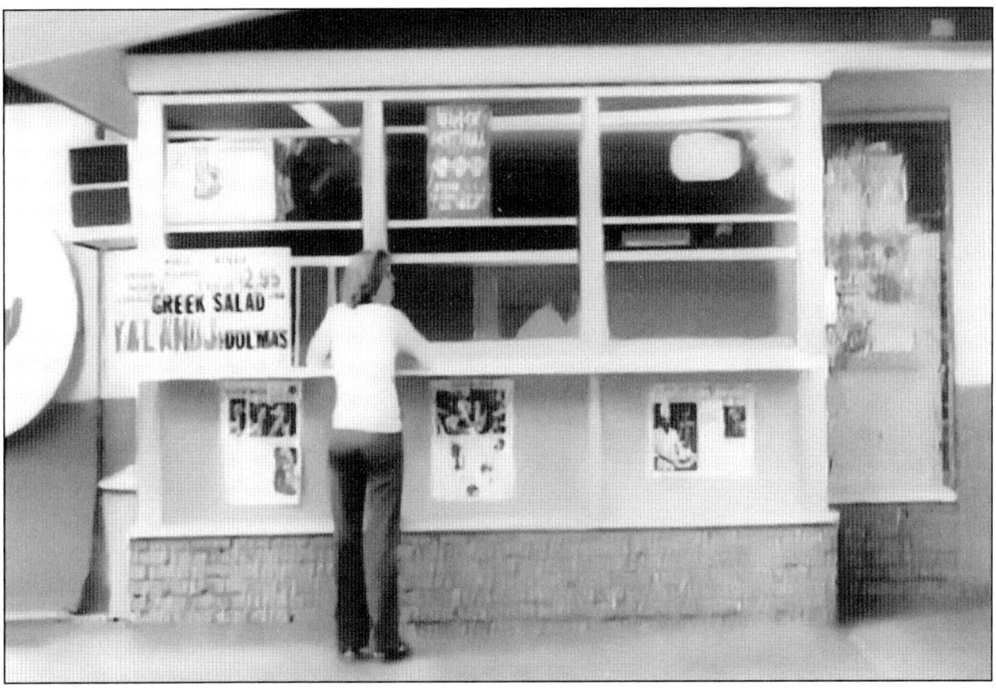

Chrysanthos and Eleni Fetokakis converted a small gas station into a neighborhood gyro stand in 1977 and named it Niko Niko's Greek & American Café. Since then, Niko Niko's has been managed by their youngest son, Dimitrios Fetokakis, and has been expanded in its original location. It continues to be a local favorite, a Houston landmark, and an institution. (Courtesy of Dimitri Fetokakis.)

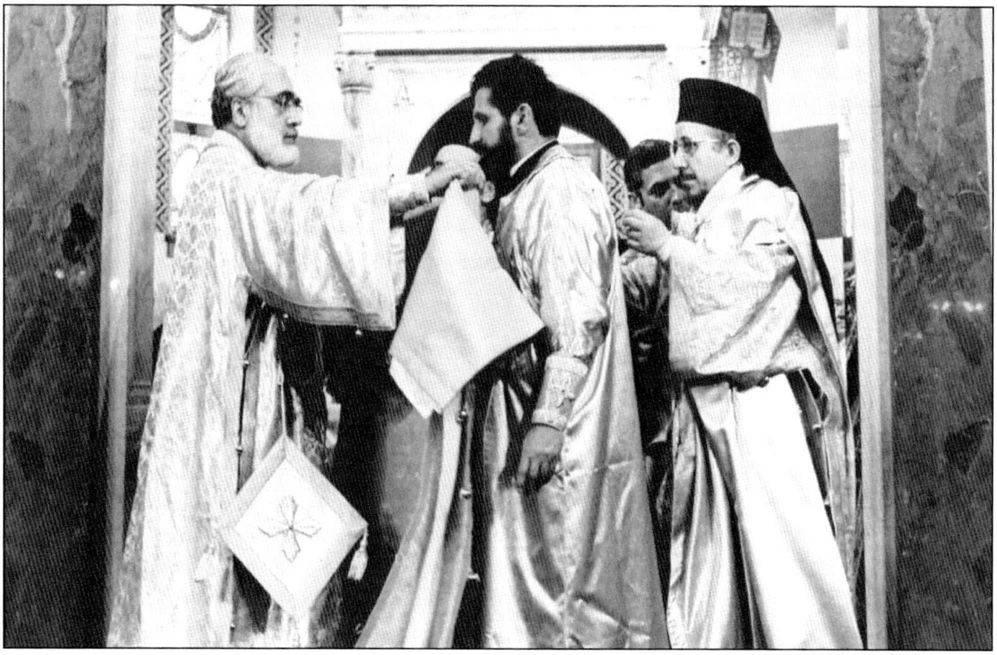

His Eminence Archbishop Iakovos, Primate of the Greek Orthodox Church of North and South America, presided over the consecration of bishop-elect, the very Rev. Archimandrite Christodoulos Kallos, first American-born Greek Orthodox priest to be elevated to the Episcopate of the Greek Orthodox Church. His consecration took place at the Annunciation Greek Orthodox Cathedral in Houston on January 17, 1971. Co-celebrant bishops were His Grace Bishop Silas of Amphipolis, of the New York Diocese, and His Grace Bishop Iakovos of Apameia, of the Detroit Diocese. (Courtesy of the AGOC archives.)

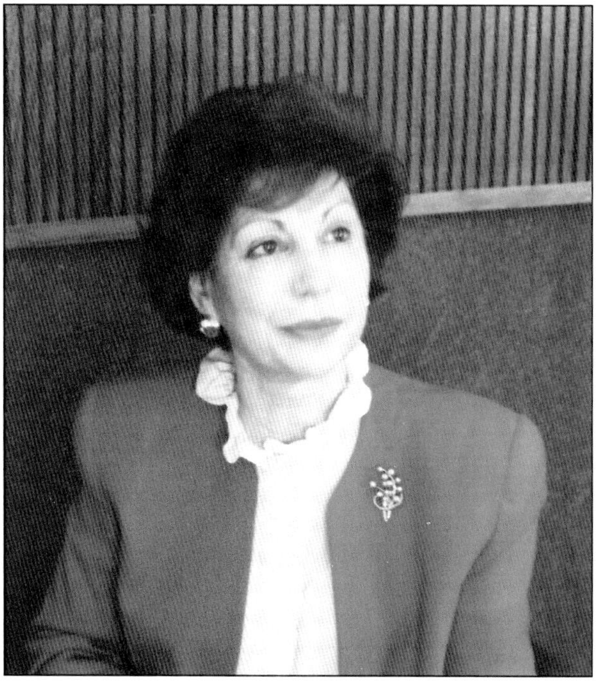

In the early years of Annunciation Church, religious education for children and adults was the responsibility of the priests and Greek school teachers. As the community flourished, Fr. Nicholas C. Triantafilou identified faithful stewards and appointed them as directors of the Sunday school program. Angelo Kasemeotes, Nick Frangakis, and Mary Bellos were the first to serve in this capacity. Mike Verges was so dedicated to the church that he taught the Bible for 50 years. Pictured is Mary Bellos, Sunday school director (1972–1987). (Courtesy of the AGOC archives.)

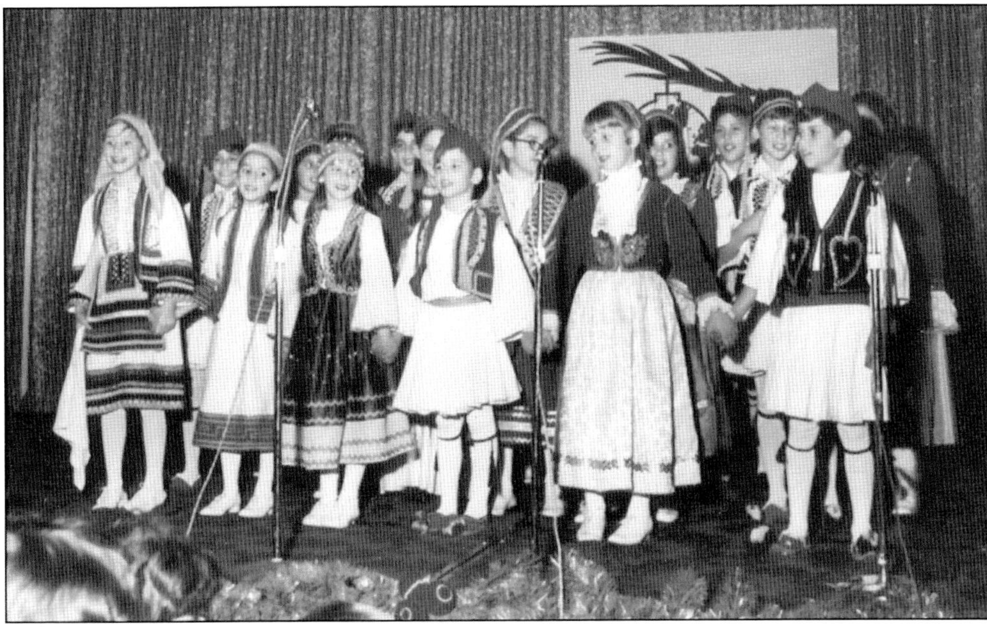

Pictured onstage is a March 25th celebration of Greek Independence Day by the Greek school students of Annunciation Cathedral. Today, Greek school is geared toward Greek American children. Greek is taught as a second language, and culture and tradition continue to be emphasized. Classes are also offered to teenagers and adults and are now held weekly for two hours. (Courtesy of the AGOC archives.)

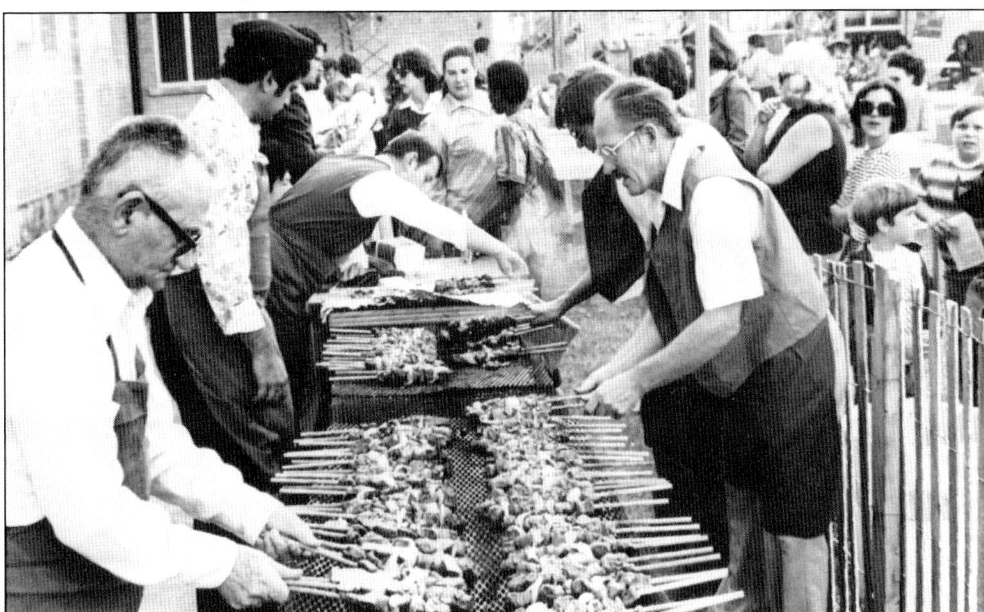

Paul Sallas (left) and James Cokins (right) grill *souvlakia* for the huge crowds at the 1976 Greek Festival. The community gathers after the Divine Liturgy the Sunday before the festival to prepare 20,000 souvlakia. Parishioners skewer meat, peppers, and onions according to diagrams posted around the Martel Auditorium, and the souvlakia marinate for several days before being grilled for the hungry Houston crowds. (Courtesy of John Cokins.)

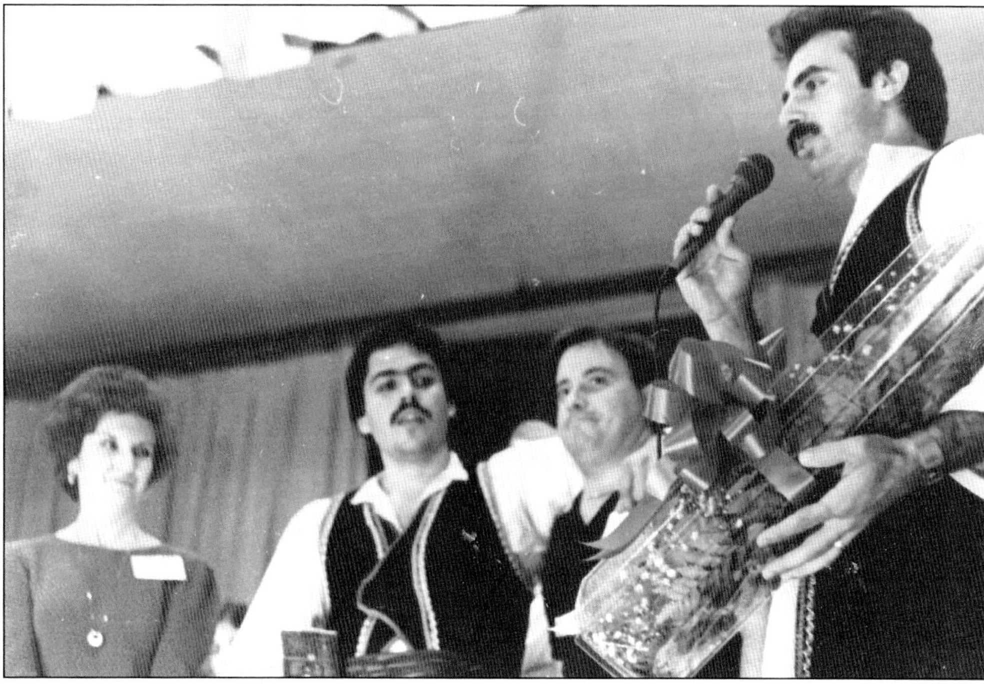

Georgia Voinis (left) directed and choreographed the Greek Festival dancers for 30 years (1973–2003). Ensuring that every detail was authentic, Georgia wrote about this ministry: "The purpose of the festival is to offer our Greek culture to the greater Houston Community, but mostly it provides an opportunity for young adults to show the love they have for their church, and offer appreciation for the beauty and talent God has given to each of them." (Courtesy of JoAnna Nicolaou.)

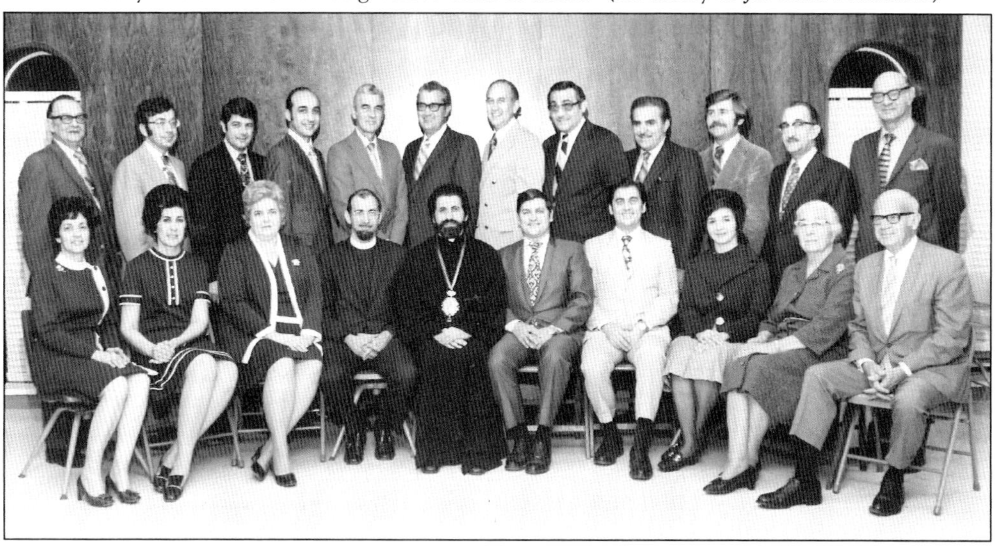

Pictured is the AGOC Clergy-Laity Congress in 1972. From left to right are (first row) Connie Glaros, Kiki Kantralis, Marie Harris, Fr. Nicholas C. Triantafilou, Bishop John of Thermon, chairman Deno Caloudas, Anthony Kouzounis, Presbytera Diane Triantafilou, Glykeria Brailas, and choir director Basil Semos; (second row) Nick Jelson, Louis Karvelas, Chris Nickolas, Paul Voinis, John Poulos, Charles Stamos, Jerry Kaler, Alec Kantralis, Victor Pappas, Artie Tropoli, John Janes, and Alex Skandalis. (Courtesy of the AGOC archives.)

CONCLUSION

Be strong and bold; have no fear or dread . . . because it is the Lord your God who goes with you.
—Deuteronomy 31:6

When the first Greek immigrants arrived in Houston in 1889, they did not imagine they would be laying the foundation for the fourth largest city in America. They came, instead, to make better lives for themselves and their families. In the process, however, they contributed to the growth and success of their new home by maintaining their Greek identity as they adapted to their new community.

These arrivals, mostly men, worked hard and eventually became prominent entrepreneurs. They learned English quickly, even Americanizing their names to make them easier to pronounce. But they never compromised who they were. First in their hearts was the establishment of a church, the centerpiece of their spiritual identity. With dedication and perseverance, the community worked to make this dream a reality. The Annunciation Greek Orthodox Church at Walker Street celebrated its first liturgy in 1918. By providing Greek language lessons, religious education classes, and fellowship to its parishioners, the church ensured that the faith and heritage of its founders would flourish in Houston. Flourish it did, and by 1952, the church moved to its present location on Yoakum Boulevard.

The cathedral community initiated dramatic changes over the decades: creation of the altar fund; transition to the Fair Share Commitment program; founding of the Annunciation Orthodox School; construction of the Greek Orthodox Community Center; formation of charitable, fraternal, social, and academic organizations; outreach ministries to the greater Houston community; liturgies in Greek and in English to accommodate the numerous converts and non-Greek speaking members; and, of course, the Greek Festival. Maintaining their Greek heritage, the immigrant pioneers and their families confirmed through their hard work and adaptability that they were also good Americans. Outreach to the Houston community included military service and stateside contributions by the women during the great wars, participation in the Houston Council of Churches and Houston Metropolitan Ministries, the Ladies Philoptochos Society Philocardiac Ministry in the Texas Medical Center, and even a radio program, "Religion on the Line."

The founders of the Annunciation Greek Orthodox Cathedral did not know how their community would grow and thrive. They had a simple dream—a new home, extraordinary opportunities, and a church that would eternally sustain them. Generations later, the faith and character of their descendants and new arrivals in Houston honor that dream with their dedication to their church and their Greek heritage.

Consistent with our mission to preserve history on a local level, this book was printed in South Carolina on American-made paper and manufactured entirely in the United States. Products carrying the accredited Forest Stewardship Council (FSC) label are printed on 100 percent FSC-certified paper.

MADE IN THE USA